Swan Electric Engraving Co. Ltd.

John Dee

JOHN DEE

JOHN DEE
(1527–1608)

Charlotte Fell Smith

Introduction by R. A. Gilbert

Ibis Press
An Imprint of Nicolas-Hays, Inc.
Berwick, Maine

First published in 2004 by
Ibis Press, and imprint of
Nicolas-Hays, Inc.
P. O. Box 1126
Berwick, ME 03901-1126
www.nicolashays.com

Distributed to the trade by
Red Wheel/Weiser, LLC
P. O. Box 612
York Beach, ME 03910-0612
www.redwheelweiser.com

Library of Congress Cataloging-in-Publication Data
available on request.

Cover design by Kathryn Sky-Peck.
Printed in the United States of America
10 09 08 07 06 05 04
7 6 5 4 3 2 1
MV

The paper used in this publication meets the minimum requirements of the American National Standard for Information Sciences—Permanence of Paper for Printed Library Materials Z39.48–1992 (R1997).

For the suggestion to write this book, and for valuable and kind assistance in reading the final proofs, I am greatly indebted to Professor Silvanus P. Thompson, D.Sc., F.R.S., etc.

C. F. S.

London, *July*, 1909.

CONTENTS

CHAPTER XI

CHAPTER XII

CHAPTER XIII

CHAPTER XIV

ILLUSTRATIONS

Frontispiece and between pages 166 and 167

1. **Portrait of John Dee—Frontispiece**

From the original (artist unknown) in the Ashmolean Museum, Oxford. It is inscribed on the face "*Johannes Dee Anglus Londinensis Aet^s suæ 67.*" The portrait was acquired by Ashmole from Dr. John Dee's grandson Rowland, and was left by him to Oxford University with his collections. It has been engraved by Scheneker and W. P. Sherlock.

2. **Title-page of Dee's "General and Rare Memorials Pertaining to the Perfect Art of Navigation," Printed by John Day, 1577.**

The motto "Plura latent quam patent" surrounds the title; above, the Queen's arms, a rose branch through a loop at each end. Allegorical drawing in a square; the date 1576 in Greek in the corners. The Queen seated at the helm of a "capital," i.e., first-class, ship; arms of England on the rudder; three noblemen standing in the waist. On the vessel's side Jupiter and Europa. Signs of famine on shore: a wheat ear upside down and a skull. A Dutch ship is anchored in the river; four more lie at its mouth; soldiers, a small boat, a man offering a purse, and in the corner a walled town. On the rock at the river's mouth stands Lady Opportunity; the angel Raphael overhead with flaming sword, and shield bearing St. George's Cross. The sun, moon, and ten stars; rays of glory proceeding from the name of Jehovah. (See Ames, *Typographical Antiquities*, ed. Herbert, vol. i., p. 66.)

3. **Picture of an Alchemist with his Assistant Tending Stills.**

From an engraving by Robert Vaughan in Ashmole's *Theatrum Chemicum Britonum* (1652), where it illustrates the first English translation of Thomas Norton's *Ordinall of Alchemy*, a metrical treatise in Latin, which Dee transcribed in the year 1577. His copy, bound in purple velvet, and with the index made by himself, is now Ashmolean MS. 57.

INTRODUCTION

Why, when we know so much about him, do we need another biography of John Dee, specifically one written almost a hundred years ago? To answer this question, we must ask others: What do we really know about Dr. Dee? How accessible is that knowledge? How much of it is relevant for the general reader?

Within the last forty years, John Dee's life and work have attracted much scholarly and popular attention. They have been dissected, analyzed, interpreted, re-interpreted, and presented to the public in many different ways. His published works, his autobiography, his private diaries and his magical records have all been ransacked, and, for the most part, have been either reprinted or published for the first time. Most of these texts, certainly all that have any significance, are readily available so that we can now discover more about his life than we may ever want or need to know.

And yet Dr. Dee still has the power to fascinate. He has been presented, correctly, as the perfect model of a Renaissance Man. As early as 1677 he was described, by John Webster, as the "greatest and ablest Philosopher, Mathematician, and Chymist" of his day,[1] and the image of Dee as among the foremost scientists of the Elizabethan era has, at least in academic circles, overtaken the view of him as an occultist. It is true that in his own lifetime he was perceived as a "conjuror" who trafficked with evil spirits, but this perception was not established in educated circles, and even then not universally until the publication, by Meric Casaubon in 1659, of *A True & Faithful relation of What passed for many Yeers between Dr. John Dee . . . and Some Spirits*. And yet, while Casaubon found Dee guilty of both spiritual pride and spiritual delusion, and ready to "pawn his soul" for the spirits with whom he sought to speak, he had to admit that spiritual wickedness did not preclude genius, for he also describes him as "A Mathematician of Great Fame."

This view of Dee as a scholar gone spiritually astray was perpetuated in Thomas Smith's dismissive biography of 1707. Smith, who had access to manuscripts unearthed after those of Casaubon, condemns Dee for "deplorable stupidity" and "execrable insanity" in following the advice of "daemons [who] most miserably deluded him."[2] Other writers on Dee followed sheepishly in Smith's track: William Godwin, in *Lives of the Necromancers* (1834); Elihu Rich in Smedley's *The Occult Sciences* (1855); and even Reverend W. A. Ayton, in the preface to his translation of Smith's *Life* (1907) all condemn Dee for his wickedness. For Ayton, who was an active member of the Hermetic Order of the Golden Dawn and who happily engaged in magical practices, to have held such views is especially surprising. Ayton evidently felt himself to be free from selfish motives and thus justified in his activities, while "Dr. Dee was an eminent and melancholy example of the great dangers incurred by those who rush into the practice of any form of Occultism whilst retaining the egoism which is a part of the lower instincts of human nature." And, because of his conceit, Dee fell from a "pure and blameless" state, "to the lowest depths of degradation and charlatanry, because he indulged himself in the idea that he was selected above all others to receive communications from Spirits."[3]

By the end of the nineteenth century, however, the negative view was beginning to crumble. A. E. Waite, who followed Ayton into the Golden Dawn, maintained that such a perception of Dee was "demonstrably unjust."[4] He argued also that Dee, for all that he was an astrologer, and "profoundly and lastingly interested in the mysteries of visions in the crystal," should be recognized not as "an alchemist on the one hand, nor a necromancer and a dealer with devils on the other," but as a "learned mathematical philosopher, who was to some extent absorbed by the physics and metaphysics of the Hermetic tradition."[5] This is very close to modern academic attitudes regarding Dee.

Waite also rejected the notion that Dee had been "the founder and head of the mysterious Rosicrucian Fraternity," not only because he died before the Rosicrucian manifestos appeared, but also because Dee was clearly not the author of the manuscript *Treatise on the Rosie Crucian Secrets* attributed to him.[6] In this, subsequent opinion has parted company with Waite.

Frances Yates, in her day the foremost cultural historian of the Renaissance, saw Dr. Dee as a true Magus: "John Dee . . . is a very clear example of how the will to operate, stimulated by Renaissance magic, could pass into, and stimulate, the will to operate in genuine applied science."[7] She would later present Dee as a "Christian Cabalist," on the basis of his numerological theory and his involvement in the conjuring of angels.[8] More significantly, she identified Dee's true—if unconscious—role in the formation of the Rosicrucian movement, setting out her argument in her book *The Rosicrucian Enlightenment* (1972).

The second of the Rosicrucian manifestos, the *Confessio Fraternitatis R.C.*, was published in 1615 as a supplementary text to Philip à Gabella's *Consideratio Brevis*, which is a reworking with substantial quotation of Dee's *Monas Hieroglyphica*. For readers of the manifestos the association of Dee's philosophy with the elusive Rosicrucians could not have been clearer. In addition, the symbol of Dee's "Hieroglyphic Monad" appears twice in Andreae's *Chymische Hochzeit* [*Chemical Wedding*] (1616), the third and last of the manifestos. One does not have to accept all of Yates's theorizing to be convinced that for Rosicrucians, Dee and his ideas were of supreme significance

Of course, a Renaissance Magus was a very different figure from that of a magician as conceived within the Hermetic Order of the Golden Dawn. For members of the Golden Dawn, Dee was the source of their knowledge of both the angelic world and the Enochian language that was used by its inhabitants. That Dee relied almost entirely on Edward Kelley for his conversations with angels did not concern them: Dee had the fame and respectability, at least to some degree, that was denied to the shifty Kelley. As the members of the Second Order carried out their curriculum of practical magic, scrying, calls, and the Enochian language were constantly with them.

Indeed, it is the ubiquity of Dee's "angel magic" and the use of Enochian within the Golden Dawn that have ensured his continuing fame in the popular mind, and not simply because the rituals and teaching of the Golden Dawn have become so widespread. After he was ignominiously ejected from the Order, Aleister Crowley cast off its rituals but retained his fascination, or rather obsession, with Enochian magic. Details of Enochian workings and phrases in the language are scattered throughout his works, and in his *Confessions* he states that, "It was part of my plan for *The Equinox* to prepare a final edition of the work of Dr. Dee and Sir Edward Kelly."[10] This never appeared, but others have taken up the task and almost all of Dee's records of his "Conference with Angels" and the Enochian texts have now been published. But for all their undeniable fascination they have obscured the true essence of Dee's spiritual philosophy.

Students of Dee who are not magically inclined have tended to see the scrying episodes as a form of proto-Spiritualism, with Kelley as a medium of singularly dubious moral worth. Thus E.M. Butler saw Kelley as a "most ambiguous person [who] was either one of the greatest mediums who have ever lived, or the world's most accomplished fraud."[11] Similarly, Frank Podmore, in *Modern Spiritualism*, his critical history of the subject, comments on the visions and on Kelley's checkered career: "Crystal vision is not, of course, necessarily associated with moral excellence; but it is clearly impossible, with such a dossier to have much confidence in Kelly's good faith." And then he makes an interesting remark: "But after all the interest of the revelations does not depend on the seer's veracity."[12]

The real interest of the visions lies in the nature of the communicators. They are described as angels, but they are not human spirits: they are spiritual beings of another order. Their language is the primeval tongue of Eden, "the original speech of man, and that of angels now,"[13] but they are essentially non-human. This does not make them some form of extra-dimensional aliens, as many contemporary "Enochian" magicians seem to believe, because they clearly act under God, part of whose creation they are. And this brings us to the matter of Dee's philosophy.

John Dee was a committed Christian and a faithful member of his native church, and his spiritual and philosophical studies were directed entirely toward an understanding of the true relationship between God, humans, and the created universe. The essence of this relationship is set out—elliptically and opaquely—in Dee's *Monas Hieroglyphica* [The Hieroglyphic Monad], which was published in 1564, seventeen years before his first foray into the world of spirits and angels. He describes it as a work explaining "mathematically, magically, cabbalistically, and anagogically"[14] the geometric symbol that is engraved on the title page and which had first appeared in his earlier book, *Propaedeumata aphoristica* (1558). The explanations are set out in a series of twenty-four theorems, with appropriate diagrams in the text, but they are extremely difficult to interpret.[15] Dee did not intend it to be understood by all, and calls upon God "to forgive me, if now I have sinned against Thy Majesty by revealing so great a secret in published writings, but I hope that only those who are worthy will really understand."[16] Essentially, then, the *Monas Hieroglyphica* is a mystical text to be grasped not by the rational mind but by the soul, and only after deep contemplation of both the symbol and Dee's words.

Are we then to see the real Dr. Dee as a Christian mystic? Perhaps, but even this is only a part of his life. He was truly a many-faceted man, but every aspect of his work was dedicated to helping his fellow men. His mathematics and astronomy were directed toward providing aids to navigation; he sought to improve the commerce of his country and to encourage the strengthening of its navy; he devoted time and energy in an attempt to reassemble the monastic libraries of England that had been scattered with the dissolution of the monasteries; and he sought to discover the wisdom of the angels for the benefit of this material world. There are gaps in the chronology of his life and much about his work that is still not fully understood.

No one biographer can do justice to every aspect of his life and thought and the student of Dee must look to specialist texts. But what of the reader who is simply curious?

And so we come back to our first question. The general reader does not want a specialist study; he or she needs simply a sound, sympathetic, and objective overview of John Dee's life, set in the context of his time and place. Charlotte Fell Smith's biography was the standard, indeed, the only substantial life of Dee for almost sixty years. It makes no pretence of providing an analysis of Dee's intellectual achievements, but it does offer a satisfying and rounded view of his life, and it possesses a freshness and charm that reflect the author's considerable skill as a biographer. Indeed, it is as a tribute to that skill, as much as for its subject, that *John Dee* deserves its reappearance.

Charlotte Fell Smith was a professional historian and a talented biographer: she became the most prolific female contributor to the English *Dictionary of National Biography*, supplying a total of 231 articles, mostly on minor religious figures of the seventeenth and eighteenth centuries—especially Quakers. She was born in 1851 at Pattiswick Hall, in Essex and died in the same county, at Felsted, in 1937. Throughout her life she was a tireless researcher into local history and from 1898 to 1933 she was the editor of an antiquarian journal, the *Essex Review*.

Her first book, an edition of the letters of Stephen Crisp, was published in 1892, while her first biography, *Mary Rich, Countess of Warwick (1625–1678): Her Family and Friends*, appeared in 1901. Over the next fifteen years she produced five more books, three of them biographies, and all save one of purely local, Essex interest. That one, published in 1909, was *John Dee (1527–1608)*. Miss Fell Smith—she never married—wrote her study of Dee at the suggestion of Silvanus Phillips Thompson (1851–1916), a prominent physicist and electrical engineer who was also a biographer. Thompson had written biographies of Michael Faraday and Lord Kelvin, and felt that Dee, whom he viewed as a scientist, deserved a better memorial for his tercentenary than being thought of as a magician and charlatan (Ayton's translation of Smith's *Life of John Dee* had appeared in 1908).

Reviews of the book were generally favorable, although G. F. Abbott, writing in *The Athenaeum* (13 November, 1909, p. 590) seized on the author's concentration on the esoteric activities of Dee's life, and noted that "Miss Smith has told the story of his failure: we should have been glad to hear more of his achievement." Others were more kind—and more just—in their criticism, A. E. Waite praised the book extravagantly in *The Occult Review* (vol. XI, no. 1, January 1910, pp. 52–53). He found it to be "a delight to the student as an instance of what simple pains can effect to elucidate an obscure matter," and noted that Miss Smith has "the especial advantage of not writing as a professed occultist; that disposition is a pool of thought which bends many straight staves of fact." She is, he added, "usually sympathetic and she is always faithful." So excellent did he find the biography that he felt it difficult to imagine that we should ever "have any need for another."

That, of course, could never be so, but it is an excellent study and we can only agree with her concluding comments on Dee: that we "must acknowledge his sincere and good intentions; his personal piety; his uncommon purity of thought and mind. . . . he was no conscious charlatan, . . . but a devout believer in man's power and purpose to wrest scientific secrets from the womb of the future."

R.A. Gilbert,
Bristol, England
October, 2004

Notes

1. John Webster, *The Displaying of Supposed Witchcraft* (London: J.M., 1677), p. 7.
2. Thomas Smith, *The Life of John Dee*, translated from the Latin by W. A. Ayton (London, 1907), pp. 54, 78. The Latin text was first published in *Vitae quorundam eruditissimorum et illustrium virorum* (London, 1707).
3. Smith, *Life of John Dee*, p. vii.
4. A. E. Waite (ed.), *The Alchemical Writings of Edward Kelly* (London, 1893; reprint, York Beach: Weiser, 1976) "Biographical Preface" p. x. Note: Kelley's name has ocassionally been spelled without the second "e" in various publications.
5. Ibid. p. lx.
6. British Library, Harleian MS 6485. This has been published as *The Rosie Crucian Secrets* (Wellingborough, Aquarian Press, 1985), edited by E. J. Langford Garstin, who firmly believed that Dee was the author.
7. Frances A. Yates, *Giordano Bruno and the Hermetic Tradition* (London: Routledge & Kegan Paul, 1964), p. 150.
8. Yates, *The Occult Philosophy in the Elizabethan Age* (London: Routledge & Kegan Paul, 1979), p. 82.
9. Yates, *The Rosicrucian Enlightenment* (London: Routledge & Kegan Paul, 1972), see especially Chapter III, "John Dee and the Rise of 'Christian Rosencreutz,'" pp. 30–40; also the bibliographical note, p. 236.
10. Aleister Crowley, *The Confessions of Aleister Crowley: An Autohagiography*, John Symonds and Kenneth Grant, eds. (London: Johnathan Cape, 1969), p. 595.
11. E. M. Butler, *The Myth of the Magus*. (Cambridge: Cambridge University Press, 1948), p. 163.
12. Frank Podmore, *Modern Spiritualism: A History and a Criticism,* 2 vols. (London: Methuen & Co., 1902), vol. 1, p. 12.
13. Ibid., p. 14.
14. C. H. Josten, "A Translation of John Dee's 'Monas Hieroglyphics'" (Antwerp, 1564), with an Introduction and Annotations, in *Ambix, The Journal for the Society for the Study of Alchemy*

and Early Chemistry XII, nos. 2 and 3 (June and October 1964): 84–221, see p. 155.

15. Nicholas Clulee, in *John Dee's Natural Philosophy* (London: Routledge & Kegan Paul, 1988), describes the text as being "exceptionally opaque" and notes that it "has remained largely unintelligible to modern commentators."
16. Josten, "A Translation of John Dee's 'Monas Hieroglyphics,'" p. 183.

Life of Dr. John Dee

CHAPTER I

BIRTH AND EDUCATION

> "O Incredulitie, the wit of fooles
> That slovenly will spit on all thinges faire,
> The coward's castle and the sluggard's cradle,
> How easy 'tis to be an infidel!"
>
> —GEORGE CHAPMAN.

IT seems remarkable that three hundred years should have been allowed to elapse since the death of John Dee in December, 1608, without producing any Life of an individual so conspicuous, so debatable, and so remarkably picturesque.

There is perhaps no learned author in history who has been so persistently misjudged, nay, even slandered, by his posterity, and not a voice in all the three centuries uplifted even to claim for him a fair hearing. Surely it is time that the cause of all this universal condemnation should be examined in the light of reason and science; and perhaps it will be found to exist mainly in the fact that he was too far advanced in speculative thought for his own age to understand. For more than fifty years out of the eighty-one of his life, Dee was famous, even if suspected and looked askance at as clever beyond human interpretation. Then his Queen died. With the narrow-minded Scotsman who succeeded her came a change in the fashion of men's minds. The reign of the devil and his handmaidens—the witches and possessed persons—was set up in order to be piously overthrown, and the very bigotry of the times gave birth to independent and rational thought—to Newton, Bacon, Locke.

But Dee was already labelled once and for all. Every succeeding writer who has touched upon his career, has followed the leaders blindly, and has only cast another, and yet another, stone to the heap of obloquy piled upon his name. The fascination of his psychic projections has always led the critic to ignore his more solid achievements in the realms of history and science, while at the same time, these are only cited to be loudly condemned. The learned Dr. Meric Casaubon, who, fifty years after Dee's death, edited his *Book of Mysteries*—the absorbing recital of four out of the six or seven years of his crystal gazing—was perhaps the fairest critic he yet has had. Although he calls Dee's spiritual revelations a "sad record," and a "work of darkness," he confesses that he himself, and other learned and holy men (including an archbishop), read it with avidity to the end, and were eager to see it printed. He felt certain, as he remarks in his preface, that men's curiosity would lead them to devour what seems to him "not parallelled in that kind, by any book that hath been set out in any age to read." And yet on no account was he publishing it to satisfy curiosity, but only "to do good and promote Religion." For Dee, he is persuaded, was a true, sincere Christian, his *Relation* made in the most absolute good faith, although undoubtedly he was imposed upon and deluded by the evil spirits whom he sometimes mistook for good ones.

It may be well here to remark that this voluminous *Book of Mysteries*, or *True and Faithful Relation* (fol. 1659), from which in the following pages there will be found many extracts, abounds in tedious and unintelligible pages of what Casaubon calls "sermon-like stuff," interspersed with passages of extraordinary beauty. Some of the figures and parables, as well as the language used, are full of a rare poetic imagery, singularly free from any coarse or sensual symbolism. Like jewels embedded in dull settings, here and there a gem of loftiest religious thought shines and sparkles. There are descriptive touches of costume and appearance that possess considerable dramatic value. As the story is unfolded in a kind of spiritual drama, the sense of a gradual moving development, and the choice of a fitting vehicle in which to clothe it, is striking. The *dramatis personæ*, too, the "spiritual creatures" who, as Dee believed, influence the destinies of man, become living and real, as of course they were to the seer. In many respects these "actions" were an exact counterpart of the dealings inaugurated by psychical scientists 275 years later, if we omit the close investigation for fraud.

Casaubon's successor in dealing with the shunned and avoided subject of John Dee was Thomas Smith, Fellow of Magdalen College, Oxford, who, in 1707, wrote the first connected Life of him, in a book of the Lives of Learned Men.[1] It was based upon some of Dee's autobiographical papers, and out of a total of a

[1] *Vitæ Quorundam Eruditissimorum et Illustrium Virorum* (1707).

hundred pages, gave fifty to letters already printed by Casaubon.

After this no sustained account of Dee's romantic career is to be found outside the pages of biographical dictionaries and magazine articles, or among writers upon necromancy, hermetic philosophy, and alchemy. Many of these decorate their collections with apocryphal marvels culled from the well-worn traditional stories of Dee and his companion, Edward Kelley. Thus, throughout his lifetime and since, he has continued to run the gauntlet of criticism. "Old imposturing juggler," "fanatic," "quack," are mild terms: in the *Biographia Britannica* he is called "extremely credulous, extravagantly vain, and a most deluded enthusiast." Even the writer on Dee in the *Dictionary of National Biography* says his conferences with the angels are "such a tissue of blasphemy and absurdity that they might suggest insanity." Many more such summary verdicts might be quoted, but these will suffice for the present.

It has been said that no Life of Dee exists. And yet the materials for such a Life are so abundant that only a selection can be here used. His private diary, for instance, if properly edited, would supply much supplementary, useful, and interesting historical information.

It is the object of this work to present the facts of John Dee's life as calmly and impartially as possible, and to let them speak for themselves. In the course of writing it, many false assertions have disentangled themselves from truth, many doubts have been resolved, and a mass of information sees the light for the first time. The subject is of course hedged about with innumerable difficulties; but in spite of the temptations to stray into a hundred bypaths, an endeavour has been strictly made to do no more than throw a little dim light on the point where the paths break off from the main road. If, at the end of the way, any who have persevered so far, feel they have followed a magnetic and interesting personality, the labour expended will not have been in vain. With a word of apology to serious historical readers for the incorrigibly romantic tendency of much of the narrative, which, in spite of the stern sentinel of a literary conscience, would continually reassert itself, the story of our astrologer's strange life may now begin.

John Dee was the son of Rowland Dee; he was born in London, according to the horoscope of his own drawing, on July 13, 1527.

His mother was Jane, daughter of William Wild. Various Welsh writers have assigned to Dee a genealogical descent of the highest antiquity, and the pedigree[1] which he drew up for himself in later life traces back his family history from his grandfather, Bedo Dee, to Roderick the Great, Prince of Wales. All authorities agree that Radnor was the county from whence the Dees sprang.

Rowland Dee, the father, held an appointment at Court, as gentleman server to Henry VIII., but was very indifferently treated by the King. This may partly account for the persistence with which Dee exhibited before Queen Elizabeth his claims to preferment at her hands. To be in habitual attendance at Court in those

[1] *Cotton Charter*, xiv. I.

days, however, bred in men a great desire for place, and a courtier was but a mendicant on a grand scale.

The boy, John Dee, was early bred in "grammar learning," and was inured to Latin from his tender years. Perhaps he was not more than nine or ten when he was sent to Chelmsford, to the chantry school founded there seven years before the great school at Winchester came into existence. The master who presided over Dee's school hours in Essex was Peter Wilegh, whom the chantry commissioners in 1548 reported as a man "of good conversation" who had kept the school there for sixteen years. Dee has always been claimed by the Grammar School at Chelmsford as one of their most famous *alumni*, whose extraordinary career with its halo of mystery and marvel they perhaps feel little qualified to explore. Dee's testimony that at Chelmsford he was "metely well furnished with understanding of the Latin tongue" is an unconscious tribute to Peter Wilegh's teaching.

In November, 1542, Dee, being then fifteen years and four months old, left Chelmsford to enter at St. John's College, Cambridge, where, as he tells us in his autobiography, he soon became a most assiduous student.[1] "In the years 1543, 1544, 1545, I was so vehemently bent to studie, that for those years I did inviolably keep this order: only to sleep four houres every night; to allow to meate and drink (and some refreshing after) two houres every day; and of the other eighteen houres all (except the tyme

[1] *Compendious Rehearsall.* "The Entrance and Ground Plat of my First Studies." Chetham Society, vol. i., p. 4.

of going to and being at divine service) was spent in my studies and learning." Early in 1546 he graduated B.A. from St. John's College. At the close of the same year, Trinity College was founded by Henry VIII., and Dee was selected one of the original Fellows. He was also appointed under-reader in Greek to Trinity College, the principal Greek reader being then Robert Pember. The young Fellow created the first sensation of his sensational career soon after this by arranging some mechanism for a students' performance of the Εἰρήνη (Eirene — Peace) of Aristophanes, in which he apparently acted as stage manager and carpenter.

For this play he devised a clever mechanical and very spectacular effect. Trygæus, the Attic vine-dresser, carrying a large basket of food for himself, and mounted on his gigantic beetle or scarab (which ate only dung), was seen ascending from his dwelling on the stage to enter the palace of Zeus in the clouds above. One has only to think of the scenic effects presented by Faust and Mephistopheles at Mr. Tree's theatre, for instance, to realise how crude and ineffective these attempts must have been; but thirty or forty years before Shakespeare's plays were written, so unusual an exhibition was enough to excite wild rumours of supernatural powers. We hear no more of theatrical performances, although several references in his after-life serve to show that his interest in the English drama, about to be born, lagged not far behind that of his greater contemporaries. He does mention, however, a Christmas pastime in St. John's College, which seems to have been inspired by this same dramatic spirit. Of details we are totally ignorant; he only relates that the custom of electing a "Christmas Magistrate" was varied at his suggestion by crowning the chosen victim as Emperor. The first imperial president of the Christmas revels in St. John's College "was one Mr. Thomas Dunne, a very goodly man of person, stature and complexion, and well learned also," evidently a presence fit for a throne. Dee adds: "They which yet live and were hearers and beholders, they can testifie more than is meete here to be written of these my boyish attempts and exploites scholasticall."

He turned to sterner studies, and became a skilful astronomer, taking "thousands of observations (very many to the hour and minute) of the heavenly influences and operations actual in this elementall portion of the world." These he afterwards published in various "Ephemerides."

In May, 1547, Dee made his first journey abroad, to confer with learned men of the Dutch Universities upon the science of mathematics, to which he had already begun to devote his serious attention. He spent several months in the Low Countries, formed close friendships with Gerard Mercator, Gemma Frisius, Joannes Caspar Myricæus, the Orientalist Antonius Gogava, and other philosophers of world-wide fame. Upon his return to Cambridge, he brought with him two great globes of Mercator's making, and an astronomer's armillary ring and staff of brass, "such as Frisius had newly devised and was in the habit of using." These he afterwards gave to the Fellows and students of Trinity College; he cites a letter of acknowledgment from John Christopherson (afterwards Bishop of Chichester), but upon search being made for the objects recently, through the kindness of the Master, it appears they are not now to be found. Dee returned to Cambridge in the year 1548 to take his degree of M.A., and soon after went abroad. "And never after that was I any more student in Cambridge." Before he left, he obtained under the seal of the Vice-Chancellor and Convocation, April 14, 1548, a testimonial to his learning and good conduct,[1] which he proposed to take with him abroad. Many times did he prove it to be of some value.

In Midsummer Term, 1548, he entered as a student at the University of Louvain, which had been founded more than a hundred years before in this quaint old Brabantian town of mediæval ramparts and textile industries. At Louvain, Dee continued his studies for two years, and here he soon acquired a reputation for learning quite beyond his years. It has been presumed that he here graduated doctor, to account for the title that has always been given him.[2] "Doctor Dee" certainly possesses an alliterative value not to be neglected. At Cambridge he was only M.A.

Long after, when he had passed middle life, and when his remarkable genius in every branch of science had carried him so far beyond the dull wit of the people who surrounded him that they could only explain his manifestations by the old cry of "sorcery and magic," Dee made a passionate appeal to the Queen, his constant patron and employer, to send two

[1] *Autobiogr. Tracts of Dr. John Dee.* Chetham Society, vol. i., p. 82.

[2] By the courtesy of M. le Secrétaire de l'Université Catholique, at Louvain, I am informed no such degree appears

emissaries of her own choosing to his house at Mortlake, and bid them examine everything they could find, that his character might be cleared from the damaging charges laid against him. He prepared for these two commissioners, to whose visit we shall revert in its proper place, an autobiographical document of the greatest value, which he calls "The Compendious Rehearsal of John Dee: his dutiful declaration and proofe of the course and race of his studious life, for the space of half an hundred years, now (by God's favour and help) fully spent."[1] It is from this narrative that the facts of his early life are ascertainable. Perhaps we discern them through a faint mist of retrospective glorification for which the strange streak of vanity almost inseparable from attainments like Dee's was accountable. But there is every reason to rely upon the accuracy of the mathematician's story.

"Beyond the seas, far and nere, was a good opinion conceived of my studies philosophicall and mathematicall." People of all ranks began to flock to see this wonderful young man. He gives the names of those who came to Louvain, a few hours' journey from Brussels, where the brilliant court of Charles V. was assembled, with evident pride. Italian and Spanish nobles; the dukes of Mantua and Medina Celi; the Danish king's mathematician, Mathias Hacus; and his physician, Joannes Capito; Bohemian students, all arrived to put his reputation to the test. A distinguished Englishman, Sir William Pickering, afterwards ambassador to France, came as his pupil,

[1] The original, partly burned, is in *Cotton MS.*, Vitell, C. vii., ff. 1—14. Ashmole's copy was printed by Hearne in *Johannis Glastoniensis Chron.*, Oxford, 1726; and in Chetham Soc., vol. i. (1851).

to study astronomy "by the light of Mercator's globes, the astrolabe, and the astronomer's ring of brass that Frisius had invented." For his recreation, the teacher "looked into the method of civil law," and mastered easily the points of jurisprudence, even "those accounted very intricate and dark." It was at Louvain, no doubt, that his interest in the subject of alchemy became strengthened and fixed. Stories were rife of course of the famous alchemist, Henricus Cornelius Agrippa, who had died there, in the service of Margaret of Austria, only a dozen years or so before. Agrippa had been secretary to the Emperor Maximilian, had lived in France, London, and Italy, and Louvain, no doubt, was bursting with his extraordinary feats of magic.

The two years soon came to an end, and a couple of days after his twenty-third birthday, young Dee left the Low Countries for Paris, where he arrived on July 20, 1550. His fame had preceded him, and within a few days, at the request of some English gentlemen and for the honour of his country, he began a course of free public lectures or readings in Euclid, "Mathematicé, Physicé et Pythagoricé," at the College of Rheims, in Paris, a thing, he says, which had never been done before in any university in Christendom. His audience (most of them older than himself) was so large that the mathematical schools would not hold them, and many of the students were forced in their eagerness to climb up outside the windows, where, if they could not hear the lecturer, they could at least see him. He demonstrated upon every proposition, and gave dictation and exposition.

A greater astonishment was created, he says, than even at his scarabæus mounting up to the top of Trinity Hall in Cambridge. The members of the University in Parisat the time numbered over 4,000 students, who came from every part of the known world. He made many friends among the professors and graduates, friends of "all estates and professions," several of whose names he gives; among them, the learned writers and theologians of the day, Orontius, Mizaldus, Petrus Montaureus, Ranconetus (Ranconnet), Fernelius, and Francis Silvius.

The fruit of these years spent in Louvain and Paris was that Dee afterwards maintained throughout his life a lively correspondence with professors and doctors in almost every university of note upon the Continent. He names especially his correspondents in the universities of Orleans, Cologne, Heidelberg, Strasburg, Verona, Padua, Ferrara, Bologna, Urbino, Rome, and many others, whose letters lay open for the inspection of the commissioners on that later visit already alluded to.

An offer was made him to become a King's Reader in mathematics in Paris University, with a stipend of two hundred French crowns yearly, but he had made up his mind to return to England, and nothing would tempt him to stay. He received other proposals, promising enough, to enter the service of M. Babeu, M. de Rohan, and M. de Monluc, who was starting as special ambassador to the Great Turk, but his thoughts turned back to England, and thither, in 1551, he bent his steps.

CHAPTER II

IMPRISONMENT AND AUTHORSHIP

"A man is but what he knoweth."—BACON.

IN December, 1551, Dee obtained, through the offices of Mr. (afterwards Sir) John Cheke, an introduction to Secretary Cecil and to King Edward VI. He had already written for and dedicated to the young King two books (in manuscript): *De usi Globi Cœlestis*, 1550, and *De nubium, solis, lunœ, ac reliquorum planetarum, etc.*, 1551. These perhaps had been sent to Cheke, the King's tutor, in the hope that they might prove useful lesson books. The pleasing result of the dedication was the gift of an annual royal pension of a hundred crowns. This allowance was afterwards exchanged for the rectory of Upton-upon-Severn, in Worcestershire, which Dee found an extremely bad bargain.

From the Beacon Hill above West Malvern Priory, the visitor may turn from inspection of the ancient British camp of Caractacus to admire the magnificent view; and across the level fields where the Severn winds, the tower of Upton church will be seen rising in the middle distance. Further west, if the day be clear, the more imposing towers of Tewkesbury and Gloucester may be discerned, while half a turn eastward will show Worcester Cathedral, not far away. Dee never lived in this beautiful place, although he was presented to the living on May 19, 1553. Even when the rectory of Long Leadenham, in Lincolnshire,[1] was added to Upton, the two together were worth only about £80 a year. Next year he declined an invitation to become Lecturer on Mathematical Science at Oxford, conveyed to him through "Mr. Doctor Smith" (Richard, D.C.L., 1528, the reformer), of Oriel College, and "Mr. du Bruarne," of Christ Church. He was occupied with literary work, and in 1553 produced, among other things, a couple of works on *The Cause of Floods and Ebbs*, and *The Philosophical and Political Occasions and Names of the Heavenly Asterismes*, both written at the request of Jane, Duchess of Northumberland.

When Mary Tudor succeeded her young brother as queen in 1553, Dee was invited to calculate her nativity. He began soon after to open up a correspondence with the Princess Elizabeth, who was then living at Woodstock, and he cast her horoscope also. Before long he was arrested on the plea of an informant named George Ferrys, who alleged that one of his children had been struck blind and another killed by Dee's "magic."[2] Ferrys also declared that Dee was directing his enchantments against the Queen's life. Dee's lodgings in London were searched and sealed up, and he himself was sent to prison. He was examined before the Secretary of State,

[1] Apparently he did sometimes visit Leadenham, for Lysons, *Env. Lond.*, 1796, gives an account of a stone found near the parsonage house there with the following inscription;—

יהוה

MISERICORDIAS DOMINI IN ÆTERNA CANTABO

◊ JOANNES △ DEE ◊

He suggests, as an explanation, that Dee escaped when the house, as a tradition records, was burned by lightning.

[2] *Cal. State Papers Dom.*, 1547–1580, p. 67.

afterwards upon eighteen articles by the Privy Council, and at last brought into the Star Chamber for trial. There he was cleared of all suspicion of treason, and liberated by an Order in Council, August 29, 1555, but handed over to Bishop Bonner for examination in matters of religion. Bonner was apparently equally satisfied. Dee was certainly enjoined by him, at John Philpot's examination on November 19, 1555, to put questions as a test of his orthodoxy. He quoted St. Cyprian to Philpot, who replied: "Master Dee, you are too young in divinity to teach me in the matters of my faith, though you be more learned in other things."[1]

Dee deserves well of all writers and students for time everlasting because of his most praiseworthy efforts to found a State National Library of books and manuscripts, with copies of foreign treasures, wherever they might be. On January 15, 1556, he presented to Queen Mary "a Supplication for the recovery and preservation of ancient writers and monuments."[2] Within a few years he had seen the monasteries dissolved and the priceless collections of these houses lamentably dispersed, some burned and others buried. He drew up a very remarkable address to the Queen dwelling on the calamity of thus distributing "the treasure of all antiquity and the everlasting seeds of continual excellency within this your Grace's realm." Many precious jewels, he knows, have already utterly perished, but in time

[1] Foxe, *Acts and Monuments*, 1847 ed., vol. vii., p. 638, *et passim*. Dee's name is suppressed after the first editions.

[2] *Autobiogr. Tracts*, p. 46. A fragment of the original, saved from fire, is in *Cotton MS.*, Vitell, C. vii. 310.

there may be saved and recovered the remnants of a store of theological and scientific writings which are now being scattered up and down the kingdom, some in unlearned men's hands, some walled up or buried in the ground. Dee uses powerful arguments to enforce his plea, choosing such as would make the most direct appeal to both Queen and people. She will build for herself a lasting name and monument; they will be able all in common to enjoy what is now only the privilege of a few scholars, and even these have to depend on the goodwill of private owners. He proposes first that a commission shall be appointed to inquire what valuable manuscripts exist; that those reported on shall be borrowed (on demand), a fair copy made, and if the owner will not relinquish it, the original be returned. Secondly, he points out that the commission should get to work at once, lest some owners, hearing of it, should hide or convey away their treasures, and so, he pithily adds, "prove by a certain token that they are not sincere lovers of good learning because they will not share them with others." The expenses of the commission and of the copying, etc., he proposed should be borne by the Lord Cardinal and the Synod of the province of Canterbury, who should also be charged to oversee the manuscripts and books collected until a library "apt in all points" is made ready for their reception.

Finally, Dee suggests that to him be committed the procuring of copies of many famous manuscript volumes to be found in the great libraries abroad: the Vatican Library at Rome, St. Mark's at Venice, and in Bologna, Florence, Vienna, etc. He offers to set to work to obtain these, the expenses only of transcription and carriage to England to be charged to the State. As to printed books, they are to "be gotten in wonderfull abundance." In this generous offer of his life to be spent in transcribing crabbed manuscripts, we cannot see the restless genius of John Dee long satisfied, but at any rate he proved himself not seeking for private gain.

Thus was the germ of a great National Library first started by the Cambridge mathematician, nearly fifty years before Thomas Bodley opened his unique collection at Oxford, and close upon 200 years before there was founded in the capital the vast and indispensable book-mine known to all scholars at home and abroad as the British Museum. The Historical Manuscripts Commission, whose labours in cataloguing private collections of archives are also foreshadowed in Dee's supplication, only came into being with the appointment of Keepers of the Public Records, by an Act signalising the first and second years of Queen Victoria's reign.

It is needless to say that nothing came of Dee's very disinterested proposition. So he became the more industrious in collecting a library of his own, which soon consisted of more than 4,000 volumes, which were always at the disposal of the friends who came often to see him.

They came also for another reason.

Astrology was a very essential part of astronomy in the sixteenth century, and the belief in the controlling power of the stars over human destinies is almost as old as man himself. The relative positions of the planets in the firmament, their situations amongst the constellations, at the hour of a man's birth, were considered by the ancients to be dominant factors and influences throughout his whole life. It is not too much to say that a belief in the truth of horoscopes cast by a skilled calculator still survives in our Western civilisation as well as in the East. Medical science to-day pays its due respect to astrology in the sign, little altered from the astrological figure for Jupiter, with which all prescriptions are still headed.

Dee, as one of the foremost mathematicians and astronomers of the time, and one employed by the Queen, became continually in request to calculate the nativity and cast a horoscope for men and women in all ranks of life. He has left many notes of people's births; his own children's are entered with the greatest precision, for which a biographer has to thank him.

When Elizabeth mounted with firm steps the throne that her unhappy sister had found so precarious and uneasy a heritage, Dee was very quickly sought for at Court. His first commission was entirely *sui generis.* He was commanded by Robert Dudley to name an auspicious day for the coronation, and his astrological calculations thereupon seem to have impressed the Queen and all her courtiers. Whether or no we believe in the future auguries of such a combination of influences as presided over the selection of the 14th of January, 1559, for the day of crowning Elizabeth in Westminster Abbey, we must acknowledge that Dee's choice of a date was succeeded by benign and happy destinies.

He was then living in London. We do not know

where his lodging was, but several of the books belonging to his library have come down to us with his autograph, "Johannes Dee, Londini," and the dates of the years 1555, 1557, and 1558.

Elizabeth sent for him soon after her accession, and invited him to her service at Whitehall with all fair promises. He was introduced by Dudley, then and long afterwards her first favourite; so he was likely to stand well. "Where my brother hath given him a crown," she said to Dudley, or to Dee's other sponsor, the Earl of Pembroke, "I will give him a noble." This was the first of innumerable vague promises made, but it was long indeed before any real and tangible gift was conferred on the astrologer, although he was continually busied about one thing and another at the fancy of the Queen. The reversion of the Mastership of St. Catherine's Hospital was promised him, but "Dr. Willson politickly prevented me."

One morning the whole Court and the Privy Council were put into a terrible flutter by a simple piece of what was common enough in ancient times and in Egypt—sympathetic magic.[1] A wax image of the Queen had been found lying in Lincoln's Inn Fields, with a great pin stuck through its breast, and it was supposed undoubtedly to portend the wasting away and death of her Majesty, or some other dreadful omen. Messenger after messenger was despatched to summon Dee, and bid him make haste. He hurried off, satisfied himself apparently of the harmless

[1] Cf. Daniel's Sonnet (1592)—

"The sly enchanter when to work his will
And secret wrong on some forspoken wight," etc., etc.

nature of the practical joke, and repaired, with Mr. Secretary Wilson as a witness of the whole proceedings and a proof of all good faith, to Richmond, where the Queen was. The Queen sat in that part of her private garden that sloped down to the river, near the steps of the royal landing-place at Hampton Court; the Earl of Leicester (as Dudley had now become) was in attendance, gorgeous and insolent as ever; the Lords of the Privy Council had also been summoned, when Dee and Mr. Secretary expounded the inner meaning of this untoward circumstance, and satisfied and allayed all their fears. Something about the calm attributes of this seasoned and travelled scholar seemed always to give moral support to the Queen and her household; this is only the first of many occasions when he had to allay their superstitious fright. That she felt it essential to keep him within reach of herself may have been one reason for not giving him the appointments for which he, and others for him, constantly sued. Dee was not an easy person to fit into a living: he required one with no cure of souls attached; for this, he says, "a *cura animarum annexa*, did terrifie me to deal with them." He is called a bachelor of divinity by Foxe in 1555, and as a matter of fact he does, both in 1558 and in 1564, add the letters S. D. T. to his name in his printed works.[1] This degree also was not from Cambridge. At last he grew tired of waiting, and a certain restlessness in his character, not incompatible with the long patience of the true follower of science,

[1] *Propædeumata Aphoristica,* 1558. Address to the Printer in *Monas Hieroglyphica,* 1564.

drove him again abroad. His intention was to arrange for printing works already prepared in manuscript. To search among out-of-the-way bookmongers and book-lovers in high-walled German towns, for rare treasures wherewith to enrich his native country, was another magnet that drew his feet. In February, 1563, after he had been thus employed for more than a year, he wrote from the sign of the Golden Angel, in Antwerp, to Cecil, to ask if he was expected to return to England, or if he might remain to oversee the printing of his books, and continue his researches among Dutch books and scholars. He had intended, he says, to return before Easter, but this was now impossible, owing to printer's delays. When we remember that a hundred years had barely elapsed since the first metal types had been cast and used in a hand press, it is not wonderful that Dee's treatise, with its hieroglyphic and cabalistic signs, took long to print. He announces in the letter to Cecil[1] a great bargain he has picked up, a work, "for which many a learned man hath long sought and dayley yet doth seek," upon cipher writing, viz. *Steganographia,* by the famous Abbot Trithemius of Würzburg. It is the earliest elaborate treatise upon shorthand and cipher, a subject in which Cecil was particularly interested. It was then in manuscript (first printed, Frankfort, 1606). Dee continues that he knows his correspondent will be well acquainted with the name of the book, for the author mentions it in his *Epistles,* and in both the editions of his *Polygraphia.* He urges its

[1] Printed by the Philobiblon Society, *Hist. Misc.,* vol. i., 1854.

claims upon the future Lord Treasurer, already a statesman of ripe experience, in the following words: "A boke for your honor or a Prince, so meet, so nedefull and commodious, as in human knowledge none can be meeter or more behovefull. Of this boke, either as I now have yt, or hereafter shall have yt, fully wholl and perfect, (yf it pleas you to accept my present) I give unto your Honor as the most precious juell that I have yet of other mens travailes recovered."

He then goes on to beg the minister and Secretary of State to procure for him that "learned leisure (*dulcia illa ocia*) the fruit whereof my country and all the republic of letters shall justly ascribe to your wisdom and honorable zeal toward the advancement of good letters and wonderful, divine, and secret sciences." Dee had copied in ten days, "by continual labour," about half of the book: a Hungarian nobleman there has offered to finish the rest, if Dee will remain in Antwerp and direct his studies for a time.

"Of this boke the one half (with contynual labour and watch, the most part of 10 days) have I copyed oute. And now I stand at the curtesye of a nobleman of Hungary for writing furth the rest; who hath promised me leave thereto, after he shall perceyve that I may remayne by him longer (with the leave of my Prince) to pleasure him also with such pointes of science as at my handes he requireth.

"I assure you the meanes that I used to cumpas the knowledge where this man and other such are, and likewise of such book as this, as for this present I have advertisement of, have cost me all that ever I could here with honesty borrow, besydes that which (for so short a time intended) I thowght needefull to bring with me, to the value of xxlib. God knoweth my zeale to honest and true knowledg; for which my flesh, blud, and bones should make the marchandize, if the case so required."

Dee did remain in the Low Countries; he completed his *Monas Hieroglyphica*, dated its prefatory dedication to the Emperor Maximilian II., at Antwerp, January 29, 1564, and added an address to the typographer, his "singular good friend, Gulielmo Silvio," dated the following day. The book appeared in April, and he at once journeyed to Presburg, to present a copy to Maximilian. Its twenty-four theorems deal with the variations of the figure represented on our title-page, which may be roughly explained as the moon, the sun, the elements (the cross), and fire as represented by the waving line below. Dee says that many "universitie graduates of high degree, and other gentlemen, dispraised it because they understood it not," but "Her Majestie graciously defended my credit in my absence beyond the seas." On his return in June she sent for him to Court and desired him to read the book with her. Dee's account of his regal pupil is given with much quaintness. "She vouchsafed to account herself my schollar in my book . . . and said whereas I had prefixed in the forefront of the book: *Qui non intelligit aut taceat, aut discat:* if I would disclose to her the secrets of that book she would *et discere et facere.* Whereupon her Majestie had a little perusion of the same with me, and then in most heroicall and princely wise did comfort and encourage me in my studies philosophicall and mathematicall."

His escort had been required for the Marchioness of Northampton, who was returning from Antwerp to Greenwich. In return for this assistance the lady begged the Queen's favour for her cavalier. Elizabeth was always Dee's very good friend, and she made a grant to him on December 8, 1564, of the Deanery of Gloucester, then void, but other counsels prevailed, and it was soon bestowed upon some other man. No doubt the appointment would have given great offence, for the popular eye was already beginning to see in Dee no highly equipped mathematician, geographer and astronomer, but a conjuror and magician of doubtful reputation, in fact, in the current jargon, one who "had dealings with the devil." What there had been at this time to excite these suspicions beyond the fact that Dee was always ready to expound a comet or an eclipse, to cast a horoscope, or explain that the Queen would not immediately expire because a wax doll with a stiletto in its heart was found under a tree, it is hard to say. But that these rumours were extremely persistent is seen by the astrologer's defence of himself in the "very fruitfull" preface which he, as the first mathematician of the day, was asked to write to Henry Billingsley's[1] first English translation of Euclid's *Elements*,[2] in February, 1570.

[1] Afterwards Sir Henry Billingsley, Sheriff and Lord Mayor of London (1596).

[2] There is a rare copy of this folio, of John Day's printing, in the King's Library, British Museum, with a fine title-page, covered with a Blake-like drawing of the Arts and Sciences. It is in the

This preface must be reckoned as one of Dee's best achievements, although, as he says, in writing it, "he was so pinched with straightness of time that he could not pen down the matter as he would." He points out that Euclid has already appeared in Italian, German, High Dutch, French, Spanish and Portuguese dress, and now at last comes to England.

In spite of its *ex parte* nature, a study of this preface alone must convince any reader that the author was no charlatan or pretender, but a true devotee of learning, gifted with a far insight into human progress. He covers in review every art and science then known, and some "until these our daies greatly missed" (his comments on music and harmony are truly remarkable), and comes back to his own predilection—arithmetic, "which next to theologie is most divine, most pure, most ample and generall, most profound, most subtele, most commodious and most necessary." He quotes Plato to show how "it lifts the heart above the heavens by invisible lines, and by its immortal beams melteth the reflection of light incomprehensible, and so procureth joy and perfection unspeakable." Speaking of the refraction of light, he foreshadows the telescope as he describes how the captain of either foot or horsemen should employ "an astronomical staffe commodiously framed for carriage and use, and may wonderfully help himself by perspective glasses; in which I trust our posterity will prove more skilfull and expert and to greater

original binding, with corners mended, and has the following interesting inscription on a flyleaf: "J'ai acheté ce livre à Oxfor en Juillet, 1598, et ma couste 16 shelins. Saint Sauveur."

purpose than in these days can almost be credited to be possible." Then he alludes to a wonderful glass belonging to Sir William P., famous for his skill in mathematics, who will let the glass be seen. The passage seems to show that looking-glasses were not common, or that this particular one was a convex mirror.

"A man," he says, "may be curstly afraid of his own shadow, yea, so much to feare, that you being alone nere a certain glasse, and proffer with dagger or sword to foyne at the glasse, you shall suddenly be moved to give back (in maner) by reason of an image appearing in the ayre betweene you and the glasse, with like hand, sword or dagger, and with like quickness foyning at your very eye, like as you do at the glasse. Strange this is to heare of, but more mervailous to behold than these my wordes can signifie, nevertheless by demonstration opticall the order and cause thereof is certified, even so the effect is consequent."

This mirror was given to Dee not long afterwards.

From optics he passes on to mechanics, and mentions having seen at Prague mills worked by water, sawing "great and long deale bordes, no man being by." He describes accurately a diving chamber supplied with air, and sums up some of the mechanical marvels of the world :—the brazen head made by Albertus Magnus, which seemed to speak; a strange "self-moving" which he saw at St. Denis in 1551; images seen in the air by means of a perspective glass; Archimedes' sphere; the dove of Archytas; and the wheel of Vulcan, spoken of by Aristotle; and comes down to recent workmanship in Nüremberg, where an artificer let fly an insect of iron, that buzzed about the guests at table, and then returned "to his master's hand agayne as though it were weary." All these things are easily achieved, he says, by "skill, will, industry and ability duly applied to proof." "But is any honest student, or a modest Christian philosopher, to be, for such like feats, mathematically and mechanically wrought, counted and called a conjuror? Shall the folly of idiots and the mallice of the scornfull so much prevaile that he who seeketh no worldly gaine or glory at their hands, but onely of God the Threasor of heavenly wisdom and knowledge of pure veritie, shall he, I say, in the mean space, be robbed and spoiled of his honest name and fame? He that seeketh, by S. Paul's advertisement in the creatures' properties and wonderfull vertues, to find juste cause to glorifie the eternall and Almightie Creator by, shall that man be condemned as a companion of Hell-hounds and a caller and conjuror of wicked damned spirits?" Then he recounts his years of study, and asks, "Should I have fished with so large and costly a nett, and been so long time drawing, even with the helpe of Lady Philosophie and Queen Theologie, and at length have catched but a frog, nay a Devill? . . . How great is the blindness and boldness of the multitude in things above their capacitie!"

Then he refers to some who have appeared against him in print.

"O my unkind countrymen. O unnatural Countrymen, O unthankfull countrymen, O brainsicke, Rashe, spitefull and disdainfull countrymen. Why oppresse you me thus violently with your slaundering of me, contrary to veritie, and contrary to your own conscience? And I, to this hower, neither by worde, deede or thought, have bene anyway hurtfull, damageable, or injurious to you or yours! Have I so long, so dearly, so farre, so carefully, so painfully, so dangerously fought and travailed for the learning of wisedome and atteyning of vertue, and in the end am I become worse than when I began? Worse than a madman, a dangerous member in the Commonwealth and no Member of the Church of Christ? Call you this to be learned? Call you this to be a philosopher and a lover of wisdome?"

He goes on to speak of examples before his time to whom in godliness and learning he is not worthy to be compared:—"patient Socrates," Apuleius, Joannes Picus and Trithemius, Roger Bacon, "the flower of whose worthy fame can never dye nor wither," and ends by summing up the people who can conceive nothing outside the compass of their capacity as of four sorts:—"vain prattling busybodies, fond friends, imperfectly zealous, and malicious ignorant." Of these he is inclined to think the fond friends the most damaging, for they overshoot the mark and relate marvels and wonderful feats which were never done, or had any spark of likelihood to be done, in order that other men may marvel at their hap to have such a learned friend.

The eloquent irony of this passage seems equalled only by its extraordinary universality, its knowledge of human character and its high philosophic spirit. At what a cost did a seeker after scientific truths follow his calling in the sixteenth century!

CHAPTER III

MORTLAKE

"In her princely countenance I never perceived frown toward me, or discontented regard or view on me, but at all times favorable and gracious, to the joy and comfort of my true, faithful and loyal heart."—DEE, of Queen Elizabeth.

THE promised benefice did not yet come, although Dee's friends at Court were all busy on his behalf. Either now or later, he was actually mentioned as Provost of Eton, and the Queen "answered favourably." Mistress Blanche Parry and Mistress Scudamore, lady-in-waiting to Anne, Countess of Warwick, urged his claims for the Mastership of St. Cross at Winchester, which it was thought Dr. Watson would soon vacate. But all he seems to have obtained was a fresh dispensation from Matthew Parker, Archbishop of Canterbury, to enjoy the two Midland rectories for ten years.

He continued his literary work, and beside writing new manuscript treatises, bethought himself of an old one, which although printed had not received great attention. This was the *Propœdeumata Aphoristica* (London, 1558), dedicated July 20, 1558, to his old and dear friend and fellow-student at Louvain, Mercator, "my Gerard," as he affectionately calls him. In January, 1568, Dee presented a copy of a new edition, with an address to the studious and sincere philosophical reader, dated December 24, 1567, from "our museum" at Mortlake, to "Mr. Secretary Cecil, now Lord Treasurer." Two copies were given at the same time to the Earl of Pembroke, one for him to use or give away at his pleasure, the other, by Cecil's advice, to be presented by him to the Queen. Within three days, Dee heard from Pembroke that she had graciously accepted and well liked his book. This gratifying information was rendered acceptable by a gift:—"He gave me very bountifully in his owne behalf xxlib. to requite such my reverent regard of his honour."

An interview with the Queen followed on February 16, at 2 o'clock, when there was talk between them in the gallery at Westminster "of the great secret for my sake to be disclosed unto her Majesty by Nicolas Grudius, sometime one of the secretaries to the Emperor Charles V." Of this alchemical secret, no doubt concerning transmutation, Dee writes after, "What was the hinderance of the perfecting of that purpose, God best knoweth."

He was now over forty, and had a natural desire to range himself and house his library. Before 1570 he took up his abode with his mother, in a house belonging to her at Mortlake, on the river Thames. It was an old rambling place,[1] standing west of the church between it and the river. Dee added to it by degrees, purchasing small tenements adjoining, so that at length it comprised laboratories for his experiments, libraries and rooms for a busy hive of workers

[1] In a survey taken 1616, eight years after Dee's death, it is called an ancient house.

and servants. Mrs. Dee occupied a set of rooms of her own. Nothing of the old premises now remains, unless it be an ancient gateway leading from the garden towards the river. After Dee's death the house passed through an interesting phase of existence, being adapted by Sir Francis Crane for the Royal tapestry works, where, encouraged by a handsome grant of money and orders from the parsimonious James, suits of hangings of beautiful workmanship were executed under the eye of Francis Cleyne, a "limner," who was brought over from Flanders to undertake the designs. At the end of the eighteenth century, a large panelled room with red and white roses, carved and coloured, was still in existence. Early in the nineteenth century the house was used for a girls' school, kept by a Mrs. Dubois.

Here Dee took up his abode. Its nearness to London and to the favourite places of Elizabeth's residence—Greenwich, Hampton Court, Sion House, Isleworth. and Nonsuch—was at first considered a great advantage, and the journey to and from London was almost invariably made by water. The Queen desired her astrologer to be near at hand. When he fell dangerously ill at Mortlake in 1571, after a tedious journey abroad into the Duchy of Lorraine on some mysterious errand, Elizabeth sent down two of her own physicians, Doctors Atslowe and Balthorp, to attend him. Lady Sidney was also despatched with kind, and gracious, and "pithy" messages from the sovereign, and delicacies, "divers rareties," were supplied from the royal table to supplement his mother's provision for the invalid. The Queen seems to have felt a special obligation to look after him, as she had sent him on some mission of her own, which probably we shall not be far wrong in thinking connected with Dee's alchemistic experiments. Every Court in Europe at this time had astrologers and alchemists in its employ, and the Queen and Burleigh were as anxious as Dee that he should really attain the ever-elusive secret of transmutation. Dee had of course carried the Queen's passport for himself and a couple of servants, with horses, and had obtained permits through foreign ambassadors in London to travel freely through various countries.[1]

Dee was now bent on rather a strange form of public service. On October 3, 1574, he wrote a very remarkable letter[2] to Lord Burleigh of four and a half folio pages in that best printed hand of his which offers no excuse for skipping. His own paramount deserts are very naturally one of the main subjects. He has spent all his money and all his life in attaining knowledge. "Certes, by due conference with all that ever I yet met with in Europe, the poor English Bryttaine (Il favorita di vostra Excellentia) hath carried the Bell away. God Almighty have the glory." If he had only a sufficiency of two or three hundred pounds a year, he could pursue science with ease. Failing that, there is another way. Treasure trouvé is a very casual thing, and the Queen is little

[1] *Compendious Rehearsal.* Chetham Soc., pp. 11, 12.

[2] *Lansdowne MS.*, xix., fo. 81, in part printed in Strype's *Annals*, 3rd ed. 1735, vol. ii., App., p. 81, and Ellis's *Letters of Eminent Lit. Men*, Camden Soc., p. 32.

enriched thereby, in spite of her royal prerogative. No one knows this better than the Lord Treasurer. Now, if her Majesty will grant him, by Letters Patent under her hand and seal, the right for life to all treasure he can find, he promises to give Burleigh one half, and of course to render to the Queen and Commonwealth the proportion that is theirs. It is not the gold, as wealth, that appeals to this man of books and stars:—

"The value of a mine is matter for King's Treasure, but a pott of two or three hundred pounds hid in the ground, wall, or tree, is but the price of a good book, or instrument for perspective astronomy, or some feat of importance."

He has spent twenty years in considering the subject; people from all parts have consulted him about dreams, visions, attractions and "demonstrations of *sympathia et antipathia rerum;*" but it is not likely he would counsel them to proceed without permission from the State. Yet what a loss is here!

"Obscure persons, as hosiers or tanners, can, under color of seeking assays of metalls for the Saymaster, enjoy libertie to dig after dreamish demonstrations of places. May not I then, in respect of my payns, cost, and credit in matters philosophical and mathematicall, if no better or easier turn will fall to my Lot from her Majestie's hands, may not I then be thought to mean and intend good service toward the Queen and this realm, yf I will do the best I can at my own cost and charge to discover and deliver true proofe of a myne, vayn, or ore of gold or silver, in some place of her Grace's kingdom, for her Grace's only use?"

The Society of Royal Mines had been incorporated May 28, 1565, and the Queen had granted patents to Germans and others to dig for mines and ores. It was well known that the country abounded in hidden treasure. The valuables of the monasteries had been, in many cases, hastily buried before the last abbot was ejected at the dissolution. The subject had a special fascination for Dee, who was conscious of a "divining rod" power to discover the hiding places. He made a curious diagram of ten localities, in various counties, marked by crosses, near which he believed treasure to lie concealed. He ends his letter to Burleigh with a more practical and much more congenial request. He has been lately at Wigmore Castle, and has seen a quantity of parchments and papers from which he has copied accounts, obligations, acquittances. Will the Treasurer give him a letter to Mr. Harley, keeper of the records there, asking permission to examine them and report as to the contents? "My fantasy is I can get from them, at my leisure, matter for chronicle or pedigree, by way of recreation." So he ends with an apology for his long letter and is "your Lordship's most bownden John Dee."

Nothing seems to have resulted from this letter at the time; later he did receive a grant of royalties from a mine.

In 1575 Dee married. He seems to have had no time for such an event before. He was now in his forty-eighth year, and did not execute the fatal folly (which, in his Court life, he had seen many times exemplified) of committing the indiscretion first and informing the Queen after. He duly laid before her his intention, and received in return a "very gracious letter of credit for my marriage." He also had congratulatory epistles from Leicester and from Christopher Hatton.

The Queen, when out riding in Richmond Park with her lords and ladies, would sometimes pass through the East Sheen Gate, down the hill towards the river, and would stop at the house between Mortlake Church and the Thames, desiring to be shown the latest invention of her astrologer, or the newest acquisition of his library. On the afternoon of one such windy day in March, 1576, she arrived at a slightly unlucky moment, for Dee's young wife, after a year of marriage, had just died, and not four hours earlier had been carried out of the house for burial in the churchyard opposite. Hearing this, Elizabeth refused to enter, but bade Dee fetch his famous glass and explain its properties to her outside in the field. Summoning Leicester to her assistance, she alighted from her horse by the church wall, was shown the wonderful convex mirror, admired the distorted image of herself, and finally rode away amused and merry, leaving the philosopher's distress at his recent bereavement assuaged for the moment by such gracious marks of royal interest and favour. And so this wraith of Dee's first wife fades away in the courtly picture, and we do not even know her name.

He turned more than ever to literary work and followed up the scholastic books dedicated to the young King Edward VI. and the studies of astrological hieroglyphs with books of another kind. To this year of historical labours, perhaps, belongs a letter from Dee to his "loving friend," Stow, the historian. Contrary to Dee's careful practice, it is undated, save for day and month, "this 5th of December." He has evidently been the means of introducing a fellow-author in influential quarters, for he says, "My friend, Mr. Dyer, did deliver your books to the two Earls, who took them thankfully, but, as he noted, there was no reward commanded of them. What shall be hereafter, God knoweth. So could not I have done." Then he adjures Stow to "hope as well as I,"[1] and turns from considering fruits to the sources of their toil. He sends a list of the various ports, including the Cinque Ports, that have a mayor or bailey, all except Gravesend, which has a portreeve. Stow may get fuller information, "the very true plat," from Lord Cobham's secretary. He returns a manuscript of Asser's *Saxon Chronicle;* "it is not of the best and perfectest copy. I had done with it in an hour. If you have *Floriacensis Wigornensis* [the Chronicle of Florence of Worcester] I would gladly see him a little."

Stow, like Dee, was a Londoner and, within a year or two, of the same age. He had already published his *Annals of England,* which had then gone through four editions.

Dee now began to keep a diary of his doings, written in the pages and margins of three fat quarto almanacs, bound in sheepskin and clasped. Quotations have perhaps already shown that his style, his spelling, his use of words, is that we expect from a

[1] Stow's labours met with small reward in spite of being granted permission by Letters Patent to collect voluntary gratuities.

man of his wide culture and reading. He was of the new learning, though before Shakespeare and Bacon. He had also two or more distinct handwritings, a roman hand with neat printed letters, and a scribbling hand. In the former all his manuscript works and his letters are written; his diary is in the last. This diary was quite unnoticed until about 1835, when the almanacs were discovered at Oxford in the Ashmolean Library, having been acquired by Elias Ashmole, a devout believer in hermetic philosophy and collector of all alchemical writings. They were transcribed (very inaccurately) by J. O. Halliwell and printed by the Camden Society in 1842.[1]

The books contain a strange medley of borrowings and lendings, births and deaths, illnesses, lawsuits, dreams and bickerings; observations of stars, eclipses and comets, above all of the weather (for Dee was a great meteorologist), of horoscopes, experiments in alchemy and topographical notes. Here are some of the earliest entries:—

"1577. Jan. 16. The Earl of Leicester, Mr. Philip Sidney, and Mr. Dyer, etc., came to my house." This was Edward Dyer, Sidney's friend, afterwards to be dramatically associated with Dee and Kelley in their reputed discovery of the secret of making gold. "Feb. 19th. great wynde S.W., close, clowdy. March 11. My fall upon my right knucklebone

[1] For the present volume the diary has been carefully collated with the originals now in the Bodleian Library. A number of entries omitted by Halliwell appear for the first time. Many names of celebrities of the time are quite unrecognisable in the printed version.

about 9 o'clock. Wyth oyle of Hypericon in 24 hours eased above all hope. God be thanked for such his goodness to his creatures! March 12. Abrahamus Ortelius me invisit Mortlakii." This interesting visit from the great Dutch map-maker is entirely omitted in the printed diary. "May 20. I hyred the barber of Chyswick, Walter Hooper, to kepe my hedges and knots in as good order as he seed them then, and that to be done with twise cutting in the year, at the least, and he to have yearlly five shillings and meat and drink."

Then he speaks of a visitor, Alexander Simon, who comes from Persia, and has promised his "service" on his return, probably to assist with information on Eastern lore and wisdom. His friend and neighbour, William Herbert, sends him notes upon his already published *Monas.* Another work is ready for press, and he is constrained to raise money, whether for the printing or other expenses. In June he borrowed £40 from one, £20 from another, and £27 upon "the chayn of gold." On August 19, his new book is put to printing (one hundred copies) at John Day's press in Aldersgate.

This was another of those works, so pithy and so alive in their remarkable application to the future, which have fallen with their author into undeserved neglect. Dee had made suggestions about supplying officers of the army with perspective glasses as part of their equipment. Now his friendship with the Gilberts, Davis, Hawkins, Frobisher, and others of the great sea-captains, drew his attention to the sister service and the sea power of "this blessed isle of

Albion." He had spent most of the previous year (1576) in writing a series of volumes to be entitled "General and Rare Memorials pertayning to the perfect art of Navigation." The first volume, *The British Monarchy*, or *Hexameron Brytannicum*, was finished in August. It was dedicated to Christopher Hatton in some verses beginning :—

> "If privat wealth be leef and deere
> To any wight on British soyl,
> Ought public weale have any peere?
> To that is due all wealth and toyle.
>
> Whereof such lore as I of late
> Have lern'd, and for security,
> By godly means to Garde this state,
> To you I now send carefully."

The intention is better than the lines. Dee was no poet, and even a bad versifier, but he would not have been a true Elizabethan had he not on special occasions dropped into rhyme, like the rest of his peers.

The second volume, *The British Complement*, "larger in bulk than the English Bible," was written in the next four months and finished in December. It was never published; its author tells us it would cost many hundreds of pounds to print, because of the tables and figures requisite, and he must first have a "comfortable and sufficient opportunity or supply thereto." The necessary funds were never forthcoming, and the book remained in manuscript. A considerable part of it is devoted to an exposition of the "paradoxall" compass which its author had invented in 1557.

The third volume was mysterious; it was to be "utterly suppressed or delivered to Vulcan his custody." The fourth was *Famous and Rich Discoveries*, a book, he thinks, "for British Honour and Wealth, of as great godly pleasure as worldly profit and delight." It was a work of great historical research which never saw the light.

The prejudice against Dee was so strong, and he was so much misunderstood, some persons openly attributing his works to other writers, others accusing him of selfishly keeping all his knowledge to himself, many perverting his meaning through ignorance, and again one, a Dutch philosopher, publishing a treatise which was in substance a repetition of his, that he determined to withhold his name from the publication. The anonymity is not, however, very well maintained, for Dee used the flimsy device of a preface to the reader by an "unknown friend," in which all the griefs and ill usages of that "harmless and courteous gentleman," "that extraordinary studious gentleman," the author, are freely aired. Under the thin disguise, Dee's high opinion of his own merits peeps, nay stares, out. Slanders have been spread against him, a damaging letter counterfeited by Vincent Murphy, his name and fame injured; he has been called "the arch-conjurer of the whole kingdom." "Oh, a damnable sklander," he bursts out, "utterly untrue in the whole and in every worde and part thereof, as before the King of Kings will appear at the dreadful day." It is no conceit on Dee's part, with his European reputation, to say that he "had at God his most mercifull handes received a great Talent of knowledge and sciences, after long and painful and costly travails." And he goes on to say that he is both warned by God and of his own disposition to enlarge the same and to communicate it to others, but now he finds himself discouraged; he cannot "sayl against the winds eye," or pen any more treatises for his disdainful and unthankful countrymen to use or abuse, or put his name to any writing. The unknown friend has no desire to flatter the studious gentleman, but considering all his contributions to learning, he may honestly say, without arrogancy and with great modesty, that "if in the foresaid whole course of his tyme he had found a constant and assistant Christian Alexander, Brytain should not now have been destitute of a Christian Aristotle"!

But he soon gets engrossed in his subject, which is to urge the importance of establishing "a Petty Navy Royall, of three score tall ships or more, but in no case fewer," of 80 to 200 tons burden, to be thoroughly equipped and manned "as a comfort and safeguard to the Realme." He shows the security it would give to our merchants, the usefulness in "deciphering our coasts," sounding channels and harbours, observing of tides. Thousands of soldiers, he says, "will thus be hardened and well broke to the rage and disturbance of the sea, so that in time of need we shall not be forced to use all fresh-water Soldyers," but we shall have a crew of "hardy sea-soldyers" ready to hand. This is interesting as showing that the word "sailor" was not yet in use. Then he touches on the question of unemployment:

"hundreds of lusty handsome men will this way be well occupied and have needful maintenance, which now are idle or want sustenance, or both." "These skilful sea-soldyers will be more traynable to martiall exploits, more quick-eyed and nimble [he quotes Pericles for this], than the landsmen." The Petty Navy Royall, as apart from the Grand Navy Royall, will look after pirates, will protect our valuable fisheries,[1] and generally serve us in better stead than four such forts as "Callys or Bulleyn." Coming to the financial side, he asserts that every natural born subject of this "British Empire" will willingly contribute towards this "perpetuall benevolence for sea security" the hundredth penny of his rents and revenues, the five hundredth penny of his goods valuation, for the first seven years, and for the second seven the hundred and fiftieth penny and the seven hundred and fiftieth penny of goods valuation, the same, after fourteen years, to be commuted for ever to half the original contribution. He calculated this tax would amount to £100,000 or over. If that is not sufficient, he would exact a second tax (exempting all such counties, towns, and the five ports, as have Letters Patent for such immunity) of the six

[1] He says the "Flemish" herring fishery is worth £490,000 a year, but is conducted almost entirely on our coasts, and we have to buy our own commodity of strangers. He cites the success of the Yarmouth herring fishery, founded only thirty-six years before, and gives details of the numbers of the foreign fishing fleets, Spanish, French, Flemish, and Dutch. Whether as a result of Dee's book or no, an Act was passed by James I., in 1609, a year after Dee's death, requiring foreign fishing vessels to obtain a licence to ply on our coasts.

hundredth penny of every one's goods and revenues. He would have twenty victualling ports, in every part of the kingdom, "the incredible abuses of purveyors duly reformed." He would have a stop put to carrying our gunpowder and saltpetre out of the realm. "Good God," he cries, "who knoweth not what proviso is made and kept in other Common Weales against armour carrying out of their Limits?" He speaks of many hundred pieces of ordnance lately carried out of the kingdom, so that we must make new; and deplores the wholesale destruction of our forests and timber (which is needed for ships) to keep the iron works going. Then he foreshadows the Trinity House by asking for a "Grand Pilot generall of England." He outlines a scheme of navy pensions, and in relation to the fisheries quotes sanitary statutes of Richard II. He devotes a chapter to the history of "that peaceable and provident Saxon, King Edgar," his "yearly pastime of sailing round this island in summer, guarded by his fleet of 4,000 sail," and speaks of the efficiency of Edgar's navy and the maintenance of his forts upon the coast.[1] Then he passes to his final argument. We must attain this "incredible political mystery"—the supremacy of our sea power. We must be "Lords of the Seas" in order that our "wits and travayles" may be employed at home for the enriching of the kingdom, that "our commodities (with due store reserve) may be carried abroad," and that peace and justice may reign. "*For we must keep*

[1] Hakluyt incorporated the whole of this in his *Principal Navigations* (1589), with due acknowledgment to Dee.

our own hands and hearts from doing or intending injury to any foreigner on sea or land."

Enough has been said of this book, perhaps, to show that it is a remarkable contribution towards the history of the navy and the fishing industries of Britain.[1] It may be contended that if within twelve years England could offer a crushing defeat to the greatest sea power of the world, and establish herself mistress of the seas, she was not in need of theoretical advice from a landsman on the subject, but at any rate Dee's treatise voices the ideals of the times, the hopes that inspired all true lovers of their country and of their Queen in the sixteenth century. In the thunders of the Armada they were to be realised.

[1] Dee sent it to his cousin William Aubrey, at Kew, for criticism. Aubrey returned it with a quaint letter dated June 28 (? 1576) (*Lives*, ed. Clark, i. 61): "I have herewith returned you my young cosen [*i.e.*, the book—Dee's offspring] in a bagge." He is rather sceptical about the willingness of Englishmen to contribute to the tax. He wants to know how those "whelps of yours"—the sailors—are to be occupied, "for they will never be idle, and if you don't find them employment they will find what is not to be desired." He praises the method, order, perspicuity, and elocution of the book, which he did not believe "our tongue, I mean the Englishe, to be capable of." "See, how boldie," he adds, "upon one soddeyne readinge, I poure my opinion to your bosome."

CHAPTER IV

JANE DEE

> "Content I live, this is my stay,
> I seek no more than may suffice;
> I press to bear no haughty sway,
> Look, what I lack my mind supplies:
> Lo! thus I triumph like a king,
> Content with that my mind doth bring."
>
> —SIR EDWARD DYER.

THAT October the Queen and the whole Court were thrown into a perturbed state of mind by a strange appearance in the heavens. This was the comet which the Swedish astronomer, Kepler, declared to predict the appearance in the north of Europe of a prince who should lay waste all Germany, and should vanish in 1632. It was lucky for his prognostications that Gustavus Adolphus was really born in Finland, did embroil Central Europe in the Thirty Years' War, and did die in 1632.

What the "blazing star," as they called it, foreboded, no one at Court could tell; Dee was summoned forthwith to expound the phenomenon. "Her Majestie took great pleasure to hear my opinion, for the judgment of some had unduly bred great fear and doubt in many of the Court, being men of no small account. For three diverse dayes she did use me.' Dee did not forget to urge his suit to the Queen, not so much this time for preferment but for protection.

"Her Majestie promised unto me great security against any of her kingdom that would by reason of any my rare studies and philosophical exercises unduly seek my overthrow. Whereupon I again to her Majestie made a very faithful and inviolable promise of great importance. The first part whereof, God is my witness I have truely and sincerely performed; tho' it be not yet evident, how truely, or of what incredible value. The second part, by God his great mercies and helps, may in due time be performed, if my plat for the meanes be not misused or defaced."

Nearly two years passed before Dee married his second wife, Jane Fromond, of East Cheam, Surrey. She was a lady-in-waiting at the Court to Lady Howard of Effingham, wife of the Lord Admiral (Charles Howard) who was afterwards in command of the fleet victorious against the "invincible" Spanish Armada. Lady Howard proved a true friend both to Jane and her elderly but learned husband throughout the rest of her life.

He paid a long visit to the Court at Windsor a couple of months before the marriage, staying there from November 22 to December 1, 1577, and records interviews with the Queen on various days, and with "Mr. Secretary Walsingham." It may be presumed that the marriage was then arranged, for without the Queen's consent it could never have taken place. Just before leaving, he had a conversation with Sir Christopher Hatton, the newly-made knight of that day (December 1).

The marriage took place on February 5, 1578, at one o'clock, as the bridegroom tells in his diary, but at what church he omits to say. Perhaps it took place in a Royal Chapel at Court. The young bride was twenty-two. She was a clever, well-born woman, hasty and quick-tempered, but of a steadfast and thorough faithfulness. It was no easy task to be the wife of a brilliant and erudite mathematician nearly thirty years her senior, but to the end of her days Jane proved herself a true and fitting helpmate, a most careful and devoted mother to her eight children. Little could she have foreseen at this bridal hour into what strange paths the coming years would lead her. Dee's devotion to his Jane, his growing respect for her force of character, is faithfully reflected in his diary, where every detail of her doings and her health is studiously entered.

Before the end of the year, he had to leave home and undertake a sudden journey abroad at the command of the Queen's ministers. Elizabeth, in spite of an iron constitution, was ill and distracted with toothache and rheumatic pains. She had come to Richmond from Greenwich on September 25, and the next day the fine weather broke up. "The first rayn that came for many a day," says Dee, "all pasture about us was withered. Rayn in afternone like Aprile showres." A week or two after this he was summoned to Hampton Court, and had a conference of two hours with the Queen, from nine to eleven in the morning. Dr. Bayly, the Queen's physician, came to Mortlake on October 16 to consult with him, for his profound hermetic studies gave him all the prestige of a super-doctor. On the 22nd Jane (Dee still writes of her as "Jane Fromonds," probably to distinguish her from his mother, Jane Dee) went to Hampton Court. She found the Queen no better, in fact a worse fit of pain than ever occurred on the 25th, lasting from nine in the evening till after midnight. On the 28th, Leicester and Walsingham decided to send Dee abroad to consult with some foreign physician about the malady. He was given his instructions at nine o'clock on November 4th; on the 7th he reached Gravesend, and sailed from Lee on the 9th. By three o'clock on the 14th, he was in Hamburg; in Berlin on December 6; and on the 11th at Frankfort-upon-Oder. The entry on the 15th, "newes of Turnifer's comming, 8 o'clock, by a speciall messenger," looks as if the object of his journey was attained. There are no more details of the business.

The diary is resumed in March, 1579, with some trivial entries about his showing Mr. John Lewis and his son, the physician, how to draw aromatical oils, and a note of his cat getting a young fledgling sparrow that 'had never had but one—the right—wing, naturally."

Dee's mother surrendered to him on June 15, 1579, the house and lands at Mortlake, with reversion to his wife Jane, and to his heirs and assigns after him, for ever. The document was delivered to him by a surveyor from Wimbledon (in which parish Mortlake was included) under the tree by the church. The fine for the surrender—twenty shillings—was paid to the Queen, as Lady of the Manor, on October 31.

A month later, on his fifty-second birthday, July 13, 1579, Dee's eldest son, Arthur, was born. The event was coincident with another, for that same night, at ten o'clock, Jane's father, Mr. Fromond (Dee always adds an "s" to the name), was seized with a fit and rendered speechless; he died on Tuesday, the 14th, at four in the morning. Arthur was christened at three o'clock on the 16th; Edward Dyer and "Mr. Doctor Lewis, judge of the Admiralty," were his godfathers; his godmother was one of Dee's Welsh relations, "my cosen, Mistress Blanche Parry, of the Queen's Privy Chamber." She was represented by another cousin, Mistress Aubrey, from Kew. "August 9. Jane Dee churched," is almost the next thing recorded.

Dyer was already a person in considerable favour with the Queen. He was Sidney's great friend, and after the poet's death on the field of Zutphen, was legatee of half his books. Dyer was no mean poet himself, even among his greater compeers. He is the author of those immortal verses on "Contentment," beginning "My mind to me a kingdom is," which were set to music in 1588 by William Byrd. We shall meet him again in these pages.

Dee of course knew all about Elizabeth's long flirtation with the King of France's brother, Duc d'Alençon, and her diplomatic holding off from the match. He notes Mr. Stafford's arrival as an emissary from "Monsieur" on February 16, 1580, and his return in June. On August 16, "Monsieur cam secretly to the Court from Calais." In ten days he mentions the departure of "Monsieur." The Queen kept a very tender spot in her heart for this ugly little deformed suitor, and Dee has a remarkable note of a call from her at Mortlake as she returned from Walsingham s on February 11, 1583: "Her Majesty axed me obscurely of Monsieur's state I said he was βιοθανατος" (dead-alive).

Pupils now began to resort to Dee. "John Elmeston, student of Oxford, cam to me for dialling." "Mr. Lock brought Benjamin his sonne to me: his eldest sonne also, called Zacharie, cam then with him." This was Michael Lock, the traveller. Zachary was the eldest of Lock's fifteen children; Benjamin afterwards wrote on alchemy—*A Picklock for Ripley's Castle.*

It was a stormy October, of continuous rains and floods for three or four days and nights, and a "raging wynde at west and southerly." Six persons were drowned in the Kew ferry boat, "by reason of the vehement and high waters overwhelming the boat uppon the roap, by the negligens of the ferryman set there to help." Mrs. Dee had a strange dream that "one cam to her and touched her, saying, 'Mistress Dee, you are conceived of child, whose name must be Zacharias; be of good chere, he sal do well, as this doth.'" This, meaning Arthur, had a sharp illness soon after, however, and when the next child arrived, in two years' time, it chanced to be a girl, who was named Katherine. So the dream went by contraries after all. Arthur was weaned in August, and his nurse discharged, with her wages, ten shillings, for the quarter ending at Michaelmas, paid in full. Dee is an exact accountant as well as diarist, and enters every payment with precise care.

The Queen came riding down from Richmond in her coach, to see what her astrologer was doing, on September 17, 1580, and put the household in a flutter. She took

"The higher way of Mortlake field, and when she came right against the church, she turned down toward my house. And when she was against my garden in the field, her Majestie stayed there a good while, and then came into the field at the great gate of the field, where her Majestie espied me at my door, making reverent and dutiful obeysance unto her; and with her hand, her Majestie beckoned for me to come to her, and I came to her coach side; her Majesty then very speedily pulled off her glove and gave me her hand to kiss; and to be short, her Majestie willed me to resort oftener to her Court, and by some of her Privy Chamber to give her to weete when I am there."

One can picture the gorgeously dressed and pearl-bedecked Queen, her auburn hair glistening in the sun, beckoning majestically to her astrologer, bidding him attend and swell her troops of courtiers and admirers, demanding imperiously to be let know when he came, and to be kept informed of all he did. Dee was a handsome man, tall and slender; he wore a beard, pointed and rather long. Among the crowd of personable courtiers in their rich and most becoming suits, he would be no inconspicuous figure.

It was perhaps the publication of the first volume of the "General and Rare Memorials pertayning to the art of perfect Navigation" that brought Dee into intimate relations with the navigators of the time. Or it may have been his intimacy with them that suggested the work. The *Hexameron* appeared in September, 1577, and in November the diarist first records a visit from one of them: "Sir Umfrey Gilbert cam to me at Mortlake." Gilbert was then living at Limehouse, engaged in writing discourses on naval strategy and discovery. A few months later,

Dee mentions a suggestion he gave to Richard Hakluyt, the author of the fascinating histories of the voyages: "I told Mr. Daniel Rogers, Mr. Hakluyt of the Middle Temple being by, that Kyng Arthur and King Maty, both of them, did conquer Gelindia, lately called Friseland, which he so noted presently in his written copy of Monumethensis, for he had no printed book thereof."[1] On August 5, one of Gilbert's company, "Mr. Reynolds of Bridewell, tok his leave of me as he passed toward Dartmouth to go with Sir Umfrey Gilbert toward Hochelaga."[2] The expedition sailed from Dartmouth on September 23, Sir Humphrey having obtained his long-coveted charter to plant a colony in the New World in June. All his money was sunk in this unfortunate expedition, which only met disaster at the hands of a Spanish fleet. Undaunted, however, Sir Humphrey set to work to collect more funds and information to pursue his end. With the first Dee could not help him much; with the last he believed he could, and in return he exacted a stake in the results: "1580, Aug. 28th. my dealing with Sir Humfrey Gilbert for his graunt of discovery. Sept. 10th. Sir Humfrey Gilbert graunted me my request to him made by letter, for the royalties of discovery all to the north above the parallell of the 50 degree of latitude, in the presence of Stoner, Sir John Gilbert his servant or reteiner; and thereupon took me by the hand with

[1] Geoffrey of Monmouth, *Historia Britonum* (c. 1147). Hakluyt (now about twenty-six years old) also says he had only a manuscript copy.

[2] The country bordering the St. Lawrence and the site of the present Montreal was so called.

faithful promises, in his lodging of Cooke's house in Wichcross Streete, where we dyned, onely us three together, being Satterday."

It was more than two years before Gilbert succeeded in getting enough other persons to embark their capital in his project, and then he set out on his final voyage, the second to Newfoundland (the first having been assisted by Raleigh, his half-brother, in 1578). We all know the end, how, after he had planted "his raw colony of lazy landsmen, prison birds and sailors," he set out in his little vessel, *The Squirrel*, to explore the coast and sandbanks between Cape Breton Island and Newfoundland, and then headed for England. In a storm off the Azores, the little ship foundered and was lost, its captain's last words being, "We are as near Heaven by sea as by land."

With another brother, Adrian Gilbert, Dee had much closer relations, as we shall shortly see. This younger half-brother of Sir Walter Raleigh was reputed "a great chemist in those days," which of course meant something of an alchemist. He is associated in one's mind with "Sidney's sister, Pembroke's mother," that accomplished and beautiful inspirer of the most exquisite epitaph ever penned, for he was one of the "ingenious and learned men" who filled her house at Wilton "so that it was like a college." The Countess of Pembroke spent a great deal yearly in the study of alchemy, and kept Adrian as a laborant for a time.[1] He is described as a buffoon who cared not what he said to man or woman of any quality. Bringing John Davis, another

[1] Aubrey, *Lives*, ed. Clark, vol. i., 311.

of the breezy Devon sea captains, Adrian came to Mortlake to effect a reconciliation after some uncomfortable passages caused, as they found, by dishonest dealings on the part of William Emery, whom they now exposed. "John Davis say'd that he might curse the tyme that ever he knew Emery, and so much followed his wicked counsayle and advyse. So just is God!" Here again we suspect Dee's reputation for "magic" had been the trouble.

With the discovery of so many new coasts and islands across in the Western seas, the Queen was anxious to know what right she had to call them hers, and what earlier navigators had sailed to them before. After Frobisher's three voyages in search of the North-West Passage, she sent for the author of the *Hexameron* and bade him set forth her title to Greenland, Estoteland (Newfoundland) and Friseland.[1] This document he calls "Her Majestie's title Royal to many foreign countreys, kingdomes and provinces: in twelve vellum skins of parchment, fair written for her Majestie's use and by her Majestie's commandment—Anno 1578." Either he prepared another, or did not present this to the Queen for two years.

1580.—"On Monday Oct. 3, at 11 of the clock before none, I delivered my two Rolls of the Queene's Majestie's title unto herself in the garden at Richmond, who appointed after dynner to heare furder of the matter. Therfore betweene one and two afternone, I was sent for into her highness Pryvy Chamber, where the Lord Threasurer allso was, who having the matter slightly then in consultation, did

[1] An imaginary island which long puzzled the navigators, really the southern extremity of Greenland.

seme to doubt much that I had or could make the argument probable for her highnes' title so as I pretended. Wheruppon I was to declare to his honor more playnely, and at his leyser, what I had sayd and could say therein, which I did on Tuesday and Wensday following, at his chamber, where he used me very honorably on his behalf."

The next day Dee fancied that Burleigh slighted him. He called to see him, and was not admitted; he stood in the ante-chamber when the great man came out, but the Lord Treasurer swept by and "did not or would not speak to me." Probably he was pondering deeply on important matters of state. Dee's hopes of preferment fell to the ground, and he was persuaded that "some new grief was conceyved." Dee was ambitious; he was not yet surfeited with fame; of wealth he had none, hardly even a competency; he was vain, and he knew that he had gifts which few of his countrymen could rival or even understand; and he was no longer young. Such advantages as he could attain must be secured quickly, if they were to be enjoyed at all.

"On the 10th, at four o'clock in the morning my mother Jane Dee dyed at Mortlake; she made a godlye ende: God be praysed therfore! She was 77 yere old."

News of this event quickly travelled to the Court at Richmond, and the Queen determined to signalise her favour to Dee and her gratification at Burleigh's report of his geographical labours, which reached her on the same day as the news of his loss, by a personal visit of condolence.

"Oct. 10th. The Quene's Majestie, to my great cumfort (hora quinta), cam with her trayn from the court, and at my dore graciously calling me to her, on horsbak, exhorted me briefly to take my mother's death patiently, and withall told me that the Lord Threasurer had greatly commended my doings for her title, which he had to examyn, which title in two rolls he had brought home two hours before; and delivered to Mr. Hudson for me to receive at my coming from my mother's burial at church. Her Majestie remembered allso how at my wive's death, it was her fortune likewise to call uppon me."

So the fancied slight was nothing. The Queen's second remarkably-timed visit was followed up by a haunch of venison from my Lord Treasurer, and an atmosphere of satisfaction reigned. One of the rolls of which Dee writes is still in existence. It has on one side of the parchment a large map of "Atlantis," or America, drawn with the skill of a practised cartographer. At the top is his name, "Joannes Dee," and the date, "Anno 1580."[1] Among his papers is a smaller map, upon which large tracts in the Polar regions are marked "Infinite yse." The other side of the roll is devoted to proving the Queen's title to lands she would never see or hear of, under the four following heads: "1. The Clayme in Particular. 2. The Reason of the Clayme. 3. The Credit of the Reason. 4. The value of that Credit by Force of Law."

Dee was also busied this summer attending at the Muscovy House and writing instructions and drawing a chart for the two captains, Charles Jackson and

[1] Reproduced in Hakluyt's *Principal Navigations*, Glasgow ed. (1904), vol. viii.

Arthur Pett, for their North-East voyage to "Cathay," or China.[1]

He had perhaps joined the Company of the Merchant Venturers, for in March, 1579, he had signed a letter with Sir Thomas Gresham, Martin Frobisher (as every one knows, he was knighted in the thick of the Armada fight), and others, to the Council of State, desiring that those Adventurers who have not paid shall be admonished to send in contributions without delay.[2] Another very interesting remark tells how "Young Mr. Hawkins, who had byn with Sir Francis Drake, came to me to Mortlake, in June, 1581; also Hugh Smith, who had just returned from the Straits of Magellan." In November, Dee is observing "the blasing star," or comet, of which, with its long tail, he makes a drawing on the margin of his diary. By the 22nd it had disappeared: "Although it were a cler night, I could see it no more."

On June 7, 1581, at half-past seven in the morning, Dee's second child and eldest daughter, Katherine, was born. She was christened on the 10th, her sponsors being Lady Katherine Crofts, wife of Sir James Crofts, Controller of the Queen's Household; Mistress Mary Scudamore, of the Privy Chamber, the Queen's cousin; and Mr. Packington, also a court gentleman. The infant was put out to nurse, first at Barnes with Nurse Maspely, then transferred to Goodwife Bennett. On August 11

"Katherine Dee was shifted to nurse Garret at

1 Reproduced in Hakluyt's *Principal Navigations*, Glasgow ed. (1904), vol. iii., 262.

2 *Cal. State Pap. Dom.*, 1547—1580, p. 621.

Petersham, on Fryday, the next day after St. Lawrence day, being the 11th day of the month. My wife went on foot with her, and Ellen Cole, my mayd, George and Benjamin, in very great showers of rain."

Nevertheless the little Katherine seemed to flourish, and there are entries of monthly payments of six shillings to her nurse, with allowance for candles and soap, up to August 8 of the following year, when "Kate is sickly," and on the 20th is reported as "still diseased." Four or five days after, she was taken from nurse Garret, of Petersham, and weaned at home. The mother had several times been over to see the child, sometimes on foot, attended by George or Benjamin, the servants, and once by water with "Mistress Lee in Robyn Jackes bote." The children seemed in trouble at this time, for about seven weeks before Arthur "fell from the top of the Watergate Stayres, down to the fote from the top, and cut his forhed on the right eyebrow." This was at the old landing-place at Mortlake. Their childish ailments are always most carefully recorded in the diary, even when the cause is a box on the ears—probably well earned—from their quick-tempered mother. Jane's friends Mr. and Mrs. Scudamore, and their daughter, and the Queen's dwarf, Mrs. Tomasin, all came for a night to Mortlake. Jane went back with Mistress Scudamore to the Court at Oatlands. A number of other visitors are named, including "Mr. Fosker of the wardrobe."

CHAPTER V

THE SEARCH FOR A MEDIUM

"Truth is within ourselves; it takes no rise
From outward things, whate'er you may believe
There is an inmost centre in us all
Where truth abides in fulness; and around
Wall upon wall, the gross flesh hems it in,
This perfect clear perception, which is truth.
A baffling and perverting carnal mesh
Binds it and makes all error; and to KNOW
Rather consists in opening out a way
Whence the imprisoned splendour may escape
Than in effecting entry for a light
Supposed to be without."

—BROWNING, *Paracelsus.*

DEE had always, working with and under him, a number of young students and assistants, who were admitted more or less to his inner counsels. If they proved apt and diligent, he would reward them with promises of alchemical secrets, "whereby they might honestly live"; once he promised £100, "to be paid as soon as of my own clere hability, I myght spare so much." This was a very safe proviso. Generous as he was, lavish to a fault, money never stuck near him, nor was it of the least value in his eyes, except as a means of advancing science and enriching others.

Naturally, jealousies arose among the assistants. They would suddenly depart from his service, and spread ignorant and perverted reports of his experiments. Roger Cook, who had been with his master fourteen years, took umbrage "on finding himself barred from vew of my philosophical dealing with Mr. Henrick." He had imagined himself the chosen confidant, for to him Dee had revealed, December 28, 1579, what he considered a great alchemical secret "of the action of the elixir of salt, one upon a hundred." Roger was now twenty-eight, "of a melancholik nature, and had been pycking and devising occasions of just cause to depart on the sudden," for he was jealous of a newer apprentice. "On September 7th, 1581, Roger went for alltogether from me." But it was not "alltogether," for Roger returned when Dee was old and infirm and poor, and remained serving him almost to the end. There was always something patriarchal in Dee's care for the members of his large household, evidenced abundantly in his diary. No doubt their loyalty to him was often severely tried by harsh and cruel outside rumours, but as they knew and loved his real nature they only drew closer towards him.

A new phase of his character is now forced upon us. He has appeared hitherto as the man of learning, astronomer and mathematician, a brilliant lecturer and demonstrator, diligent in probing the chemical and alchemical secrets of which his vast reading, his foreign correspondence, and his unique library gave him cognisance. Interested in geographical discovery and history, a bibliographical and mathematical writer, his genuine contributions to science had been considerable. He had written upon navigation and history, logic, travel, geometry, astrology, heraldry, genealogy, and many other subjects. He had essayed to found a National Library, and was contemplating a great work upon the reformation of the Calendar. But these purely legitimate efforts of his genius were discounted in the eyes of his contemporaries by the absurd suspicions with which his name had been associated ever since his college days. After his arrest and trial by Bonner, he never really succeeded in shaking off this savour of something magical. The popular idea of Dee in league with evil powers was, of course, the natural result of ignorance and dull understanding. To a public reared in superstition, untrained in reasoning, unacquainted with the simple laws of gravitation, the power to raise heavy bodies in the air at will, to see pictures in a simple crystal globe, or converse with projections of the air, to forecast a man's life by geometric or planetary calculations, and to discern the influence of one chemical or mineral substance upon another, seemed diabolically clever and quite beyond human agency. Even to study Nature and her secrets was to lay oneself open to the suspicion of being a magician. We must remember that in the early years of Queen Elizabeth's reign it was thought necessary to pass an Act of Parliament decreeing that all who practised sorcery causing death should suffer death; if only injury was caused, imprisonment and the pillory should be the punishment. Any conjuration of an evil spirit was to be punished by death as a felon, without benefit of clergy or sanctuary. Any discovery of hidden treasure by magical means was punishable by death for a second offence.

But if "magic" was tottering on its throne, the reign of alchemy was still uncontested. Belief in it was universal, its great votaries in the past were of all nations. St. Dunstan of Glastonbury, Roger Bacon, Raymond Lully, Canon George Ripley of Bridlington, Albertus Magnus, Cornelius Agrippa, Arnold de Villa Nova and Paracelsus, all their writings, and hundreds of others, Dee had in his library and constantly upon his tongue. Alchemy was not only a science, it was a religion and a romance. It was even then enduring the birth-throes and sickly infancy of modern chemistry, and the alchemists' long search for the secret of making gold has been called one of its crises. Long after this it was still an article of faith, that such a man as Robert Boyle did not deny. We cannot forget that even that great chemist, Sir Humphry Davy, reverenced the possibility, and refused to say that the alchemist's belief in the power to make gold was erroneous. How unlike Dante's keen irony of the dark and groping men who seek for "peltro," or tin whitened with mercury. But alchemy was bursting with many other secrets beyond the manufacture of gold. The spiritual element abounding in all minerals, and the symbolism underlying every actual substance, were deeply imbedded in it. It was a science of ideals. It ever led its followers on to scale illimitable heights of knowledge, for in order to surpass all material and rational nature, and attain the crowning end, did not God delegate His own powers to the sage? So the art of healing was thought the noblest, the most Godlike task, and no means of attaining hermetic wisdom were untried. The psychical world became every bit as real to these religious mystics as the physical and rational, which they understood so vaguely. Even the strange shapes which escaped from the retorts of the old alchemists were known to them as "souls." Their successors called them spirits. Paracelsus named them as mercury, and it was left to his pupil, Van Helmont, the true founder of all modern chemistry, to give the name of gas.

It is easy to see how Dee, the astrologer, grew into close touch with those psychic phenomena which, though they have become extremely familiar to us, as yet continue to baffle our most scientific researches. When he first became conscious of his psychic powers, and how far he himself was mediumistic, is harder to discern. It is on May 25, 1581, that he makes in his diary the momentous entry:—"I had sight in Chrystallo offered me, and I saw." We may take it that he "saw" through a medium, for he never afterwards seems to have been able to skry without one. Perhaps his first crystal had then been given him, although, as we have seen, he already owned several curious mirrors, one said to be of Mexican obsidian such as was used for toilet purposes by that ancient race. He had made a study of optics, and in his catalogue of the manuscripts of his library are many famous writings on the spectrum, perspective and burning glasses, etc. Then came the trouble with Roger, "his incredible doggedness and ungratefulness against me to my face, almost ready to lay violent hands on me."[1] Dee hears strange rappings and knockings in his chamber. A gentleman came from Lewisham to consult him about a dream many times repeated. Dee prays with him, and "his dream is confirmed and better instruction given." A mysterious fire breaks out for the second time in "the maydens" chamber at night. The knocking is heard again, this time accompanied with a voice repeated ten times. No words apparently, but a sound like "the schrich of an owl, but more longly drawn and more softly, as it were in my chamber." He has a strange "dream of being naked and my skyn all over wrought with work like some kinde of tuft mockado, with crosses blew and red; and on my left arm, abowt the arm in a wreath, these words I read:—'Sine me nihil potestis facere.' And another the same night of Mr. Secretary Walsingham, Mr. Candish and myself." Then he was ten days from home, at "Snedgreene, with John Browne, to hear and see the manner of the doings." Evidently some remarkable manifestation. He was becoming more interested in psychic problems, but he was not able to proceed without a medium, and the right one had not yet appeared.

Meanwhile, he fills his diary with all manner of interesting news. Vincent Murphy, the "cosener" who had defamed him, and against whom in September, 1580, he had instituted a troublesome law-suit, was condemned by a jury at the Guildhall to pay

[1] This entry and many other similar ones are written in Greek characters, but the words are English. It was a natural precaution of the diarist, whose house was the abode of many servants.

£100 damages. "With much adoe, I had judgment against him." Five or six months later, he agreed with Mr. Godolphin to release the cosener. Jean Bodin, the famous French writer on witches, and publicist, had come to England with "Monsieur," and Dee was introduced to him by Castelnau, the French ambassador, in the "Chamber of Presence at Westminster." Letters came from Doctor Andreas Hess, the occult philosopher, sent through Dee's friend, Richard Hesketh, agent at Antwerp. There are also letters from Rome. John Leonard Haller, of Hallerstein by Worms, came to him to say he had received instructions for his journey into "Quinsay [or Northern China], which jorney I moved him unto, and instructed him plentifully for observing the variation of the compass in all places as he passed." He notes, as if it were a common occurrence, a "fowl falling out" between two earls at Court, Leicester and Sussex [the Lord Chamberlain], tells how they "called each other traytor, wheruppon both were commanded to keepe to theyre chambers at Greenwich, wher the Court was." It sounds like a schoolboys' quarrel, but the royal schoolmistress would have them both know that they were in disgrace for a time. In July, there was an eclipse of the moon, but it was "clowdy, so as I could not perceyve it." In August, about half-past eight on the night of the 26th, "a strange Meteore in forme of a white clowde crossing galaxium, lay north and sowth over our zenith. This clowde was at length from the S. E. to the S. W., sharp at both ends, and in the West it was forked for a while. It was about sixty degrees high, it lasted an howr, all the skye clere abowt and fayr star-shyne."

Dee made a journey into Huntingdonshire, by St. Neots, to Mr. Hickman's at Shugborough, in the county of Warwick. Young Bartholomew Hickman was afterwards to become the companion and servant of his old age, and manifested some slight mediumistic powers. On the way home, a month or two later, Dee rode into Sussex to Chailey, probably to the glass works there. The Queen and "Monsieur" were at Whitehall.

A pretty little scene was enacted at Mortlake at the New Year, when "Arthur Dee and Mary Herbert, they being but 3 yere old, the eldest of them, did mak as it were a shew of childish marriage, of calling each other husband and wife." Then Dee essays a harmless little play upon words. "The first day Mary Herbert cam to her father's house at Mortlake, the second day she came to her father's house at East Shene." Mrs. Dee went the same day to see the baby Katherine at Nurse Garret's, and Mistress Herbert went with her. So the two families were in great unity.

Sir George Peckham, who sailed with Sir Humphrey Gilbert, came to consult Dee about exploration in North America, and promised a share in his patent of the new lands. He also sent down his sea-master, Mr. Clement, and another gentleman, Mr. Ingram, to see the mathematician. For Sir John Killigrew, Dee devised "a way of protestation to save him harmless for compounding for the Spaniard who was robbed: he promised me fish against Lent." Haller came again to get instructions how to transfer his money to Nüremberg, and to get letters of introduction to Constantinople. By him, Dee sent letters to correspondents in Venice, where the German explorer was to winter.

Mr. Newbury, who had been in India, came early in the New Year. Dee recounts how the stage in that well-known old London place of amusement, the Paris Garden, on Bankside, Southwark, fell down suddenly while it was crammed with people beholding the bear-baiting. "Many people were killed thereby, more hurt, and all amazed. The godly expound it as a due plague of God for the wickedness there used, and the Sabbath day so profanely spent." Sunday was the great day for the bear-fights.

"1583.—Jan. 23. Mr. Secretarie Walsingham cam to my howse, where by good luk he found Mr. Awdrian Gilbert, and so talk was begonne of North-west Straights discovery.

"Jan. 24. Mr. Awdrian Gilbert and John Davis went by appointment to Mr. Secretary, to Mr. Beale his house, where only we four were secret, and we made Mr. Secretarie privie of the N. W. passage, and all charts and rutters were agreed uppon in generall.

"Feb. 3. Mr. Savile, Mr. Powil the younger, travaylors, Mr. Ottomeen his sonne cam to be acquaynted with me.

"Feb. 4. Mr. Edmunds of the Privie Chamber, Mr. Lee, Sir Harry Lee, his brother, who had byn in Moschovia, cam to be acquaynted with me.

"Feb. 11. The Queene lying at Richmond went to Mr. Secretarie Walsingham to dynner;[1] she

[1] Walsingham's house at Barn Elms is now pulled down, and its park forms part of the beautiful pleasure grounds of the Ranelagh Club.

coming by my dore gratiously called me to her, and so I went by her horse side as far as where Mr. Hudson[1] dwelt.

"Feb. 18. Lady Walsingham cam suddenly to my house very freely, and shortly after that she was gone, cam Syr Francis himself, and Mr. Dyer.

"March 6. I and Mr. Adrian Gilbert and John Davis did mete with Mr. Alderman Barnes, Mr. Townson and Mr. Yong and Mr. Hudson, about the N. W. passage.

"March 17. Mr. John Davys went to Chelsey with Mr. Adrian Gilbert to Mr. Radforths, and so, the 18th day from thence, to Devonshyre.

"April 18. The Queene went from Richmond toward Greenwich, and at her going on horsbak, being new up, she called for me by Mr. Rawly his putting her in mynde, and she sayd 'quod defertur non aufertur,' and gave me her right hand to kisse."

While these every-day events were going on and being chronicled, Dee was also occupying himself with the search for a medium. He first tried one named Barnabas Saul (he seems to have been a licensed preacher), who professed himself an occultist. Saul gives news of buried treasure—great chests of precious books hidden somewhere near Oundle in Northamptonshire, but the disappointed book-lover finds the hoard an illusion. Then Saul, who slept in a chamber over the hall at Mortlake, is visited at midnight by "a spiritual creature."

The first real *séance* that Dee records, "Actio Saulina," took place on December 21, 1581. The

[1] Thomas Hudson, of Limehouse, a traveller in Persia and Astrakhan. He had probably a country house by the river.

skryer was bidden to look into the "great crystalline globe," and a message was transmitted by the angel Annael through the percipient to the effect that many things should be declared to Dee, not by the present worker, "but by him that is assigned to the stone." After New Year's tide, on any day but the Sabbath, the stone was to be set in the sun, the brighter the day the better, and sight should be given. The sitters might "deal both kneeling and sitting." When we consider how very real to a devout person in the Middle Ages apparitions of the devil and of evil spirits were, there seems nothing at all extraordinary in Dee's belief that good spirits also might be permitted to come to his call, for purposes of good.

A month or two after this, Saul was indicted on some charge and tried in Westminster Hall, but, thanks to Mr. Serjeant Walmesley and a couple of clever lawyers, he was acquitted. There was an end of his clairvoyance, however: "he confessed he neyther herd or saw any spirituall creature any more." If the accusation against him had been that of sorcery, he was wise to risk no further appearances in Westminster Hall. He seems to have spread abroad many false reports about Dee, who reproached him bitterly when he called at Mortlake a few months later. Dee had, however, gained psychical experience by these early and tentative experiments.

The field was now open for a maturer applicant. When he arrived, he was to change the whole current of Dee's life and outlook, to become at once a helper and a stumbling-block, a servant and a master, loving as a son, treacherous as only a jealous foe. It was a strange fate that sent Edward Kelley to Dee at this moment, when everything was ripe for his appearance. And it was characteristic of the man that he was ushered into Dee's life under a feigned name.

On March 8, two days after Saul had confessed he saw and heard no more of the spirits, Dee writes in his diary, "Mr. Clerkson and his frende cam to my howse." He makes the visit very emphatic by repeating the information: "Barnabas went home abowt 2 or 3 o'clock, he lay not at my howse now; he went, I say, on Thursday, and Mr. Clerkson came." At nine o'clock the same night, there was a wonderful exhibition of the aurora in the northern and eastern heavens, which Dee describes minutely in Latin in the diary. The next day, March 9, he mentions Clerkson's friend by name as "Mr. Talbot," and shows how that individual appears to have begun ingratiating himself with his new patron by telling him what a bad man his predecessor was. Barnabas had said that Dee would mock at the new medium; Barnabas had "cosened" both Clerkson and Dee. This, Talbot professed to have been told by "a spiritual creature."

The pair proceeded at once to business. On the 10th, they sat down to gaze into "my stone in a frame given me of a friend," with very remarkable results. Information was vouchsafed that they should jointly together have knowledge of the angels, if the will of God, viz., conjunction of mind and prayer between them, be performed. They were bidden to "abuse not this excellency nor overshadow it with vanity, but stick firmly, absolutely and perfectly in the love of God for his honour, together." There were forty-nine good angels, all their names beginning with B, who were to be answerable to their call.

The first entry that Dee makes in his *Book of Mysteries* concerning Talbot is as follows :—[1]

"One Mr. Edward Talbot cam to my howse, and he being willing and desyrous to see or shew something in spirituall practise, wold have had me to have done something therein. And I truely excused myself therein: as not, in the vulgarly accownted Magik, neyther studied or exercised. But confessed myself long tyme to have byn desyrous to have help in my philosophicall studies through the cumpany and information of the blessed Angels of God. And thereuppon, I brought furth to him my stone in the frame (which was given me of a frende), and I sayd unto him that I was credibly informed that to it (after a sort) were answerable *Aliqui Angeli boni.* And also that I was once willed by a skryer to call for the good Angel Annael to appere in that stone to my owne sight. And therefore I desyred him to call him, and (if he would) Anachor and Anilos likewise, accounted good angels, for I was not prepared thereto.

"He [Talbot] settled himself to the Action, and on his knees at my desk, setting the stone before him, fell to prayer and entreaty, etc. In the mean space, I in my Oratory did pray and make motion to God

[1] *MS. Diary. Sloane,* 3188. In a note Dee says that he came to his house two days before, and tried to entrap him into owning he had dealings with wicked spirits.

and his good creatures for the furdering of this Action. And within one quarter of an hour (or less) he had sight of one in the stone."

The one to appear was Uriel, the Spirit of Light. On the 14th, the angel Michael appeared, and gave to Dee a ring with a seal. Only on two other occasions does a tangible object pass between them. Dee was overjoyed at the success of his new "speculator" or "skryer"; the sittings were daily conducted until March 21, when the medium was overcome with faintness and giddiness, and Michael, who was conversing with him, bade them rest and wait for a quarter of an hour. The next day, Talbot departed from Mortlake, being bidden by Michael to go fetch some books of Lord Monteagle's which were at Lancaster, or thereby, and which would else perish.

He returned before long, and all through April, instructions were being given at the sittings for the future revelations. Elaborate preparations were needed, and they were described in minute detail.

By April 29, a square table, "the table of practice," was complete. It was made of sweet wood, and was about two cubits high ("by two cubits I mean our usual yard"), with four legs. On its sides certain characters, as revealed, were to be written with sacred yellow oil, such as is used in churches. Each leg was to be set upon a seal of wax made in the same pattern as the larger seal, "Sigilla Æmeth," which was to be placed upon the centre of the table, this seal to be made of perfect, that is, clean purified wax, 9 inches in diameter, 27 inches or more in circumference. It was to be an inch and half a quarter of an inch thick, and upon the under-side was to be a figure as below.

It was a mystical sign, similar to those in use in the East, and also used by contemporary astrologers.

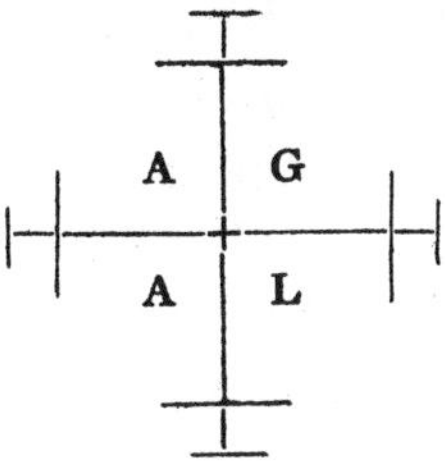

The four letters in the centre are the initials of the Hebrew words, "Thou art great for ever, O Lord," which were considered a charm in the Middle Ages.

The upper side of the seal was engraved with an elaborate figure obtained in the following manner. First, a table of forty-nine squares was drawn and filled up with the seven names of God—"names not known to the angels, neither can they be spoken or read of man. These names bring forth seven angels, the governors of the heavens next unto us. Every letter of the angels' names bringeth forth seven daughters. Every daughter bringeth forth her daughter, every daughter her daughter bringeth forth a son. Every son hath his son."[1]

The seal "was not to be looked upon without great reverence and devotion."

It is extremely curious and interesting to relate that two of these tablets of wax, "Sigillum Dei," and one of the smaller seals for the feet of the table, with a crystal globe, all formerly belonging to Dee, are still preserved in the British Museum, having come there from Sir Thomas Cotton's library, where the table of practice was also long preserved.[2]

[1] *Cf.* an article by Mr. O. M. Dalton in *Proc. Soc. Antiq.*, March 14, 1907. Casaubon, Preface to *True Relation.*

[2] The seals were seen there by Mr. Thomas Northmore in 1692 (*Hist. MSS. Commission, Report* V. p. 383).

The spirits were kind enough to say: "We have no respect of cullours," but the table was to be set upon a square of red silk as changeable (*i.e.*, shot) as may be, two yards square, and a red silk cover, with "knops or tassels" at the four corners, was to be laid over the seal, and to hang below the edge of the table. The crystal globe in its frame was then to be set upon the centre of the cover, resting on the seal with the silk between.

The skryer seated himself in "the green chair" at the table, Dee at his desk to write down the conversations. These were noted by him then and there at the time, and he is careful to particularise any remark or addition told him by the skryer afterwards. Once a spirit tells him: "There is time enough, and we may take leisure." Whereupon Dee rejoins: "I make speed to write." Sometimes Dee conversed directly with the visitant; sometimes apparently only Talbot hears and repeats to him what is said. A golden curtain was usually first seen in the stone, and occasionally there was a long pause before it was withdrawn. Once Dee writes: "He taketh the darkness and wrappeth it up, and casteth it into the middle of the earthen globe." The spirits generally appeared in the stone, but sometimes they stept down into a dazzling beam of light from it, and moved about the room. On some occasions a voice only is heard. At the close of the action, the "black cloth of silence is drawn," and they leave off for the present.

There are very few comments or general impressions of the actions left by Dee, but on one occasion he does use expressions that show his analytical powers to have been actively at work to account for the phenomena. He brought his reason to bear upon the means of communication with the unseen world in a remarkable manner. In speaking to the angels one day he said: "I do think you have no organs or Instruments apt for voyce, but are meere spirituall and nothing corporall, but have the power and property from God to insinuate your message or meaning to ear or eye [so that] man's imagination shall be that they hear and see you sensibly."

As Plotinus says, "Not everything which is in the soul is now sensible, but it arrives to us when it proceeds as far as sense."

The minute descriptions of the figures seen are of course characteristic of clairvoyant or mediumistic visions. In the case of Bobogel, the account of his "sage and grave" attire—the common dress of a serious gentleman of the time—may be quoted.

"They that now come in are jolly fellows, all trymmed after the manner of Nobilitie now-a-dayes, with gylt rapiers and curled haire, and they bragged up and downe. Bobogel standeth in a black velvet coat, and his hose, close round hose of velvet upper-stocks, over layd with gold lace. He hath a velvet hat cap with a black feather in it, with a cape on one of his shoulders; his purse hanging at his neck, and so put under his girdell. His beard long. He had pantoffolls and pynsons.[1] Seven others are apparelled like Bobogel, sagely and gravely."

[1] Pinsons, thin slippers without heels.

CHAPTER VI

EDWARD KELLEY

> "Kelley did all his feats upon
> The Devil's looking-glass, a stone
> Where, playing with him at bo-peep,
> He solv'd all problems ne'er so deep."
>
> —BUTLER, *Hudibras*.

IT is now time to inquire who this Talbot, this seer and medium, was. Where did he come from, and what was his previous history?

That he came to the Mortlake philosopher under a feigned name is perhaps not so damning an accusation as might at first sight appear. There was in his case, certainly, every reason why he should change his identity, if possible, but an *alias* in those days was so common a thing that perhaps more stress has been laid upon Kelley's than is strictly fair.

The whole of Kelley's story is so wildly and romantically coloured, it is so incredible, and so full of marvels, that it is extremely difficult to know what to believe. There is no disentangling the sober facts of his life from the romance attributed to him; indeed, there are no sober facts, as the reader will see when the accepted traditions of this extraordinary man's career are laid down.

From March 8 to November, 1582, Edward Talbot, the skryer, came and went in the Mortlake establishment, gazed in the crystal, and ingratiated himself into his employer's liking. Then he disappeared, and Edward Kelley took his place. There had been a quarrel of some kind, precursor of many others, and Dee opens his fourth *Book of Mysteries*, on November 15, "after the reconciliation with Kelley." Henceforth "E. K." is his name.

Kelley was born at Worcester, on August 1, 1555, as appears by the horoscope drawn for him by the astrologer. He began life as an apothecary's apprentice, and showed some aptitude for his calling. It has been stated that, under the name of Talbot, he studied for a short time at Oxford, but left abruptly under a cloud. A few years later, he was exposed in the pillory in Lancaster for having either forged ancient title deeds or coined base money. Both feats are accounted to him. The next incident in his career is a charge of having dug up a newly buried "caitiff's" corpse in Walton-le-Dale churchyard, Lancashire, for the purpose of questioning the dead, or "an evil spirit speaking through his organs," respecting the future of "a noble young gentleman," then a minor. After this savoury episode, Kelley is reported to have been wandering in Wales (it is suggested that he was hiding from justice), when he stumbled accidentally upon an old alchemical manuscript and two caskets or phials containing a mysterious red and white powder. Another version of this discovery is that Dee and Kelley together found the powder at Glastonbury.[1] This we may dismiss.

[1] The *Life of Kelley*, by A. E. Waite (1893), prefixed to his three alchemical treatises, is largely an imaginary story based upon

Wherever he procured it, Kelley undoubtedly owned a small quantity of some substance which he regarded as of priceless value, inasmuch as, if properly understood and manipulated, it could be used for transmuting baser metals into gold.

The reputation of the learned doctor of Mortlake, who was known all over the Continent, was a favourite at Court, and in touch with every adventure by sea or land, had of course reached Kelley. Dee's parsonage of Upton-on-Severn, near Worcester, did not trouble him much with responsibility, but it must have been on one occasional visit to it that he received from the Dean of Worcester Cathedral a Latin volume, in which he inscribed the gift thus: "Johannes Dee, 1565, Februarii 21. Wigorniæ, ex dono decani ecclesiæ magistri Beddar."

With the powder that he did not know how to use, and the alchemical manuscript which he could not decipher, and which yet might contain the invaluable secret (if indeed there is any truth in the story of his find), Kelley, the adventurer, sought out some means of introduction to the man so likely to

Lenglet du Fresnoy's (1742) and Louis Figuier's in *L'Alchemie et les Alchemistes* (Paris, 1856). He is called a skilled paleographer and alchemist, a notary in London, and a neighbour and old friend of Dee there. But Dee never lived in London after 1568, when Kelley was aged thirteen, and the astrologer has carefully described Talbot's first appearance as a stranger in 1582. Mr. Waite, whose learned writings on the mystics and alchemists are well known, has not consulted historical sources, such as Strype, nor the earliest MS. diary, and the voluminous *True Relation* printed by Casaubon fifty years after Dee's death. He invents a graceful story of his own, as others have done before him. The apocryphal account by "John Roby" in the *Romantic History of Lancashire* is even more unreliable.

help him. He had dabbled in alchemy, and came to Mortlake with something of a reputation, for Dee speaks of him as "that lerned man." It is utterly unlikely that Dee had heard anything of Kelley's exploits in the north. Such doings would scarcely penetrate the solemn recesses of the laboratory on the Thames side. So Kelley arrived, and was received in all good faith. He told Dee that the last seer, Barnabas, had "cosened" him, and seems to have at once impressed himself favourably upon the astrologer, who at the moment was without a reliable assistant. The sittings began, as we have seen, in March, and were successful immediately. In May the message comes that "none shall enter into the knowledge of these mysteries but this worker," and Kelley's position is secured.

Kelley was now about twenty-seven years old, and unmarried. He was bidden by the spirits on April 20 to take a wife, "which thing to do," he told Dee, "I have no natural inclination, neither with a safe conscience may I do it." But Michael had made him swear on his sword to follow his counsel, so he married reluctantly, not long after, Joan, or Johanna, Cooper, of Chipping Norton, who was eight years his junior, and about nineteen.

There was little love on his side apparently, but the girl seems at any rate to have essayed to do her duty as a wife. She was apparently a complete stranger to the Dees, although soon to become a part of their household. What were Jane's feelings at the thought of this invasion of her domestic peace we can only guess from an entry in Dee's diary made two days after one of these first sittings. Dee does not write much about his wife in his diary, save only entries relating to her health, and this one he has carefully erased, as if he thought some disloyalty to her was involved in it. It is, however, possible to make it out almost entirely. "1582, 6 May. Jane in a merveylous rage at 8 of the cloke at night, and all that night, and next morning till 8 of the cloke, melancholike and ch[? ided me] terribly for . . . ." Something illegible follows, and then this: "that come to me only honest and lerned men." Finally, "by Mr. Clerkson his help was [? pacified]." What can this mean save that she had taken a violent dislike to, and disapproval of, Kelley; that she mistrusted his honesty and wished they might have no more to do with him; that it was only by his friend Clerkson's help that she was at last quieted? Her woman's intuition was scarcely at fault; however kindly she came to treat her husband's medium afterwards, however charitable she showed herself, she was right in suspecting no good to come to Dee through association with Kelley.

The accounts of the actions with the spirits which took place under Kelley's control were minutely written down by Dee, as we have seen, mostly during the time of the sittings. The papers had a romantic history. The last thirteen books, which were in Sir Thomas Cotton's library, were printed by Dr. Meric Casaubon about fifty years after Dee's death, under the title of *A True and Faithful Relation of what passed for many Yeers between Dr. John Dee, a Mathematician of Great Fame in Q. Elizabeth and K. James their Reigns, and some Spirits: Tending (had it succeeded) To a General Alteration of most*

States and Kingdomes in the World . . . With a Preface confirming the reality (as to the Point of Spirits) of this Relation ; and shewing the several good Uses that a sober Christian may make of all" (folio 1659). Casaubon in his learned preface maintains stoutly that the visions were no distempered fancy, that Dee acted throughout with all sincerity, but that he was deluded. His book sold with great rapidity; it excited so much controversy, and incurred such disapproval from Owen, Pye, and the other Puritan divines, that it came near being suppressed; only the excellent demand for it prevented its confiscation, for not a copy could be found. *The True Relation* contains the record of all actions after the beginning of June, 1583. The earlier conversations, from the first with Barnabas, and Talbot's appearance on the scene, are still to be found in manuscript,[1] they having in some way parted company from those of which Cotton had possession.

These earlier papers were acquired by the antiquary, Elias Ashmole, in a rather romantic way. Ashmole had been visiting William Lilly, the astrologer, at Horsham, in August, 1672, when on his return his servant brought him a large bundle of Dee's autograph MSS. which a few days before he had received from one of the warders of the Tower. The warder called on Ashmole at the Excise Office, and offered to give them in exchange for one of Ashmole's own printed works. The Windsor Herald cheerfully agreed, and sent him a volume " fairly bound and gilt on the back," of which of his works we know not.

[1] *Sloane MSS.*, 3188.

Now for the history of the papers. Mrs. Wale, the warder's wife, had brought them with her dower from her lamented first husband, Mr. Jones, confectioner, of the Plow, Lombard Street. While courting, these young people had picked up among the "joyners in Adle Street" a large chest whose "very good lock and hinges of extraordinary neat work" took their fancy. It had belonged, said the shopman, to Mr. John Woodall, surgeon, father of Thomas Woodall, surgeon to King Charles II. and Ashmole's friend. He had bought it probably at the sale of Dee's effects in 1609, after his death. The Joneses owned the chest for twenty years without a suspicion of its contents. Then, on moving it one day, they heard a rattle inside. Jones prized open the space below the till, and discovered a large secret drawer stuffed full of papers, and a rosary of olive-wood beads with a cross, which had caused the rattle. The papers proved to be the conferences with angels from December 22, 1581, down to the time of the printed volume; the original manuscripts of the (unprinted) books entitled, "48 Claves Angelicæ," "De Heptarchia Mystica," and "Liber Scientiæ Auxiliis et Victoriæ Terrestris." We may imagine Ashmole's excitement when he found he had in his hand the earlier chapters of the very remarkable book that was still in every one's mouth, published only thirteen years before.

We may now briefly examine this remarkable and voluminous *Book of Mysteries*. In view of the fact that it is perhaps the earliest record of mediumistic transactions, the first attempt to relate consecutive psychic transmissions, in fact a sort of sixteenth century Proceedings of a Society for Psychical Research, it seems to warrant investigation at some length.

The first book (still in manuscript) opens with a Latin invocation to the Almighty, and an attribution of all wisdom and philosophy to their divine original source. It ends "O beata et super benedicta omnipotens Trinitas, concedas mihi (Joanni Dee) petitionem hanc modo tali, qui tibi maxime placebit, Amen." Then comes a table of the four angels—Michael, Gabriel, Raphael, and Uriel, their particular attributes, and their descent from Annael. A long prayer in English follows, which gives a remarkable insight into Dee's attitude of mind. Unfeigned humility towards God, a certain unconsciousness of self and of his own particular acquirements, are mingled with a calm assumption of authority and power to enter into the heart of knowledge. This was perhaps the chief characteristic of the exalted mysticism so prevalent at the time in a small section of alchemists, especially on the Continent. Dee was its representative in England, having, of course, imbibed much of it during his residence abroad. Paracelsus had been dead but forty years. His disciples everywhere were seeking three secrets which were to fulfil his teaching—the secret of transmutation, the elixir of life, and the philosophic stone, key to all wisdom. Bruno was still alive, developing his theories of God as the great unity behind the world and humanity. Copernicus was not long dead, and his new theories of the solar system were gradually becoming accepted. Galileo was still a student at Pisa, his inventions as yet slumbering in his brain.

Montaigne was writing his gentle satires on humanity. Everywhere and in every sphere new thought was beginning to stir.

Dee did not scruple to claim in his prayer gifts like those bestowed upon the prophets. He deprecates any kind of traffic with unauthorised or unreliable spirits, and acknowledges again the only Source of wisdom. But since he has so long and faithfully followed learning, he does think it of importance that he should know more. The blessed angels, for instance, could impart to him things of at least as much consequence as when the prophet told Saul, the son of Kish, where to find a lost ass or two! A spirit afterwards told him that ignorance was the nakedness wherewith he was first tormented, and "the first plague that fell unto man was the want of science."

He had reached that state of mind when he seemed unable to discern any boundary line between finite and infinite. His hope and his confidence were alike fixed on nothing less than wresting all the secrets of the universe from the abyss of knowledge, or, at any rate, as many of them as God willed. He explains how from his youth up he has prayed for pure and sound wisdom and understanding,

"such as might be brought, under the talent of my capacitie, to God's honour and glory and the benefit of his servants, my brethren and sisters. And forasmuch as for many yeres, in many places, far and nere, in many bokes and sundry languages, I have wrought and studyed, and with sundry men conferred, and with my owne reasonable discourse Laboured, whereby to fynde or get some ynkling, glimpse, or beame, of such the aforesaid radicall truthes: . . . And seeing

I have read in thy bokes and records how Enoch enjoyed thy favor and conversation, with Moses thou wast familiar, And also that to Abraham, Isaac, and Jacob, Josua, Gedeon, Esdras, Daniel, Tobias, and sundry other, the good angels were sent, by thy disposition, to instruct them, informe them, help them, yea in worldly and domesticall affairs; yea and sometimes to satisfy theyr desyres, doubts and questions of thy secrets; and furdermore, considering the Shewstone which the high priests did use by thy owne orderinge, wherein they had lighte and judgments in their great doutes, and considering allso that thou (O God) didst not refuse to instruct the prophets (then called seers), to give answers to common people of things œconomicall, as Samuel for Saul, seeking for his father's asses, being gon astray: and as other things, vulgar true predictions, whereby to wyn credit unto ther waightier affayres. And thinking within myself the lack of thy wisdom to me to be of more importance than the value of an Asse or two could be to Cis (Saul his father): And remembering what good counsayle thy apostle James giveth, saying *Si quis autem vestrum*[1] etc. And that Solomon the wise, did so, even immediately by thyselfe, atteyne to his wonderfull wisdome: Therefore, Seeing I was sufficiently taught and confirmed that this wisdome could not be come by at mans hand, or by human powre, but onely from thee (O God) mediately or immediately. And having allwayes a great regarde and care to beware of the filthy abuse of such as willingly and wittingly did invocate and consult (in divers sorte) Spirituall Creatures of the damned sort: Angels of darknes, forgers and patrons of lies and untruths; I did fly unto thee by harty prayer, full oft, and in sundry manners: sometymes cryinge unto

[1] James i. 5.

thee *Mittas Lucem tuam et veritatem, tuam quæ me ducant*, etc."

Then he goes on to say that his slight experience with two different persons has convinced him of God's wish to enlighten him through His angels. He has heard of a man accounted a good seer and skryer, a master of arts and preacher of the Word, and through his means he has seen spiritual apparitions "either in the christalline receptacle, or in open ayre." He hopes to have help from this person until "some after man or meanes are sent him from on high." But Saul—for it is Saul he means—is not devout, sincere and honest. Evil spirits have come to him, much to Dee's terror "but that thou didst pitch thy holy tent to my defence and comfort." He has quoted to Saul Roger Bacon's warning to wicked devil-callers; but the man cannot brook rebuke, and is angry at being further debarred from the mysteries "which were the only things I desired, through thy grace." He begs, most humbly and deprecatingly, for leave to note down the actions, and asks that Annael may come to his help.

Barnabas having proved so unreliable, he rejoiced at having found another skryer. The one accessory wanting, when all the table and seals were complete, was a "shewstone." Dee seems already to have owned several. He had used a crystal before this time, but a new one was desirable. One evening, towards sunset, a little child angel appears standing in the sunbeams from the western window of the study, holding in its hand a thing "most bright, most clere and glorius, of the bigness of an egg."

Michael with his fiery sword appeared and bade Dee "Go forward, take it up, and let no mortall hand touch it but thine own."

Michael tells them, too, that he and Kelley are to be joined in the holy work, united as if one man. But one is to be master, the other minister; one the hand, the other the finger. They are to be contented with their calling, for vessels are not all of one bigness, yet all can be full. Dee is reminded that all his knowledge is "more wonderful than profitable, unless thou art led to a true use of the same."

Another spirit, Medicus Dei, or Medecina, says, "Great are the purposes of him whose medecine I carry," and on one of the early March days utters some remarkable words on the precious doctrine of the universality of the Light:—

> "Your voices are but shadows of the voices that understand all things. The things you look on, because you see them not indeed, you also do name amiss. . . .
>
> "We are fully understanding. We open the eyes from the sun in the morning to the sun at night. Distance is nothing with us, unless it be the distance which separateth the wicked from His mercy. Secrets there are none, but that are buried in the shaddow of man's souls. . . . Iniquitie shall not range where the fire of his piercing judgment and election doth light."

Calvin had been dead but twenty years, but with his scheme of election and eternal reprobation Dee had no affinity. His mind was far more in harmony with the ancient hermetic teaching that medicine, healing, was the true road to all philosophy.

CHAPTER VII

THE CRYSTAL GAZERS

> "To follow knowledge like a sinking star
> Beyond the utmost bound of human thought."
>
> —TENNYSON, *Ulysses*.

IT is a curious picture to call up, that of the strangely assorted pair seated in the inner room at Mortlake, acting out this spiritual drama. Dee had asked for instructions about the room for the sittings: "May my little fartherest chamber serve, if the bed be taken down?" The table, covered with its cloth, stood in the centre upon the seals. Kelley, perhaps with the black cap he is credited with having always worn, pulled close over his cropped ears, was seated at it. Dee at his desk sat writing in the great folio book. He was now fifty-six years old; his beard was long, but perhaps not yet "as white as milk," as Aubrey describes it. He did not apparently ever see the visions himself. Once he reproachfully said, "You know I cannot see or skry." He conversed with the spirits and sometimes heard what they said; but to the eye and ear of his body they were invisible; hence his dependence upon a skryer.

The sole object of his ambition was the attainment of legitimate wisdom. When conversing with the angels, how near within his grasp it seemed! Michael's exposition seemed almost to promise it to him:—

"'Wilt thou have witt and wisdom? Here it is.'

"Michael points each time to a figure of seven squares shown within a circle of light.

"'The exaltation and government of princes is in my hand.

"'In counsayle and Nobilitie, I prevayle.

"'The Gayne and Trade of Merchandise is in my hand. Lo! here it is.

"'The Qualitie of the Earth and Waters is my knowledge, and I know them. And here it is.

"'The motion of the Ayre and those that move in it, are all known to me. Lo! here they are.

"'I signifie wisdom. In fire is my government. I was in the beginning and shall be to the end.

"'Mark these mysteries. For this knowne, the state of the whole earth is knowne, and all that is thereon. Mighty is God, yea, mighty is he who hath composed for ever. Give diligent eye. Be wise, merry and pleasant in the Lord.'"

Quite early in the actions, it was told them that a third person was necessary to the complete work. Adrian Gilbert was the first selected, and permission was given for him to be made "privie of the mysteries, but not to be a practiser."

Gilbert was making ready for a voyage to the North-West. Dee and the spirits seem to think it may be a kind of missionary enterprise, and Dee asks for (but does not actually obtain) a geographical description of the country he is going to. The answer is that Dee knows about it, as indeed he did, sufficiently well, as we have seen, to draw very good charts of North America and the Frozen Seas. An angel named Me tells him he must counsel A. G. and be his father. "Who made the sun of nothing?

Who set Nature to thrust up her shoulder amongst trees and herbs like a gentle fire? How great is his power in those in whom he kindleth a soul of understanding."

In Dee's absence in London, at the Muscovy House, on Maundy Thursday (March 28), Kelley tried to summon Medicina again, but was only visited by an "illuder." Next day Dee asks for "the veritie of his doings," and is told that darkness has presumed to put itself in place of light. Kelley will not be overthrown, but he is to *brag not.* "When I yoked your feathers together, I joined them not for a while." The illuder is made to confess deception and is consumed by fire, and Dee turns to his skryer with "Master Kelley, is your doubt of the spirit taken away?"

Dee had been requested to prepare a calculation for the reformation of the Calendar, or at any rate to give his opinion on the scheme propounded by Pope Gregory. His calculations were approved by all the English mathematicians of the time, but the Queen, advised by the bishops, did not see her way to adopt them in effect. Dee tells his angel friends how "grieved" he is that "Her Majestie will not reform the Kalendar in the best terms of veritie." He desires counsel what to do.

Easter Day passed, and the crystal gazing still went on. The sittings were often long. On April 3, Dee ventured to tell his visitor that "it will be dark soon, and our company will expect our coming down to supper. If without offence we might now leave off, it might seem good to do so." Three days after, he again offered a slight remonstrance, asking why they had not been warned of Mistress Frances Howard's coming, a gentlewoman of Her Majestie's Privy Chamber. She had caused interruption of their exercise for a full hour, or two. Was this to be forgiven her because of her great charity, and goodness in procuring the Queen's alms for many needy people?

The Queen was then at Richmond, and Dee was several times at Court. He seems to have been there to bid her adieu when she left for Greenwich on the 18th:—"At her going on horseback, being new up, she called for me, by Mr. Rawly his putting her in mynde, and she sayd, '*quod defertur non aufertur*,' and gave me her right hande to kisse."

Dee was now puzzling over some mysterious papers brought him by Kelley, whether those he is reported to have found in Wales or Glastonbury we can scarcely decide, but they seem to concern ten places in England where treasure was supposed to be hid. There is a curious drawing of them in the MS. diary: "After coming from the Court, I thought I would try to discover the cipher of the paper E. K. brought me as willed to do, found at Huets Cross, with a book of magic and alchemy, to which a spiritual creature led them." Dee was by no means the easy dupe of Kelley that he has been called. Two or three months after he first knew him he writes in his diary of his "abominable lyes"; and he here makes a very telling remark, an aside, so to speak: "Of this K., I doubt yet."

Kelley's hot, uncontrollable nature and his overbearing ways had already begun to appear. There was an outbreak at supper one night because Charles Sled had "done him an injurie in speeche at my table." Probably some story of his early career had been raked up. A voice next morning says to him appropriately: "Serve God and take hold of nettles."

The manuscript in crabbed signs puzzled the astrologer desperately, and he was unhappy at the delay. An angel tells him they are to be "rocks in faith." "While sorrow be measured thou shalt bind up thy fardell." He is not to seek to know the mysteries till the very hour he is called. "Can you bow to Nature and not honour the workman?"

A new spirit visits them, Il, "a merie creature, apparelled like a Vyce in a [morality] play. He skipped here and there." Dee asks where is his Arabic book of tables that he has lent and lost. Il says it is in Scotland and is nothing worth. Then Dee asks about the Lord Treasurer's books, for he had not seen Burleigh's library, and had all the rival collector's jealousy over his own treasures. He was never quite sure that Burleigh was his friend; there seemed always a suspicion in his mind where the Lord Treasurer was concerned. The feeling was reflected in a curious dream that he had soon after the beginning of his partnership with Kelley: "I dreamed on Saturday night that I was deade, and afterwards my bowels wer taken out. I walked and talked with divers, and among other with the Lord Thresorer, who was com to my howse to burn my bookes when I was dead. I thought he looked sourely on me." Now, Il tells him that Burleigh has no books "belonging to Soyga," and explains that name as in "the language of Paradise, before Babel's aery tower." Dee takes up a lexicon to look for the word, but Il points to another book on "the mysteries of Greek, Latin and Hebrew." Then Il becomes very practical, and says: "Your chimney will speak against you anon," and Dee remembers that he had hidden there "in a cap-case" the records of his doings with Saul and the others. Il advises Kelley to communicate to his employer the book and the powder, and all the rest of the roll. "True friends are not to hide anything each from the other."

This was perhaps the cause of the "great and eager pangs" that now took place between Dee and Kelley. The medium pretends to fear they are dealing with evil spirits. He bursts into a passion, declares he is a cumber to the house, and dwells there as in a prison. He had better be far away in the open country, where he can walk abroad, and not be troubled with slanderous tongues. He is wasting his time there, and must follow some study whereby he may live. As for these spirit mysteries, Adam and Enoch knew them before the Flood. Dee responds gravely to this tirade: He will wait God's time, and he will not believe a stone will be given them and no bread. As to Kelley's necessities, are not his own far greater? At the present moment, he owes £300, and does not know how to pay it. He has spent forty years, and travelled thousands of miles, in incredible forcing of his wit in study, to learn, or bowel out, some good thing, yet he would willingly go up and down England in a blanket, begging his bread, for a year or more, if at the end he might be sure of attaining to godly wisdom, whereby to do God service for His glory. He was resolved either willingly to leave this world, to enjoy the fountain of all wisdom, or to pass his days on earth in the enjoyment of its blessings and mysteries.

Another violent scene occurred before long; this time the mistress of the house was the one offended. Dee says: "By A[drian] G[ilbert] and Providence, E. K.'s vehement passions were pacified. He came back again to my house, and my wife was willing and quiet in mind and friendly to E. K. in word and countenance. A new pacification in all parts confirmed and all upon the confidence of God his service faithfully performed." Kelley's wife had not yet joined him at Mortlake, but he had occasional letters from her. One found him in a tender religious mood, about to "pray in his bedchamber, on a little prayer book which Mr. Adrian Gilbert had left here, and it lay on the table during the action." It was *Seven Sobbes of a Sorrowful Soul for Sinne*, in English metre, "made by Mr. William Harris." When he opened it, he found some automatic script in the end, or, as he calls it, a counterfeit of his own hand. He took it to Dee, who saw in it the work of a wicked spirit trying to shake their confidence. The next evening, both prayed against their enemy, Kelley on his knees before the green chair standing at the chimney. Uriel appeared and said temptation was requisite. "If it were not, how should men know God to be merciful?" He speaks to Kelley:—"Thou, O yongling, but old sinner, why dost thou suffer thy blindness to increase?

Why not yield thy Limbs to the service and fulfilling of an eternal veritie? Pluck up thy heart, and follow the way that leadeth to the knowledge of the end." He explains how the trouble is caused by Belmagel, "the firebrand who hath followed thy soul from the beginning."

The whole of this spring, the pair of partners had been busily engaged in preparing the various things—the table, the wax seals, the ring and lamin—required for use. Most complicated diagrams of letters and figures had also been dictated to them, and Kelley, whose mathematical training had been slight, was sometimes very exhausted. Once fire shoots out of the crystal into his eyes, and when it is taken back, he can read no more. As Dee remarks one day to a spirit, apologising for his many questions: "For my parte I could finde it in my heart to contynue whole days and nights in this manner of doing, even tyll my body should be ready to synk down for weariness before I could give over, but I feare I have caused weariness to my frends here." A journey is foretold, but first of all Kelley is to go to the places of hidden treasure, and bring earth, that it may be tested. He may be away ten days. He bought a "pretty dun mare" for the journey, of "good man Penticost," for which he paid £3 ready money in angels. A day or two after, he took boat to London to buy a saddle, bridle, and "boote-hose."

At supper the night before he started, in a clairvoyant state, he had an extraordinary prophetic sight of the execution of Mary Queen of Scots, a beautiful woman having her head cut off by a tall black man.

He also speaks of seeing the sea, covered with many ships. Uriel warns them that foreign Powers are providing ships "against the welfare of England, which shall shortly be put in practice." It is hardly necessary to remind the reader that the Queen of Scots' execution and the defeat of the Spanish Armada took place in two following years, 1587, 1588, four years after this vision.

CHAPTER VIII

MADIMI

"Therefore for spirits I am so far from denying their existence that I could easily believe that not only whole countries but particular persons have their tutelary and guardian angels. It is not a new opinion, but an old one of Pythagoras and Plato. There is no heresy in it, and if not manifestly defined in Scripture, yet it is an opinion of good and wholesome use in the course and actions of a man's life, and would serve as an hypothesis to solve many doubts whereof common philosophy affordeth no solution."
—Sir Thomas Browne, *Religio Medici.*

Dee's costly apparatus and experiments, his large establishment and generous treatment of his servants and assistants, his entertainment of great folk, were all heavy drains upon his resources. He spent lavish amounts upon books and manuscripts for his library; he contributed as able to some of the Adventurers' funds. He borrowed freely, and he had sometimes to run long bills. Beside the rent of the two livings (about £80 a year) he had no fixed income. The Queen was ever promising him benefices which either never fell vacant, or when they did, had to be bestowed elsewhere. At the time he first fell in with Kelley, he knew not where to turn for money. Almost at this very moment, however, a rich patron appeared unexpectedly on the horizon and changed Dee's outlook for several years.

On March 18, 1583, Mr. North came to Mortlake bringing a "salutation" from Albert or Adelbert

Laski, Count Palatine of Siradia, a Polish Prince then about to arrive on a visit to the Queen. He wished to make Dee's acquaintance, to see his library, and discuss magic, of which he had made a study. Laski was one of the most powerful of the Polish nobles reconverted to Catholicism. He had taken a very prominent part in the patriotic movement of a few years before in Poland, when almost every European sovereign had made a bid for the Polish crown. Elizabeth's old suitor, the Duc d'Alençon, had actually worn it a month or two before escaping in the night to his brother of France. Laski was a dashing adventurer of heroic courage, quite unscrupulous as to cost; and although he had favoured the claims of the Emperor of Austria, he had, openly at least, agreed in the people's victorious choice of Stephan Báthory. When that Transylvanian Prince had been elected King in 1576, Laski had taken a prominent part in affairs. He was popular and ambitious, not without aspiration towards the Polish crown himself. Burleigh, in writing of him to Hatton, called him "a personage of great estimation, few in the Empire of the greatest exceed him in sovereignty and power." He is described by contemporary writers as a most learned man, handsome in stature and lineaments, richly clothed, "of very comely and decent apparel," and of graceful behaviour. He wore his beard very long, not clipped close like the English courtiers.[1] He arrived in London by Harwich on May Day, and proceeded to Winchester House,

[1] Nicolas, *Life of Sir Christopher Hatton*, quoting Camden, p. 324; Darcy, *Annals of Elizabeth* (1625), Book III., p. 42.

Southwark, where he made his headquarters during his stay. There seemed some doubt about how he was to be received, whether he was actually in favour or in disgrace with King Stephan. Burleigh desired Hatton to get some Essex nobleman—Lord Rich or Lord Darcy—to meet him at Harwich with proper state, "if he is the very Count Palatine of the House of Laski." Hatton replied that he must wait to hear more from Leicester, for in his letter to the Queen the visitor has called her "the refuge of the disconsolate and afflicted," so perhaps he is out of favour after all.

Dee first saw Laski on May 13, at half-past seven in the evening, in the Earl of Leicester's apartments at the Court at Greenwich, when he was introduced by Leicester himself.

Five days after the first meeting, Laski "came to me at Mortlake with only two men. He cam at afternone and tarryed supper, and [till] after sone set." Near a month elapsed before his next visit, when he made a sort of royal progress down the Thames from Oxford to Mortlake.

"June 15 about 5 of the clok, cam the Polonian Prince, Lord Albert Lasky, down from Bissham, where he had lodged the night before, being returned from Oxford, whither he had gon of purpose to see the universitye, wher he was very honorably used and enterteyned. He had in his company Lord Russell, Sir Philip Sydney and other gentlemen: he was rowed by the Queene's men, he had the barge covered with the Queene's cloth, the Queene's trumpeters, etc. He cam of purpose to do me honor, for which God be praysed!"

The visit was repeated on the 19th, when the distinguished foreigner was hospitably entertained for the night. The Queen was then at Greenwich, but on July 30 she and her court proceeded in great splendour up the river to Sion House. She passed by Dee's door, and probably paused as usual for a greeting. Next morning Leicester rode over to Mortlake, and put the household in commotion by announcing that Laski and others would come to dine at Mortlake on the next day but one. These festivities were a great tax on the astrologer's means, and he confessed sincerely that he was "not able to prepare them a convenient dinner, unless I should sell some of my plate or some of my pewter for it. Whereupon her Majestie sent unto me very royally, within one hour after, forty angells of gold [£20] from Sion, whither her Majestie was now come from Greenwich." Leicester's secretary, Mr. Lloyd, was despatched post-haste with the gift, prompted, as Dee adds, "through the Erle his speech to the Queene." One imagines Leicester's somewhat peremptory suggestion and the Queen's impulsive acquiescence. In minor matters she was woman enough to relish being sometimes dictated to. The secretary also brought what was hardly less acceptable to Dee, viz., "Mr. Rawligh his letter unto me of her Majestie's good disposition unto me." Raleigh was then in great favour with the Queen.

In the intervals between these visits of the Prince, the spirits had been consulted about Laski's prospects. They had at once interested themselves in him, and Madimi, one of the most fascinating of these psychical projections, had vouchsafed some kind of genealogical information, connecting him with the Lacys and Richard, Duke of York. She was the first of the female angels who appeared to Dee, as it seemed in answer to his arguments reproving Trithemius, who had asserted that no good spirits ever took the shape of women. Madimi, who suddenly appeared on May 28, was "like a pretty girle of 7 or 9 years, attired in a gown of Sey, changeable green and red, with a train"; her hair was "rowled up before and hanging down very long behind." She came into the study and played by herself; "she seemed to go in and out behind my books; . . . the books seemed to give place sufficiently, one heap with the other, while she passed between them." She announced that her elder sister would come presently, and corrected Dee's pronunciation of her name. "My sister is not so short as you make her: Eseméli not Esémeli." Madimi was a very clever and accomplished little fairy. She learned Greek, Arabic, and Syrian on purpose to be useful to Dee. On June 14 Dee asked the spirit Galvah, or Finis, what she had to say about the "Polandish Lord Albertus Laski." The reply came, "Ask me these things to-morrow." But when the next day came, Kelley, the seer, "spent all that afternoon (almost) in angling, when I was very desirous to have had his company and helping hand in this action." So at the next sitting Galvah administers to Kelley a sharply pointed reproof: "You, sir, were best to hunt and fish after Verity." Dee adds that "she spake so to E. K. because he spent too much time in Fishing and Angling." Then he asked if Laski should return to Poland in August, if his relation with the Prince should bring him credit, and how should he "use himself therin to God's liking, his country's honour, and his own credit." Galvah replied oracularly: "He shall want no direction in anything he desireth." "Whom God hath armed, no man can prevaile against." Again, on June 19, Dee asked if it would be best for the Prince to take the first opportunity of going homeward.

"It shall be answered soon," replied Galvah.

"May he be present at the action?"

"Those that are of this house are not to be denied the Banquets therein."

"May I request you to cause some sensible apparition to appear to him, to comfort him and establish his minde more abundantly in the godly intent of God his service?"

"If he follow us, let him be governed by us. But whatsoever is of flesh is not of us."

"You perceive how he understandeth of the Lord Treasurer his grudge against him. And perhaps some others also are of like malicious nature. What danger may follow hereof, or encombrance?"

"The sum of his life is already appointed; one jot cannot be diminished. But he that is Almighty can augment at his pleasure. Let him rejoice in poverty, be sorry for his enemies, and do the works of justice."

Then "the cloud of invisibility"—a drop scene between the acts—came over Galvah, and she disappeared.

Next day Laski was present at the action. An angel named Jubanladec appeared, and said he was appointed the Prince's "good governour or Angel," "the keeper and defender of this man present." He bade him "look to the steps of his youth, measure the length of his body, live better and see himself inwardly." Excellent advice, which might have been continued had not a man named Tanfield, attached to the Prince, arrived suddenly at Mortlake with a message from the Court, and, contrary to all good manners, burst into the study. Laski had gone out another way through the oratory to meet him. The angel was annoyed, and prophesied rather unkindly that in five months the rash interrupter should be devoured by fishes of the sea. Was he drowned then or ever? Then the thread was resumed.

"What do ye seek after? Do ye hunt after the swiftness of the winds? Or are you imagining a form unto the clouds? Or go ye forth to hear the braying of an Asse, which passeth away with the swiftness of the air? Seek for true wisdom, for it beholdeth the highest and appeareth unto the lowest."

Then Laski's guardian angel becomes extremely practical and interesting: "Cecil hateth him [Laski] to the heart, and desireth he were gone hence. Many others do privily sting at him."

Dee endeavours to keep him to the point.

"For his return, what is your advice? Perhaps he wanteth necessary provision, and money."

"He shall be helpen, perhaps miraculously. Let him go so soon as he can conveniently."

"I say again, perhaps he wanteth money; but the Treasures of the Lord are not sent to them whom he favoureth."

"His help shall be strange. The Queen loveth him faithfully and hath fallen out with Cecil about him. Leicester flattereth him. His doings are looked into narrowly. But I do alwayes inwardly direct him. I will minister such comfort to him as shall be necessary in the midst of all his doings."

Mingled with these sayings were some prophetical utterances about Laski overcoming the Saracens and Paynims with a bloody cross shown in his hand, and about Dee's passing to his country and aiding him to establish his kingdom. Then the familiar spirit sank through the table like a spark of fire, "seeming to make haste to his charge, I mean the Lord Laski."

On Wednesday, the 26th, Laski again being present, the good angel Il appeared with a besom in his hand. The Prince's pedigree was then barely begun, but on June 29 the clever little Madimi promised to finish the book exactly as Dee would have written it. It was no matter where the book was left, she told him, locked up or lying about. "Your locks are no hindrance to us."

"You have eased my heart of a thousand pound weight," ejaculated Dee, fervently. "Now I shall have leisure to follow my sute, and to do all Mr. Gilbert's businesse."

Madimi was much too learned a scholar for Kelley, who on this same day grew very angry with her for speaking to him in Greek, of which he knew nothing, not even the alphabet. As an alternative she gave him Arabic. "Unless you speak some language which I understand, I will expresse no more of this Gibberish," he said, rudely.

Poor Dee! His skryer was a constant anxiety to him. Like every medium since known, he would sometimes apply himself and sometimes not, was often honest and yet frequently a cheat.

Dee writes:—

"My heart did throb oftentimes this day, and I thought E. K. did intend to absent himself from me, and now upon this warning, I was confirmed, and more assured that it was so. Whereupon seeing him make such haste to ride to Islington, I asked him why he so hasted to ride thither. And I said if it were to ride to Mr. Harry Lee, I would go thither also, to be acquainted with him; seeing now I had so good leisure, being eased of the book writing [through Madimi's good offices]. Then he said that one told him the other day that the Duke[1] did but flatter him, and told him other things, both against the Duke and me. I answered for the Duke and myself, and also said that if the forty pound annuity which Mr. Lee did offer him was the chief cause of his mind feeling that way (contrary to some of his former promises to me), that then I would assure him of fifty pounds yearly, and would do my best by following of my sute [with the Queen] to bring it to passe as soon as possibly I could, and thereupon did make him promise upon the Bible. Then E. K. again, upon the same Bible, did swear unto me constant friendship and never to forsake me: And moreover said that unless this had so faln out, he would have gone beyond the Seas, taking ship at Newcastle, within eight days next. And so we did plight our faith to one another, taking each other by the hands upon these points of brotherly and friendly fidelity during life, which Covenant I beseech God to turn to his honour, glorie and service, and the comfort of our brethren (his children) here on earth."

[1] Laski. They were all uncertain about his titles.

This reconciliation was not for long, in spite of the promised salary, and soon another scene occurred. On June 5 Dee writes that from nine in the morning Kelley was "in a marvellous great disquietness of mind, fury and rage," because his brother Thomas Kelley brought him word, first, that a commission was out to attach and apprehend him as a felon for coining money; second, that his wife, whom he had left at Mistress Freeman's house at Blockley, having heard from Mr. Hussey that he was a cosener, had gone home to her mother, Mrs. Cooper, at Chipping Norton. Dee is "touched with a great pang of compassion," grieved that any Christian should use such speeches and be of so revenging a mind, even more than he is distressed that his own credit shall be endangered for embracing the company of such a disorderly person, especially if he be arrested at Mortlake, "which will be no small grief and disgrace." But he generously resolves to stand by his friend. Kelley, it seems, had been met coming from Islington with his scroll, book and powder, and had been threatened to "be pulled in pieces" if he brought them to Dee. A drawing in the margin of the MS. shows the book to have had a cross on the cover, one clasp, and deep metal bands across its two sides. Presumably these were some of the treasures reported to have been found at Glastonbury.

A day or two after, June 18, Kelley again simulated great fear and distress at seeing evil spirits. He protested he would skry no more, and was so excited that he brought on himself the wise rebuke from Galvah: "He that is angry cannot see well." He seems to have wished to show Laski some reprobate spirits in Dee's study, but the older man wisely kept the crystal and the "table of communion" under his own control. It was, perhaps, partly cunning that made Kelley, although he really possessed extraordinary mediumistic powers, so sceptical. "I am Thomas Didymus," he says to the spirits. "How can ye persuade me ye are no deluders?"

Three days after this, Dee was writing letters to Adrian Gilbert, in Devonshire, when Madimi suddenly appeared to Kelley, who was seated in the green chair.

Dee said, "How is the mind of Mr. Secretary toward me? Methinketh it is alienated marvellously."

Dee had long been on neighbourly terms with Sir Francis and Lady Walsingham. If any cause existed for supposing both Burleigh's and Walsingham's attitude toward him was changed, it may have been that the Lord Treasurer, the great financier of the time, resented his constant applications for a salary from the exchequer, while Walsingham, with his intimate knowledge of foreign affairs, perhaps misdoubted this intimacy between Dee and the scheming Polish Prince. Curiously enough, it was through this very intimacy with Laski that both Burleigh and Walsingham came later to regard the alchemists in the light of a valuable national asset.

Madimi replied—

"The Lord Treasurer and he are joyned together, and they hate thee. I heard them when they both said, thou wouldst go mad shortly. Whatever they can do against thee, assure thyself of. They will shortly lay a bait for thee, but eschew them."

D.—"Lord have mercy upon me, what bait, I beseech you, and by whom?"

M.—"They have determined to search thy house, but they stay untill the Duke be gone."

D.—"What would they search it for?"

M.—"They hate the Duke, both, unto death."

Then with a sharp caution to Kelley to deal uprightly with Dee, and a protestation from him of his "faithful mind" to his master, she goes on to reveal the suspicions attached to Laski:—

M.—"Look unto the kind of people about the Duke in the manner of their diligence."

D.—"What mean you by that? His own people? Or who?"

M.—"The espies."

D.—"Which be those?"

M.—"All. There is not one true."

D.—"You mean the Englishmen."

M.—"You are very grosse if you understand not my sayings."

D.—"Lord! what is thy counsel to prevent all?"

M.—"The speech is general. The wicked shall not prevail."

D.—"But will they enter to search my house or no?"

M.—"Immediately after the Duke his going, they will."

D.—"To what intent? What do they hope to find?"

M.—"They suspect the Duke is inwardly a traitor."

Dee replies with sincerity, " They can by no means charge me, no not so much as with a traitorous thought."

M.—" Though thy thoughts be good, *they cannot comprehend the doings of the wicked.* In summe, they hate thee. Trust them not. They shall go about shortly to offer thee friendship. But be thou a worm in a heap of straw."

D.—" I pray you expound that parable."

M.—" A heap of straw being never so great, is no weight upon a worm. Notwithstanding every straw hindereth the worm's passage. See them and be not seen of them ; dost thou understand it ? "

It now seemed certain that Dee and his skryer were to embark their fortunes with Laski. Dee begs for particular instructions when they had better take ship, what shall be done with all the furniture prepared and standing in the chamber of practice ? Is it best for the Pole to resort hither oft, or to stay quiet at his house in London ?

Madimi retorts—

" Thou hast no faith. He is your friend greatly and intendeth to do much for you. He is prepared to do thee good, and thou art prepared to do him service. Those who are not faithful shall die a most miserable death, and shall drink of sleep everlasting."

A couple of days after, on July 4, Dee returning from Court, found Kelley making preparation to go away for five days, having fixed to meet some companions in Mortlake, others in Brentford. Doubtless he found all this mystical and angelic society somewhat of a bore, and was yearning for an outburst a little more to his taste. Dee, who had seen Laski in

London, knew that he intended to come down to Mortlake within a day or two, "who also," he says, "delighted in E. K. his company." So he wrote a short note in very polite Latin to the "Nobilissimi Princeps," bidding him put off his visit, as "our Edward" was about to take a journey, and would not be home for five days, or so he says: "*Quid sit ipsa veritas.*"

He showed Kelley the letter. Kelley took great offence at these words, suspecting some secret understanding between the two against him. Dee gently referred to Kelley's own words that his return might be within, or at the end of, five days. Kelley, angry and suspicious, seized the letter and tore it up.

Soon after, Kelley beholds "a spiritual creature" by his right shoulder, telling him to go clean away, for if he stays there he will be hanged. If he goes with the Prince, he will cut off his head, and (*to Dee*)

"You mean not to keep promise with me. And therefore if I might have a thousand pound to tarry, yea, a kingdom, I cannot. Therefore I release you of your promise of 50 pounds yearly stipend to me, and you need not doubt but God will defend you and prosper you, and can of the very stones raise up children unto Abraham. And again, I cannot abide my wife, I love her not, nay, I abhor her, and here in the house I am misliked because I favour her no better."

Dee endeavoured to calm this turbulent young man, spoke of his confidence in him in his dealings with their spiritual friends, but such doings and sayings as these, he points out, are not meet and fitting.

Kelley flung out of the room in a passion, mounted his mare, and rode off furiously towards Brentford, clattering out of the house with such commotion that Jane came running up to her husband's study to know what was the matter. It was about seven o'clock in the evening.

" 'Jane,' I said, 'this man is marvellously out of quiet against his wife, for her friends their bitter reports against him behind his back, and her silence thereat, etc. He is gone,' said I, 'but I beseech the Almighty God to guide him and defend him from danger and shame. I doubt not but God will be merciful to him, and bring him at length to such order as he shall be a faithful servant unto God.' "

Then a remarkable thing happened. By ten o'clock that night (the long midsummer twilight barely over), the prodigal returned, and mounted softly up the study stairs, "unbooted, for he was come in a boat from Brentford. When I saw him, I was very glad inwardly. But I remained writing of those records as I had yet to write, of last Tuesday's action.

" 'I have lent my mare,' he said, 'and so am returned.'

" 'It is well done,' said I.

"Thereupon he sate down in the chair by my table where he was wont to sit. He took up in his hand the books which I had brought from London, of the Lord Laskie, written to him in his commendations." Evidently books sent to Kelley by way of compliment.

Almost immediately, Madimi, who seemed to have a special wardship over books, appeared. She patted the parchment cover of one and would have taken it out of Kelley's hand. Dee heard the strokes, he says. He took a paper and, greeting his visitor, noted the conversation.

D.—"Mistresse Madimi, you are welcome in God for good, as I hope. What is the cause of your coming now?"

M.—"To see how you do."

D.—"I know you see me often, but I see you onely by faith and imagination."

M. (*who is always more personal than the other spirits*)—"That sight is perfecter than his," pointing to Kelley.

D. (*with emotion*)—"O Madimi, shall I have any more of these grievous pangs?"

M. (*oracularly*)—"Curst wives and great Devils are sore companions."

D.—"In respect of the Lord Treasurer, Mr. Secretary and Mr. Rawly, I pray you, what worldly comfort is there to be looked for? Besides that I do principally put my trust in God."

M.—"Madder will staine, wicked men will offend, and are easie to be offended."

D.—"And being offended, will do wickedly, to the persecution of them that mean simply."

M.—"Or else they were not to be called wicked."

D.—"As concerning Alb. Laski, his pedigree, you said your sister would tell all."

M.—"I told you more then all your Dog painters and Cat painters can do."[1]

Kelley interrupts Dee's questions about Laski's pedigree and parentage, impatiently, with

K.—"Will you, Madimi, lend me a hundred pounds for a fortnight?"

[1] No explanation of this curious remark can be offered.

M.—"I have swept all my money out of doors."
D.—"As for money, we shall have that which is necessary when God seeth time."

Then Madimi, becoming serious, addresses to Kelley a beautiful exposition of the unity of all things: "Love is the spirit of God uniting and knitting things together in a laudable proportion." She turns sharply to him, with

"What dost thou hunt after? Speak, man, what dost thou hunt after? . . . Thou lovest not God. Lo, behold, thou breakest his commandments: thy bragging words are confounded. . . . If thou hast none of these [faith, hope, love] thou hast hate. Dost thou love Silver and Gold? The one is a Thief; the other is a Murderer. Wilt thou seek honour? So did Cain. But thou hast a just God that loveth thee, just and virtuous men that delight in thee. Therefore be thou virtuous."

Next follows a remarkable scene. Madimi summons Barma and his fourteen evil companions, who have assumed possession of Kelley, with the words "*Venite Tenebræ fugite spirito meo,*" and orders them to return to the Prince of Darkness: "Depart unto the last cry. Go you thither. . . . The hand of the Lord is like a strong oak. When it falleth it cutteth in sunder many bushes. The light of His eyes shall expel darkness."

Kelley sees the whole crew sink down through the floor of the chamber: "A thing like a wind came and pluckt them by the feet away." He professes his deliverance: "Methinketh I am lighter than I was, and I seem to be empty and to be returned from a great amazing. For this fortnight, I do not well remember what I have done or said."

"Thou art eased of a great burden. Love God. Love thy friends. Love thy wife."

And with this parting injunction, and a psalm of thanksgiving from Dee, the story of Kelley's wild attack of temper, or as it was regarded in the sixteenth century, his possession, for the present ends. Nor is there any record of further dealings with spirits for more than two months.

CHAPTER IX

A FOREIGN JOURNEY

"Friends are everywhere to him that behaves himself well, and a prophet is not esteemed in his own country."

—ROBERT BURTON.

THERE is a hiatus in the *Liber Mysteriorum* after this tempestuous scene with Kelley. We can, however, slightly fill it up from Dee's other diary.[1] It seems as if the skryer went away, leaving behind at Mortlake the poor slighted wife, who must have joined him there, for Dee notes on July 7 payment of wages to a servant he dismissed, "in the presens of Goodman Hilton and Mistress Kelley in my study."

On the 30th, as we have seen, the Queen came in grand procession, heralded with music and song, down the river to Sion. The next day, Leicester's secretary brought letters and gifts. On August 1, John Halton, a London minister, called; also a Worcestershire man, "a wicked spy came to my howse, whom I used as an honest man, and found nothing wrong, as I thought. He was sent to E. K."

This entry is characteristic of the philosopher who, in spite of all his learning, was, as regards men, of so confiding and innocent a nature that he ended by being infinitely more deceived by another

[1] Edited by the Camden Society, 1842.

Worcestershire man—Kelley, for whom he entertained to the last a most faithful friendship.

Then we come on a very entertaining remark in the diary: "Aug. 18. A great tempest of wynde at midnight. *Maxima era E. K. cum uxore ejus.*" Kelley had returned, and his wife was treated to another of his outbreaks, by comparison with which the gale outside was slight.

This is the last entry in the diary before Dee's departure for Poland with Laski.

The Prince proposed to take the whole party from Mortlake back with him to the Continent. He was reputed to be deeply in debt, and seems to have entertained wild hopes that they, aided by the spirits, would provide him with gold, and secure to him the crown of Poland. Kelley foresaw an easy and luxurious life, plenty of change and variety suited to his restless, impetuous nature. He had not as yet been out of England. There were very obvious reasons that he should quit the country now if he would escape a prison. Dee had been a great traveller, as we know, and these were not the attractions to a man of his years. He went in obedience to a supposed call, in the hope of furthering his own knowledge and the Prince's good. The notion of providing for himself and his family lay doubtless at the back of his mind also, but he had all a genius's disregard for thrift and economy, and though very precise and practical about small details, as his diary proves, his mind refused to contemplate these larger considerations of ways and means.

He disposed of the house at Mortlake to his

brother-in-law, Nicholas Fromond, but in such a loose and casual way that before his return he found himself compelled to make a new agreement with him. He took no steps about appointing a receiver of the rents of his two livings, and when he came back the whole six years were owing, nor did he ever obtain the money. He says he intended at the most to be absent one year and eight months. It was more than six years before he again set foot in England.

So, unprepared, he left Mortlake about three in the afternoon of Saturday, September 21, 1583. He met the Prince by appointment on the river, and travelled up after dark to London. A certain secrecy was observed about the journey. Laski, as we have seen, was under some suspicion of Walsingham and Burleigh, whose business it had become to learn news from every Court in Europe. He was suspected of plots against the King of Poland.

In the dead of night, Dee and Laski went by wherries to Greenwich, "to my friend Goodman Fern, the Potter, his house, where we refreshed ourselves." Probably a man whom Dee had employed to make retorts and other vessels for his chemical work. Perhaps they met there the rest of the party, but on the whole it seems more probable that all started together from Mortlake. The exit of such a company from the riverside house must have been quite an event. At Gravesend, a "great Tylte-boat" rowed up to Fern's house, on the quay, and took them out to the two vessels arranged to convey them abroad. These ships, which Dee had hired, were lying seven or eight miles down stream—a Danish double fly-boat, in which Laski, Dee, Kelley, Mrs. Dee and Mrs. Kelley and the three children, Arthur, Katherine and Rowland Dee, embarked at sunrise on Sunday morning; and a boyer, "a pretty ship," which conveyed the Prince's men, some servants of Dee, and a couple of horses. They sailed at once, but the wind coming from N.W., they anchored on the Spits. The fly-boat dragged her anchor, and the wind suddenly changing to N.E., they were in danger of grounding. However, next morning they made Queenborough Haven, and landed in small fishing boats. On the landing, the boat in which the party were seated was nearly upset. Water came in up to their knees, an oar was lost, and they were in considerable peril, but Kelley seems to have risen to the occasion by baling water out of the bottom with a great gauntlet. Dee thinks he saved their lives. Dee, poor man, was dropped from the captain's back on landing into ooze and mud, so that he was "foule arrayed" on reaching "Queenborough town, up the crooked creek." "God be praised for ever that all that danger was ended with so small grief or hurt," is his cheerful comment.

After three nights ashore, they again embarked, and at daybreak on the 27th sailed out into the Channel. On the 29th they landed at Brill. Here Laski's guardian angel, Jubanladec, seems to have granted them an interview. They only paused for two or three days, and hurried on, travelling forward each day by the sluggish Dutch canals, having exchanged their vessel for a hoy of Amsterdam at

Rotterdam. They passed through Tergowd and Haarlem to Amsterdam; here they stayed three days, and Dee despatched Edmond Hilton with his heavy goods by sea to Dantzic. By Enkhuisen they sailed up the Zuyder Zee to Harlingen, then took to the canals again in little "scuts," or small boats, to Leewarden, thence to Dokkum, in West Friesland, in some still smaller craft. On the Sunday spent at Dokkum, Gabriel appeared in the crystal, and delivered to them the most searching and exalted code of ideals for the conduct of their lives. Everything was laid bare before his relentless and unerring eyes. They were bidden to live in brotherly charity, the imperfections of each to be by the other "perfectly shadowed in charity."

"Bear your own infirmities, and so the infirmities of others, with quiet and hidden minde . . . The Cross of Christ is the comparison in mildness over thy brethren . . . He that forsaketh the world for the love of God in Christ shall have his reward, but he that forsaketh himself shall be crowned with a diadem of glory. Bridle the flesh. Riotousness is the sleep of death and the slumber to destruction. Feed the soul, but bridle the flesh, for it is insolent. Look to your servants. Make them clean. Let your friendship be for the service of God. All friendship else is vain and of no account. Persevere to the end. Many men begin, but few end. He that leaveth oft is a damned soul."

From Dokkum the travellers put out to sea again, beyond the islands, and sailed up the Western Ems to Embden. They arrived after dusk, and found the city gates shut, so they lay all night on shipboard.

Next morning, the 18th October, Laski took up his quarters at "The White Swan," on the quay, for he was to remain there to see the Landgrave, and obtain money. The others "lay at 'The Three Golden Keys,' by the English House," and left early next morning by a small boat to sail up the river Ems to Leer, and thence by a little tributary to Stickhuysen and Apen—"a very simple village," and so on to Oldenburg. A night there, and then on by Delmenhorst to Bremen, where they lodged at "an old widow, her house, at the signe of the Crown."

Here Il, the jaunty spirit who was like a Vice in a morality play, again appeared to them, clad in a white satin jerkin, ragged below the girdle. The curtain lifted, and his first words were theatrically light.

"Room for a player! Jesus! who would have thought I should have met you here?"

D. (*solemnly*).—"By the mercies of God we are here. And by your will and propriety and the power of God, you are here."

IL. "Tush, doubt not of me, for I am Il."

KELLEY (*with rebuke*).—"My thinketh that the gravity of this action requireth a more grave gesture, and more grave speeches."

IL.—"If I must bear with thee for speaking foolishly, which art but flesh and speakest of thy own wisdom, how much more oughtest thou to be contented with my gesture, which is appointed of Him which regardeth not the outward form, but the fulfilling of His will and the keeping of His commandments, etc., etc."

KELLEY.—"I do not understand your words. I do only repeat your sayings."

Il.—"It is the part of a servant to do his duty, of him that watcheth to look that he seeth . . . Do that which is appointed, for he that doeth more is not a true servant."

Il turns from Kelley to Dee. "Sir, here is money, but I have it very hardly. Bear with me, for I can help thee with no more. Come on, Andras; where are you, Andras?" he calls.

Andras, in a bare and shabby gown, "like a London 'prentice," appears, but empty-handed.

Il.—"This is one of those that forgetteth his businesse so soon as it is told him."

Andras.—"Sir, I went half-way."

Il.—"And how then? Speak on. Speak on."

Andras.—"Then, being somewhat weary, I stayed, the rather because I met my friends. The third day, I came thither, but I found them not at home. His family told me he had gone forth."

Il.—"And you returned a coxcomb. Well, thus it is. I placed thee above my servants, and did what I could to promote thee. But I am rewarded with loytring and have brought up an idle person. Go thy way, the officer shall deliver thee to prison, and there thou shalt be rewarded. For such as do that they are commanded deserve freedom; but unto those that loytre and are idle, vengeance and hunger belongeth."

Then Dee questions Il about Laski, and whether he is having any success in his efforts to obtain money, about Laski's brother-in-law, Vincent Seve, whose errand in England is not yet completed, and whether they shall all arrive safe at Cracow, or the place appointed.

Kelley has a sight of Master Vincent in a black satin doublet, "cut with cross cuts," a ruff and a long cloak, edged with black or blue. Then Il goes off into a mystical rhapsody, at the end of which he suddenly falls " all in pieces as small as ashes."

Next day, Kelley sees Master Vincent again, walking down by Charing Cross, accompanied by "a tall man with a cutberd, a sword and skie-colored cloak." He passes on towards Westminster and overtakes a gentleman on horseback with five followers in short cape-cloaks and long moustaches. The rider is a lean-visaged man in a short cloak and with a gold rapier. His horse wears a velvet foot cloth. (It sounds like a vision of Raleigh.)

They are merry. Vincent laughs heartily and shows two broad front teeth. He has a little stick in his crooked fingers. The scar on his left hand is plainly seen. He has very high straight close boots. They arrive at Westminster Church (the Abbey). Many people are coming out. A number of boats lie in the river, and in the gardens at Whitehall a man is grafting fruit trees. The lean-visaged man on horseback alights, and goes down towards, and up, the steps of Westminster Hall, Vincent with him. His companion walks outside and accosts a waterman. The waterman asks if that is the Polish bishop? The servant wants to know what business it is of his. A messenger comes down the steps of the Hall and says to Vincent's man that his master shall be despatched to-morrow. The servant saith he is glad of it. " Then all that shew is vanished away."

There are one or two allusions here to an emissary from Denmark who has brought a bag of amber. Il also says he has much business in Denmark. Frederick, the King of Denmark, was in frequent correspondence with Queen Elizabeth at this time.

At Bremen, where they stayed a week, Dee says that Kelley, when skrying by himself, was given a kind of rambling prophetical verse of thirty-two lines, which he prints, foretelling the downfall of England, Spain, France and Poland. In fact, a general *débâcle* of nations. It is very bad prophecy and still worse poetry, but evidently inspired by the highly diplomatic foreign relations of Elizabeth and her two ministers.

On leaving Bremen, the party travelled by Osterholz to Harburg, on the left bank of the Elbe. They crossed the river and went on by coach to Hamburg. Laski had then rejoined them, but stayed behind in Hamburg, at "the English house," probably the consul's. Dee and the rest reached Lübeck on November 7.

CHAPTER X

PROMISES AND VISIONS

> "Search while thou wilt; and let thy reason go
> To ransom truth, e'en to th' abyss below;
> Rally the scattered causes; and that line
> Which nature twists be able to untwine.
> It is thy Maker's will; for unto none
> But unto reason can He e'er be known."
>
> —SIR THOMAS BROWNE.

THE dealings which Kelley had in Lübeck with the spirits seem to throw a light on all his relations with Dee. Kelley is gaining confidence; he sees that he is already able to dupe his employer considerably. He has only to manipulate the conversations a little to show up often his so-called sincerity. He can pretend he is aghast at Il's levity, and he seems to have been cunning enough when the spirits very often blamed him.

But his dreams of advancement in wealth and fame were no nearer accomplishment. He had seen through Dee's ambition. It was very different from his own, but he thought he could use it to his own advantage. Dee was now flattered without stint.

So at the sitting on November 15 he sees eleven noblemen in rich sables. One, wearing a regal cap trimmed with sable, is seated on a chair beset with precious stones. "He is a goodlier man than the Lord A. L." He addresses Dee with glittering promises.

He is the King or the Emperor, and is represented in the margin of the diary by a crown. He says to Dee:—

"Pluck up thy heart and be merry, pine not thy Soul away with inward groanings, for I will open unto thee the secrets of Nature and the riches of the world, and withal give thee such direction that shall deliver thee from many infirmities both of body and mind, ease thee of thy tedious labours and settle thee where thou shalt have comfort.

"Thanks be given unto the Highest now and ever.

"Why dost thou [hesitate] within thy thought? Hast thou not need of comfort?"

"Yes, God knows, for I am half confounded."

"Then first determine within thyself to rest thee for this winter. Secondly, open thy mind to desire such things as may advance thy credit and enrich thy family, reap unto thee many friends and lift thee up to honour. For I will stir up the mindes of learned men, the profoundest in the world, that they shall visit thee. And I will disclose unto you such things as shall be wonderful and of exceeding profit. Moreover I will put to my hands and help your proceedings, that the world may talk of your wisdom hereafter. Therefore wander not farther into unknown places: contagious, the very seats of death for thee and thy children and such as are thy friends. If thou enquire of me where and how, I answer, everywhere, or how thou wilt. Thou shalt forthwith become rich, and thou shalt be able to enrich kings and help such as are needy. Wast thou not born to use the commodity of this world? were not all things made for man's use?"

Here are the old dreams of the philosopher's stone, the elixir of life, the transmutation of metals and all the works of alchemy, for which both these travellers were adventuring their lives in a foreign land. Dee does not seem exactly dazzled by these allurements. He only begs leave to ask questions, and seeks to keep the speaker to the point. "Are they to stay there and not to go on with Laski? Where are they to spend the winter?"

"Where you will," comes the answer. "Are you so unwise as to go with him now? Let him go before, and provide for himself and the better for you. In the Summer, when it is more fair, you can follow. The weather now will be hard and the travel unfit for children. Heap not up thy wife's sorrow."

"I desire to live in quiet that my spirit may the better attend to the service of God."

"Well, you are contented?"

Dee asks again, are they to part from Laski? Will it not be prejudicial to their arrangement, they having entered into a kind of covenant with him? "Are you not content?" the visitor repeats.

Then he did impart some remarkable information to Dee, in which there was certainly a grain of telepathically conveyed truth.

"Your brother is clapped up in prison. How like you that? Your house-keeper I mean."

This evidently refers to Nicholas Fromond.

"They examine him. They say that thou hast hid divers secret things. As for thy books, thou mayst go look at them at leasure. It may be that thy house may be burnt for a remembrance of thee, too. Well, if they do, so it is. I have given thee my counsel, and desired to do thee good. The choice is thine."

There is no evidence that Fromond was imprisoned, but he was a poor protector of his brother-in-law's valuable effects. He was powerless against a mob who broke into Dee's house not long after his departure from Mortlake, made havoc of his priceless books and instruments, and wrought irreparable damage. It was now nearly two months since Dee had left Mortlake, and, moving from place to place, it was unlikely that he had heard any news from thence. No date has ever been assigned to this action of the mob. It is quite conceivable that it actually took place on this day, November 15, and that by Kelley's clairvoyant or telepathic power the news was communicated across the sea and continent to Dee.

The poor astrologer was torn with doubts and misgivings. He fell upon his knees, uttering a piercing supplication to the "Author of all truth and direction of such as put their trust in him."

"I most humbly beseech thee consider these promises thus to me propounded. If they be true and from thee, confirm them. If they be illusions and not from thee, disprove them. For hardly in my judgment they do or can agree with our former precepts and order taken by thee."

And again, in an agony:

"O Lord, I doubt of these promises of ease, wealth, and honour: I suspect the whole apparition of the eleven to be an illusion. O confirm my judgment or disprove it."

So he seeks for a revelation of guidance, writes

letters to Laski, and waits. Soon he perceives these temptations to have come from "a very foolish devil." He decides that they will continue to throw in their lot with Laski, who rejoined them in Lübeck. He left again to visit the Duke of Mecklenburg, they meanwhile going by Wismar to Rostock and Stettin, which place they reached at ten o'clock on Christmas morning. Laski joined them in a fortnight. They passed on by Stayard to Posen, where Dee adds an antiquarian note that the cathedral church was founded in 1025, and that the tomb of Wenceslaus, the Christian king, is of one huge stone. It was here that Dee began to enter curious notes about Kelley in the *Liber Peregrinationis*, written in Greek characters, but the words are Latin words, or more frequently English. The supposition is that Kelley was unacquainted even with the Greek alphabet. Dee kept his other foreign diary, written in an *Ephemerides Cœlestium* (printed in Venice, 1582), secret from his partner, for Kelley had obtained possession of an earlier one kept in England and had written in it unfavourable comments, as well as erased things, about himself. Dee had the last word, and has added above Kelley's "shameful lye," "This is Mr. Talbot's, his own writing in my boke, very unduely as he came by it." The various diaries sound, perhaps, confusing to the reader, but are really quite simple. By the private diary is meant the scraps in the Bodleian Almanacs, edited by Halliwell for the Camden Society, in which he seldom alludes to psychic affairs. *The Book of Mysteries* is the diary in which he relates all the history of the crystal gazing. The printed version

(*True Relation*) begins with Laski's visit to Mortlake on May 28, 1583.

Winter had now set in with unwonted rigour, and one is amazed at the celerity with which this great caravanserai of people and goods pushed on from place to place. From Stettin to Posen, for instance, is more than 200 miles, and it was accomplished within four days and apparently with only one stop. Then southwards into the watery district between the Oder and the Warthe, where the country was so icebound that they had to employ five-and-twenty men to cut the ice for their coaches for a distance as long as two English miles. On February 3 they reached Lask, on the Prince's own property, and at last were comfortably housed in the Provost's "fair house by the Church." Here Dee was ill with ague, but the table was set up, and a new spirit called Nalvage appeared in the globe. Nalvage's "physiognomy was like the picture of King Edward the Sixth. His hair hangeth down a quarter of the length of the cap, somewhat curling, yellow." Dee, of course, had seen the young Kingwhen he presented his books, so this is a first-hand reminiscence. Nalvage stood upon a round table of mother-of-pearl, and revealed to them many cabalistic mysteries, tables of letters and names. There was a terrible vision of Mrs. Dee lying dead, with her face all battered in, and of the maid Mary being pulled out of a pool of water half drowned. But it seems to portend no more than did another piece of ill news conveyed at the same time: "Sir Harry Sidney died upon Wednesday last. A privy enemy of yours." Dee says, "I ever took him for one of my chief friends," and adds, with unconscious humour:

"Note. At Prague, Aug. 24, I understood that Sir H. Sidney was not dead in February nor March, no, not in May last. Therefore this must be considered. Doctor Hagek, his son, told me."

The note makes us realise for a moment how slowly news travelled from England to the Continent in this year of grace 1584.

The informant, Madimi, "a little wench in white," told Dee that she had been in England at his house, and all there were well. The Queen said she was sorry she had lost her philosopher. But the Lord Treasurer answered, "He will come home shortly a begging to you." "Truly," adds Madimi, "none can turn the Queen's heart from you." Then, recurring to Mortlake, she says: "I could not come into your study. The Queen hath caused it to be sealed." This no doubt after the breaking in of the rioters. Dee was counselled to go and live at Cracow. He would like to be led step by step, and begs to know what house "is in God's determination for me and mine." Madimi answers, "As wise as I am, I cannot yet tell what to say." Dee demurs to the expense, and reproaches her for not telling them sooner. Needless cost would have been saved, and he does not know if Laski will have enough money for yet another move. He had rather Kesmark had been redeemed before Laski went to Cracow. Perhaps then his credit with the people would be greater.

Laski had heavily mortgaged his estates in Poland;

he was in debt, and he had apparently raised a loan on his Kesmark property for a large sum of money. The bond was to expire on St. George's Day, April 23 next, and without the Emperor's help Dee did not see how it could be met. Kelley recurs to the Danish treasure he had found in England, hidden in ten places, which they would fain have transported to Poland now, very speedily, for Laski's use. Dee is anxious to know from Madimi whether his rents are being duly received in England by his deputy or not, "whether Her Majesty or the Council do intend to send for me again or no." They ask instructions from Gabriel about Kelley's red powder, and how they shall use it. Dee seeks for information about the Prince's wife, whom they have not yet seen, but they doubt she is not their sound friend. He begs for medicine for his ague. And again, shall he take the pedestal, being made in Lask for the holy table, on to Cracow when they go, "rather than make a new one there, both to save time and to have our doings the more secret"? This pedestal was for the crystal to rest in upon the table. Three iron hasps and padlocks were also made at Lask for the table.[1] If any answer to these questions was vouchsafed by the spirits, it was in the usual enigmas.

Part of Dee's baggage, a chest left at Toon on their way out, not having arrived, they did not immediately obey the injunction to move on to Cracow, but after about five weeks in Lask, they again journeyed forward.

[1] *Ashmolean MS.*, 1790, 56.

CHAPTER XI

CRACOW

" Sir, to a wise man all the world's his soil :
It is not Italy, nor France, nor Europe
That must bound me if my fates call me forth.
Yet, I protest it is no salt desire
Of seeing countries, shifting a religion ;
Nor any disaffection to the State
Where I was bred, and unto which I owe
My dearest plots, hath brought me out : much less
That idle, antique, stale, grey-headed project
Of knowing men's minds and manners."

—JONSON, *Volpone, or The Fox.*

AT the close of the sixteenth century, Cracow was at the height of its fame and prosperity. It was still the capital of Poland, and the residence of her kings, as well as the seat of the university founded two hundred years before by Casimir the Great. The Gothic cathedral erected under the same king, the burial place of Polish monarchs, was already adorned with sculptures and bronzes, the work of Renaissance artists from Florence and Siena. The visitor of to-day will find himself surrounded by churches and other buildings dating from the twelfth, fourteenth, and sixteenth centuries. Amid the ramparts of the Austrian fortress can still be traced here and there the older fortifications.

The city lies in the centre of a vast plain, almost

at the confluence of two rivers, the Vistula and Rudowa. Across this plain from the north-west the travellers came, and reached Cracow in the afternoon of March 13, 1584.

"We were lodged in the suburbs by the church,[1] where we remained a seven night, and then we (I and my wife) removed to the house in St. Stephen Street, which I had hired for a year for 80 gylders of 30 groschen. And Master Edward Kelley came to us on Fryday in the Easter week by the new Gregorian Kalendar, being the 27 day of March by the old Kalendar, but the sixth day of April by the new Kalendar, Easter Day being the first day of April in Poland, by the new Gregorian institution."

From the time of arriving in Poland Dee is careful to enter the dates in both old and new styles. The New Style was then extremely new, it having been introduced by Pope Gregory XIII. only a couple of years before, and universally adopted by all Roman Catholic countries. England, in all the fervour of her recently established Protestantism, would have none of it, but still desired not to lag behind in needful reforms. Dee, as already stated, had been commissioned before he left England to make calculations by which the calendar could be suitably adopted in this country. The Roman Church had assumed the chronology adopted by the Council of Nice to be strictly correct. But Dee desired to ascertain the actual position of the earth in relation to the sun at the birth of Christ, as a basis on which

[1] Probably the old Church of the Visitation.

to rectify the calendar. The result of his calculations would have omitted eleven instead of ten days.

Dee's book (which was never printed, but remains in manuscript among the Ashmolean MSS.) was entitled "A Playne discourse and humble advise for our gratious Queene Elizabeth, her most Excellent Majestie, to peruse and consider as concerning the needful Reformation of the Vulgar Kalendar for the civile yeres and daies accompting or verifying, according to the tyme truely spent." It was finished and delivered to Burleigh on February 26, 1583. To him it was inscribed with these rather playful verses:—

"Τὸ ὅτι, and Τὸ διότι,
I shew the thing and reason why,
At large, in briefe, in middle wise
I humbly give a playne advise;
For want of tyme, the tyme untrew
If I have myst, command anew
Your honour may, so shall you see
That love of truth doth govern me."

Burleigh proposed that skilful men in science, as Mr. Digges, be called from the universities to peruse the work and confer.[1] But the Council of State consulted Archbishop Grindal and three of the bishops, who recommended the rejection of Dee's scheme, chiefly on the ground that it emanated from Rome, and so their opposition delayed this desirable public reform in England for 170 years. Dee agreed to grant the ten days for the sake of conformity with the rest of the world, if his calculation that eleven were strictly accurate was publicly announced. It will

[1] *Lansdowne MS.*, xxxix. f. 28.

be remembered that in 1742, when the change was made, eleven days were omitted from the calendar.

The household at Cracow now consisted of Mrs. Dee, Arthur, Katherine, Rowland and his nurse, and the maid Mary, Mrs. Kelley and her husband, a servant named John Crocker and a boy. It was augmented before long.

The actions with the spirits soon recommenced. Kelley began very unfairly by trying sittings alone, for he was importunate to know how the Prince was going to treat them as regards money. But he seems only to have drawn reproof and much excellent counsel on himself from Nalvage.

The next few weeks were taken up with instructions from Gabriel and Nalvage, consisting of letters, numbers and words in a strange Eastern or angelic language, to which Dee probably had some key, though they appear unintelligible. The partners were bidden to keep the Sabbath, and Dee resolves to go always to church. Kelley seems to have turned restive once again. On April 17 he declared he would sit no more to receive these A. B. C. messages unless they were better explained. "There is your boy, John," he said; "he can well enough give you these simple signs. You need me no longer. I will be gone." As Casaubon remarks, "he was ever and anon upon projects to break with Dee."

Two days after, Dee heard him come upstairs to his own study, and called him in. Dee's study was an inner room through one that opened on to the stairs, at the foot of which was a door. He explained that he had now a distinct clue to the meaning of the tables of letters on which he had long been puzzling; dwelt on how essential it was to miss not a single letter, or else the words would err. He asked him, in fact, to resume his skrying, and encouraged him by saying that he knew he "would come to like better this due and methodical manner of our friends' proceeding," if only he would continue. Kelley scornfully replied that their teachers were mere deluders, and no good or sufficient teachers. In two years they had not made them able to understand, or do anything. "In two years," he said, boastingly, "I could have learned all the seven liberal arts and sciences, if I had first learned Logick." He protested he would have no more to do with the spirits in any manner or way, wished himself in England, and vowed if the books were his he would burn them all. "These spiritual creatures are not bound to me. Take John for your skryer."

Dee pathetically recapitulated his long desire for wisdom, his faith that more knowledge will be granted him. Kelley went out leaving Dee buried in prayer.

In two days, Kelley was again submissive to the spirits, who bade him not mistrust. "Let him that is a servant and is commanded to go, go. And let not the earth rise up and strive against the plowman." So they go on again with their cabalistic letters and signs. In the beginning of May, Dee notes: "E. K. is very well persuaded of these actions now, thanked be the Highest."

Later in the month he says: "There happened a great storm or temptation to E. K. of doubting and mistaking our instructors and their doings, and of contemning and condemning anything that I knew or could do. I bare all things patiently for God his sake." Kelley at the same time says: "I am contented to see and to make true report of what they will show, but my heart standeth against them."

That night after the sitting, he again swore he would not go on skrying. The morning after, Dee knocked at his study door, and bade him come, for Nalvage had left off the previous day in the middle of an interesting geographical lesson about unknown parts of the earth, and had told them to be ready to continue it next morning. Kelley was obdurate, and Dee retired to prayer. In half an hour, the skryer burst in with a volume of Cornelius Agrippa's in his hand, where he said all the countries they were told about yesterday were described and written down. "What is the use," he said, "in going on with this farce, if they tell us nothing new?" Dee replied that he was glad to see Kelley had such a book of his own; that Nalvage in giving those ninety-one new names of countries, all of seven letters, was answering his particular request; that he had verified the lands in the charts of Gerardus Mercator and Pomponius Mela, which he had at hand and produced, "and now," he said triumphantly, "we know exactly what angels govern which countries, in case we are ever called to practise there." Nalvage had described the natives of the countries and the products, suggesting that in Greenland a vein of gold might be found. "Your wilful phantasie," Dee ended to Kelley, "perverts your reason; and whereas you find fault with our instructors,

I, who much more narrowly peruse their words, know that they give direct answers to my questions, except indeed when you misreport them, or I make a mistake in hearing or writing." So three days were lost, as Dee bemoans in the margin, and then Kelley was again induced to resume his skrying.

On the 25th, Laski arrived and left again for Kesmark.[1] He now intended to redeem his property there. But King Stephan and his Chancellor were both set against him, and he wished Dee to go with him to the Emperor of Austria, Rudolph II.

Instructions were now given that they must be ready to go with Laski to the Emperor, must make themselves apt and meet, for until no remembrance of wickedness is left among them they cannot forward the Lord's expeditions. Gabriel tells Kelley at some length of his many faults. Dee did not hear this, but considerately does not ask for a repetition of the catalogue. He only bids Kelley listen well. Gabriel says if any will be God's minister, he must sweep his house clean, without spot. He must not let his life be a scandal to the will of the Lord.

"God finds thee, as he passes by in his Angel, fit in matter, but, my brother, God knows, far unfit in life. O consider the Dignity of thy creation. See how God beareth with thy infirmity from time to time. Consider how thou art now at a Turning where there lieth two wayes. One shall be to thy comfort, the other to perpetual woe."

[1] One of the oldest towns in Hungary, a royal free town since 1380. It lies in the valley of the Popper, within reach of the magnificent scenery of the Hohe Tatra, a group of the Central Carpathian Mountains.

Gabriel's dart, like a flame of fire, is upright in his hand. He pleads with Kelley in such adorable gentleness and with such tender and ecstatic weeping, that both his hearers cannot withhold their tears. Gabriel's words so moved Kelley that he professed absolute repentance for all his dealings with wicked spirits, vowed he would burn whatsoever he has of their trash and experiments, and write a book setting forth their horrible untruth, and blasphemous doctrine against Christ and the Holy Ghost. It is curious that among the other errors he renounced was the Eastern doctrine that a fixed number of souls and bodies have always been in the world, and that a man's soul goes from one body to another, viz., into the new-born child. In the light of after-events, it is significant that another belief abjured is that to the chosen there is no sin.

Dee was overjoyed, and full of thanksgiving. He believed utterly in Kelley's conversion, all the more because of his former lapses. If anything were wanting to prove it, it was to be found in the humble and patient spirit in which this impracticable, volcanic skryer of his now sat on patiently for two hours and a half before the stone without either cloud, veil, or voice appearing. This to Kelley was "no light pang." Nay, he argues that servants must wait as long as their Master pleases, and the time is better spent than in any human doings. He opens his wayward heart to Dee, the man without guile, and avows that he had fully intended at his last outburst, ten days before, to have gone away secretly with those with whom he had so long dealt had they not threatened him with beggary—a thing, adds Dee, that he most hated and feared. Therefore, till this time he had been a hypocrite. Now, in his new-found elation, he cares not for poverty; life eternal is more than riches and wealth. He that can be hired with money to forsake the devil is no Christian. He will doubt no more, but believe. Dee adds that he omits many others of his godly sayings, thinking these sufficient to write down. He had no suspicion of any ill faith. His love for Kelley was truly unbounded in its long-suffering. He offered a fervent thanksgiving for the conversion, and for Satan's defeat, and prayed for them both for "continual zeal, love of truth, purity of life, charitable humility and constant patience to the end."

The same atmosphere continued next day, June 11. Kelley protests he could sit for seven years awaiting a vision. They do wait nearly four hours. Evidently Kelley converted is not going to be so good a medium as Kelley unregenerate. Dee explains the non-appearance as retribution for the three days wasted before. But they are all rather depressed, especially the Prince.

Then a vision appears of the castle of Grodno, in Littau,[1] where the King of Poland then was. Stephan's arms are seen over the gate. A man like an Italian is beheld, carrying an iron chest within which are an image in black wax, a dead hand, and so on. The promise is that Laski shall be King of Poland.

Early next morning Kelley, lying awake in bed, had a vision which he or Dee afterwards embodied in the curious diagram facing p. 141.

It may be taken as a sample of the kind of intricate

[1] In East Bohemia, on the river March, not far from Austerlitz.

complications of theurgy which often absorbed the pair for days together.

The vision was expounded by Ave, something in the following manner:—

A Vision.

East and West, North and South, stand four sumptuous and belligerent Castles, out of which sound Trumpets thrice. From every Castle, a Cloth, the sign of Majesty, is cast. In the East it is red, like new-smitten blood. In the South, lily-white. In the West, green, garlick-bladed like the skins of many dragons. In the North, hair-coloured, black like bilberry juice. Four trumpeters issue from the Castles, with trumpets pyramidal, of six cones, wreathed. Three Ensign bearers, with the names of God on their banners, follow them. Seniors, Kings, Princes as train bearers, Angels in four phalanxes like crosses, all in their order, march to the central Court, and range themselves about the ensigns.

It Vanisheth.

The dazzling, shifting formation seems to proceed in a glorious pageant of colour, and then to rest, frozen into a minutely exact phantasticon of harmony.

Now for the meaning of the allegory. The Castles are Watch towers provided against the Devil, the Watchman in each is a mighty angel. The ensigns publish the redemption of mankind. The Angels of the Aires, which come out of the Crosses, are to subvert whole countries, without armies, in this war waged against the Powers of Darkness.

Many weeks were taken up with tables of letters for the exposition of this vision, and with explaining the names of these gates, angels, seniors, etc.

Kelley is again sometimes very much tempted to doubt the good faith of the angelic visitants, more especially as he sadly fears that good angels will not provide them with the needful money that the Prince requires for the success of his cause. One day, Dee wrote in his diary: "E. K. had the Megrom sore." Kelley read this, and "A great temptation fell on E. K., upon E. K. taking these words to be a scoff, which were words of compassion and friendship." After this Dee resorts more frequently to the use of his Greek characters.

The Dees were still living near the church of St. Stephen, where Kelley was a frequent visitor. Laski lodged with the Franciscans in their convent.[1] The revelations were now of tables of letters again, intended, Dee thinks, that they may learn the names of angels and distinguish the bad from the good. (The bad angels' names are said to be all of three letters.) He hopes Ave is about to reveal the healing medicines; the property of fire; the knowledge, finding, and use of metals; the virtues of stones, and the understanding of arts mechanical. But Ave says it is the wicked spirits who give money coined, although there are good angels who can find metals, gather them and use them. Then Madimi appears, after a long absence, and addressing Dee as "my gentle brother," tells him that Ave is a good creature and they might have made more of him. She wants to know why they have not gone to the Emperor Rudolph. The old excuse of poverty is pleaded.

[1] The refectory of this convent is now used as a technical and industrial museum.

That evening, June 26, at seven o'clock, Dee sat in his study considering the day's action, when Kelley entered and asked if he understood it. He, it seems, had burst out again, had raged and abused Michael and Gabriel, called Ave a devil, made "horrible speeches." There had been a most terrible storm of thunder and rain, and Kelley always appeared sensitive to these electric disturbances. Now he is penitent once more, acknowledges his words were "not decent," and begs forgiveness of God and Dee. The talk lasted long, and several calls to supper were unheeded; then, just as they were leaving the room, Kelley felt something warm and heavy on his shoulder, and behold! it was Ave come to acknowledge his repentance. Dee hands him his Psalter book, and with three prayers devoutly said, all is smooth again, and they go down to supper.

Dee's patience and humility seemed unending. In conversing with the spirits he is always, as it were, face to face with God. His replies are made direct to the Majesty of the Divine. When Kelley is blamed he assumes equal blame.

AVE.—"Which of you have sought the Lord for the Lord his sake?"

D.—"That God can judge. We vaunt nothing of our doings, nor challenge anything by the perfection of our doings. We challenge nothing, Lord, upon any merits, but fly unto thy mercy, and that we crave and call for. Curiosity is far from our intents."

CHAPTER XII

FROM CRACOW TO PRAGUE

"Since all men from their birth employ sense prior to intellect, and are necessarily first conversant with sensible things: some, proceeding no farther, pass through life considering these as first and last; and apprehending what is painful to be evil, what is pleasant good, they deem it sufficient to shun the one and pursue the other. Some pretending to greater reason than the rest, esteem this wisdom; like earth-bound birds, though they have wings they are unable to fly. The secret souls of others would recall them from pleasure to worthier pursuits, but they cannot soar: they choose the lower way, and strive in vain. Thirdly, there are those—divine men—whose eyes pierce through clouds and darkness to the supernal vision, where they abide as in their own lawful country."—PLOTINUS.

ALL this time, Dee is so absolutely absorbed with his spiritual visions that we know very little about his outer existence. For three years after he left England, he neglected to enter anything in his ordinary diary, and the *Liber Mysticus* contains nothing of everyday affairs.

In this July, 1584, however, at Cracow, he does enter an important piece of information about his boy Rowland, the baby then about a year and a half old.

"1584. Remember that on Saturday the fourteenth day of July by the Gregorian Calendar, and the fourth day of July by the old Calendar, Rowlande my childe (who was born Anno 1583, January 28 by the old calendar) was extreamely sick about noon or mid-day, and by one of the clock was ready to give up the ghost, or rather lay for dead, and his eyes set and sunck in his head.

"I made a vow if the Lord did foresee him to be his true servant, and so would grant him life, and confirm him his health at this danger, and from this danger, I would during my life on Saturdays eat but one meal."

Although we never find this vow referred to again, there is no doubt that Dee devoutly kept his bargain. Rowland did grow up and had other remarkable escapes.

Still the journey to Prague to the Emperor Rudolph was postponed, and it was not until the first day of August that the trio set off. Dee and Kelley were ready to go sooner, but Laski had not sufficiently recovered his finances. The party had been augmented by the arrival of Kelley's brother, Thomas, and Edmond Hilton, son of Dee's old friend, Goodman Hilton, who had sometimes lent him money, and who in 1579 had requested leave for his two sons to resort to Dee's house. Thomas Kelley accompanied the Prince and his pair of crystal gazers. The women were left behind under Edmond Hilton's charge.

Five or six days after arriving in Prague, on the day of the Assumption of the Blessed Virgin Mary, August 15, Dee was settled in the house of Dr. Hageck, by Bethlem in Old Prague (Altstadt), kindly lent him for his use. The house was not far from the old Rathhaus, the great clock tower of which, dated 1474, and the Council Chamber, still exist. It was also near the Carolinum or University, founded by Charles IV. in 1383, in whose hall John Huss a hundred and fifty years before had held his disputations. When Dee and his party arrived in the city Tycho Brahe was still alive, though not yet a resident in Prague. Prague was the city of alchemists. The sombre, melancholy Emperor himself relieved his more serious studies by experiments in alchemics and physics. A mania for collecting rare and valuable objects provided him with a still lighter pastime. He painted, read much, and worked in iron, was a good linguist, and a regular dilettante. Unmarried, and with all the weaknesses of the Habsburghs, for nearly thirty years out of his long life and far too protracted reign he was quite mad. Not many years after his reception of Dee he ceased to make any pretence of public appearance.

The excellent little study or "stove" (from "stube," German for study) in Dr. Hageck's house had been since 1518 the abode of some student of alchemy, skilful of the holy stone. The name of the alchemist, "Simon," was written up in letters of gold and silver in several places in the room. Dee's eyes also fell daily on many cabalistic hieroglyphs, as well as on drawings or carvings of birds, fishes, flowers, fruits, leaves and six vessels, all the work, he presumed, of *Simon baccalaureus Pragensis.* Over the door were the lines:

"Immortale Decus par gloriaque illi debentur
Cujus ab ingenio est discolor hic paries,"

and on the south wall of the study was a long quotation from some philosophical work ending with

"Ars nostra est Ludus puero cum labor mulierum. Scitote omnes filii artis hujus, quod nemo potest colligere fructus nostri Elixiris, nisi per introitum nostri lapidis Elementati, et si aliam viam quærit, viam nunquam intrabit nec attinget. Rubigo est opus, quod sit ex solo auro, dum intraverit in suam humiditatem."

In these congenial surroundings skrying was at once resumed. Madimi (now grown into a woman) was the first visitor, and Dee hastened to inquire for his wife and children at Cracow. He notes that his first letter from her arrived on the 21st. She joined him before long. He was told to write to the Emperor Rudolph. He did so on August 17, and he relates in the epistle the favourable attention he has received from Charles V. and his brother Ferdinand, Rudolph's father, the Emperor Maximilian II., who accepted the dedication of his book *Monas Hieroglyphica*, and others of the imperial house. He signs the letter, "Humillimus et fidelissimus clientulus Joannes Dee."

After waiting a week he sent the letter by Laski's secretary to the Spanish ambassador, Don Guglielmo de Sancto Clemente, who was to present it to Rudolph. With it he also sent a copy of his *Monas*. The same night he heard by Emerich Sontag, the secretary, that the Emperor had graciously accepted the book, and within three or four days would appoint a time for giving him audience.

He received letters from England on August 27, which were dated April 15 and 16. His brother-in-law, Nicholas Fromond, told him that Mr. Gilbert,

Mr. Sled, and his bookseller had used him very ill. Doubtless he was expecting some money from the sale of his books. Mrs. Dee was much upset at her brother's defections, and poor Dee was worried all round, for, as he writes in the margin of his diary, "Satan is very busy with E. K. about this time." Kelley seems to have been making friends with young Simon Hageck, son of "our host," as Dee calls him. To furnish his own study he had bought a clock of Mrs. Hageck for five ducats, which was so good a bargain that she requested "a quart of wine" (probably a quarter hogshead) thrown in. She herself does not seem to have benefited much by the largess, for Kelley and Laski's man Alexander proceeded to get drunk on it, and fell to fighting and quarrelling. Dee, who had stayed writing in his study instead of going to supper, was warned by the city watchman to keep better peace in his house. Looking from his window to account for the caution, he saw Laski's man sitting on a great stone, and called him to come in. When he had heard the tale he went off to Hageck's to "understand the very truth," and there found Kelley lying in a drunken sleep on a form. This was a relief. He was better pleased to think that angry words had been spoken "when wine, not wit, had rule," and persuaded Laski's man to stay in his lodgings that night instead of raging forth into the street. Already a scandal had been made which he foresaw would do him much harm. Next morning Kelley had a madder fit than ever.

"Much ado. Emerich and his brother (Thomas Kelley) and I had to stop or hold him from going on

Alexander with his weapon. At length we let him go, in his doublet and hose without a cap or hat on his head, and into the street he hasted with his brother's rapier drawn, and challenged Alexander to fight. But Alexander said 'Nolo, Domine Kelleie, Nolo.' Hereupon E. K. took up a stone and threw after him as after a dog, and so came into the house again in a most furious rage for that he might not fight with Alexander. The rage and fury was so great in words and gestures as might plainly prove that the wicked enemy sought either E. K. his own destroying of himself, or of me, or of his brother. This may suffice to notifie the mighty temptation and vehement working of the subtle spiritual enemy, Satan, wherewith God suffered E. K. to be tempted and almost overcome: to my great grief, discomfort, and most great discredit, if it should come to the Emperor's understanding. I was in great doubt how God would take this offence, and devised with myself how I might with honesty be cleared from the shame and danger that might arise if these two should fight. At the least, it would cross all good hope here with the Emperor for a time, till God redressed it."

By this time Dee had become skilled and tactful in dealing with his turbulent skryer, and he soon brought him to quietness by yielding to his humour, and saying little. At mid-day came Dee's messenger from Cracow, bringing letters from and tidings by word of mouth of his dear wife Jane, "to my great comfort." Much he was in need of comfort, and when a letter from the Emperor arrived the same day, desiring to see him, Kelley's enormities began to assume less desperate proportions.

Dee started at once to the Castle, the Palace of Prague, and waited in the guard-chamber, sending

Emericus to the Lord Chamberlain, Octavius Spinòla, to announce his coming.

"Spinòla came to me very courteously and led me by the skirt of the gown, through the dining chamber to the Privie chamber, where the Emperor sat at a table, with a great chest and standish of silver before him, and my *Monad* and Letters by him."

Rudolph thanked Dee politely for the book (which was dedicated to his father), adding that it was "too hard for his capacity" to understand; but he encouraged the English philosopher to say on all that was in his mind. Dee recounted his life history at some length, and told how for forty years he had sought, without finding, true wisdom in books and men; how God had sent him His Light, Uriel, who for two years and a half, with other spirits, had taught him, had finished his books for him, and had brought him a stone of more value than any earthly kingdom. This angelic friend had given him a message to deliver to Rudolph. He was to bid him forsake his sins and turn to the Lord. Dee was to show him the Holy Vision.

"This my commission is from God. I feign nothing, neither am I a hypocrite, an ambitious man, or doting or dreaming in this cause. If I speak otherwise than I have just cause, I forsake my salvation," said he.

Rudolph was probably very much bored by this mystical rhapsody. He excused himself from seeing the vision at this time, and said he would hear more later. He promised friendship and patronage, and Dee, who says he had told almost more than he intended of his purposes, "to the intent they might get some root or better stick in his minde," was fain to take his leave. In a few days he was informed, through the Spanish ambassador, that one Doctor Curtius, of the Privy Council, " a wise, learned, and faithful councillor," was to be sent to listen to him on the Emperor's behalf. Uriel, whose head had been bound of late in a black silk mourning scarf because of Kelley's misdoings, now reappeared in a wheel of fire, and announced favour to Rudolph.

" If he live righteously and follow me truly, I will hold up his house with pillars of hiacinth, and his chambers shall be full of modesty and comfort. I will bring the East wind over him as a Lady of Comfort, and she shall sit upon his castles with Triumph, and she shall sleep with joy."

To Dee, he says, has been given "the spirit of choice." Dee petitions that his understanding of that dark saying may be opened: "Dwell thou in me, O Lord, for I am frail and without thee very blind."

The conference between Dee and Curtius on September 15 lasted for six hours. It took place at the Austrian's house, whither Dee was permitted, it seems, to take the magic stone and the books of the dealings. Dee in all good faith promised that many excellent things should happen to Rudolph, if only he would listen to the voice of Uriel. Dee's sincerity, credulous though it appears, was as yet unshaken. He lived in a transcendental atmosphere, and trembled, as he believed, on the brink of a great revelation. The very heavens seemed opening to him, and soon, he thought, he would probe knowledge to its heart.

Kelley, on the other hand, was under no delusion. He had worked the spirit mystery for long enough without profit; already he was beginning to more than suspect that the game was played out; that their dreams of Laski as King of Poland, dispensing wealth and favour to his two helpers, were never to be realised; that the Emperor's favour would be equally chimerical and vain; and that some more profitable occupation had better be sought. At the back of his mind lay always the hope of the golden secret. Somehow and somewhere this last aspiration of the alchemist must be realised.

At the very time when the two learned doctors were holding their confabulation, Kelley, says Dee, was visited at their lodgings with a wicked spirit who told him that Dee's companion would use him like a serpent, "compassing his destruction with both head and tayle; and that our practices would never come to any fruitful end."

This was a true prophecy indeed, but many things were yet to come to pass.

Uriel now instructs Dee to write to the Emperor and tell him that he can make the philosopher's stone: in other words, that he can transmute base metal into gold. In the next breath Uriel foretells that Rudolph shall be succeeded by his brother Ernest, for when he sees and possesses gold (which is the thing he desireth, and those that counsel him do also most desire), he shall perish, and his end shall be terrible. Dee shall be brought safely home to England. Uriel used a curious simile, that Dee "shall ascend the hills as the spiders do." Dee, with his knowledge of many sciences, has never shown himself a naturalist, but he here gives us an interesting scrap of natural history. He writes in the margin: "Perhaps spiders flying in the aire, are carried by strings of their own spinning or making, or else I know not how."

Dee's suit with the Emperor did not much progress. His ministers were naturally envious of this foreigner, and many whispers, as well as louder allegations against the two Englishmen, were abroad, although, as San Clemente told him, the Emperor himself was favourable. The Spanish ambassador was friendly enough, and Dee dined several times at his table. He professed to be descended from Raymond Lully, and, of course, like every educated person of the fifteenth and sixteenth centuries, was a believer in the virtues of the philosopher's stone. He bade them not regard the Dutchmen's ill tongues, "who can hardly brook any stranger." Dee wrote again to the Emperor a letter of elaborate compliment and praise of *vestræ sacræ Cæsareæ Majestatis*, in which he offered to come and show him the philosopher's stone and the magic crystal.

Still nothing came of it, and these needy adventurers in a foreign land began to get into deadly straits. "Now were we all brought to great penury: not able without the Lord Laski's, or some heavenly help, to sustain our state any longer." Dee returned from a dinner at the Spanish ambassador's to find Kelley resolved to throw up the whole business and start for England the next day, going first to Cracow to pick up his wife. If she will not go he must set off without her, but go he will. He will sell his clothes and go to Hamburg, and so to England. It is all very well for the spirits to promise spiritual covenants and blessings; but as Kelley said to Uriel, "When will you give us meat, drink and cloathing?"

At this time the women and children did join the party from Cracow, although Dee does not record it in his diary. But on September 27 Dr. Curtius called to see him at his lodging in Dr. Hageck's house by Bethlem,[1] and he says, "saluted my wife and little Katherine, my daughter." Dee laid before him some of the slanders that he knew were going about. He had been called at Clemente's table a bankrupt alchemist, a conjuror and necromantist, who had sold his own goods and given the proceeds to Laski, whom he had beguiled, and now he was going to fawn upon the Emperor. Curtius was at last induced to spread before the Emperor his report of the conference he had held (by command) with Dee. "Rudolph," said Curtius, "thinks the things you have told him almost either incredible or impossible. He wants you to show him the books." Then the talk became the learned gossip of a couple of bookish and erudite scholars. Dee produced some rare editions which the other had never seen. Curtius offered the loan of one of his own works, *De Superficierum Divisionibus*, printed at Pesaro. After this, with mutual courtesies offered on both parts, "after the manner of the world," Curtius took his horse, and returned homeward.

[1] The street is still called Bethlehems Gasse. It runs from the Huss Strasse to the embankment on the Moldau.

Jane Dee was ailing at this time, and Dee was much distressed. Gabriel, when consulted, told him that the true medicine is trust in the God of Hosts and in His Son Christ. "The Lamb of Life is the true medecine of comfort and consolation." He did, however, condescend to give a remarkable prescription for her use, concocted of a pint of wheat, a live pheasant cock, eleven ounces of white amber, and an ounce of red wine, all distilled together. Dee, though no Christian Scientist, was willing enough to administer the strange decoction, but says he knows not where or how to get a cock pheasant. In the spring of the next year, Jane's fourth child, Michael, was born. He was always rather sickly, and died when nine years old. Theodore, her fifth child, was only thirteen when he too died, but all the six other children grew up.

Curtius and Dee became good friends. The Austrian showed his English acquaintance several of his inventions connected with the quadrant and with astronomical tables, and Dee confided to him the secret of a battering glass he had contrived for taking observations on a dark night. The glass was left at Cracow with his books and other goods, but he would gladly go and fetch it to show the Emperor. This led to Dee's request for a passport to enable him to travel, with servants, wife and children, where he would in the Emperor's dominions at any time within a year. He drew it up himself on October 8, 1584, and the Emperor granted it without demur. Dee soon started for Cracow to bring the rest of his goods to Prague, but the diary for the month of November is missing, and the following book opens on December 10, when he had set out from Cracow to return to Prague. "Master Kelley" was with him, John Crocker, and Rowland and his nurse, who had been left behind when Mrs. Dee and the two elder children joined her husband in Prague. As before, more than a week was occupied with the journey, which was made in a coach, with horses bought of "Master Frizer." In Prague a new lodging was found in a house belonging to two sisters, of whom one was married to Mr. Christopher Christian, the registrar of Old Prague. Dee hired the whole house from him at a rent of 70 "dollars" or thalers a year, to be paid quarterly.

"On Saturday afternoon, January 12, 1585, I removed clean from Doctor Hageck, his house by Bedlem, and came with all my household to the House which I had hired of the two sisters (married) not far from the Market Place in old Prage."

He announced his return to the Spanish ambassador and to Dr. Curtius, and continued his interviews with "the schoolmaster" daily.

Some of the sittings recorded at this time are really of the nature of school lessons, which to a man of Dee's acquirements must have seemed rather elementary, yet he humbled himself as a child to learn. One day geographical and ethnographical information is imparted about America, or, as Dee calls it, "Atlantis;" Cathay; the Bactrian desert; and Phalagon, a country of which Dee says he never heard. Another day, minerals and their properties form the subject of the lesson.

Much was said about the doubting, incredulous spirit of Kelley, which Dee always feels is the hindrance to further knowledge. At length he is given permission to choose another skryer if he will: "Take whomsoever thou wilt in whose face the Lord shall seem to dwell, and place him with this Seer, and let him stand seven times by him. I will take the spirit from him and will give it unto the same that standeth by, and he shall fulfill my word that I have begun."

But Dee was strangely reluctant to part with Kelley. He loved him like a son, he yearned over his soul, and he entertained more lively hopes than ever of his real conversion, for Kelley had at last consented to partake of the sacrament with his older friend. Dee uttered aloud a solemn prayer:—

"O God, thou hast coupled us two together in thy election, and what the Lord hath joyned, no fleshly fancy of mine shall willingly separate. But if it be thy will, seeing he is so hard to give credit to thy holy messengers, without some proof in work first past, as for example this doctrine of the philosophers stone, that so he may come to be allowed, though he imitate Thomas Didymus in his hard and slow belief. And because he is to receive the pledge of thy mercies, and mystery of the heavenly food, we would gladly hear of that holy sacrament some discourse for our better instruction, and his better encouragement to the mystery receiving."

Then was delivered a remarkable homily expounding Protestant Christian belief upon several points: the Creation, the fall of Adam (because he wanted[1]

[1] *I.e.*, acked.

the beauty and excellency of God's spirit for which he was created); of the sacrament of Christ's body, "the holy sign of peace between God and man"; and the mystery and wonder of the rite as shown to the disciples, not, as the wicked do, "tying the power and majesty of God and His omnipotence to the tail or end of reason, to be haled as she will. . . . It is a holy miracle, and thou must believe, as the Disciples did, that thou partakest of the true Body of Christ *sub forma panis.* But receiving ceasing, the Sacrament ceaseth also." This in answer to Dee's interposed question. The Hussite doctrine of the permanence of the sacred element in the common food when once blessed was of course much in men's minds in Prague. So with an injunction to "share this doctrine with your wives," this exposition ends.

CHAPTER XIII

A DREAM OF GOLD

> "Now, Epicure,
> Heighten thyself, talk to her all in gold,
> Rain her as many showers as Jove did drops
> Unto his Danaid, shew the gold a miser
> Compared with Mammon. What! the stone will do't.
> She shall feel gold, taste gold, hear gold, sleep gold."
>
> —JONSON, *The Alchemist.*

ON February 27, 1585, Dee and Kelley, with Thomas Kelley, rode with great secrecy to Limburg, six miles from Prague, in obedience to Madimi, who however told them on arriving that Rudolph knew of their departure. Dee suspected Laski's man, Sontag, of treachery. Michael appeared to them there, and instructed Dee to name his new-born child Michael. The infant was baptised by the Court chaplain in Prague Cathedral (which is dedicated to the very unpopular Saint Vitus) on March 18, the Spanish ambassador being godfather and the Lady Dietrichstein, wife of the Emperor's major-domo, godmother.

Kelley was still murmuring under the mystical dealings of the angels. "Let them give me somewhat profitable to my body, or some wisdom to my mind's behoof, and then I will believe in them," he says. Then he protests he will confess all to the priest, and if the holy father does not allow their doings or counsel to be genuine, neither will he.

The remarkable answer that Dee gives again shows us how in advance he was of his times in matters spiritual as well as scientific. "The authority of good angels or messengers from God is greater," says he, "than the authority of the Pope, or priests."

So the weeks went on. Kelley postponed the day of taking the sacrament. At Easter will be a fit time. He will wait till then. He is tired of skrying: "I pray you deal with another. Here is John, a boy in the house. You may use him." Thus, for the third time, a boy is suggested.

It is a curious piece of psychology, or crystallomancy, that Kelley, who possessed the mediumistic powers, was always so reluctant to use them, while Dee, who, as Madimi told him, had clearer sight than his skryer, was entirely unable to open up communication with the unseen.

Money was scarcer than ever. "My wife being in great perplexity, requested E. K. and me that the annexed petition might be propounded to God and his good angels, to give answer or counsel in the cause." Jane's petition set out simply that they had no provision for meat and drink for their family, that it "would discredit the actions wherewith they are vowed and linked unto the heavenly majesty" to lay the ornaments of their house or coverings of their bodies in pawn to the Jews, and that the city was full of malicious slanders. Aid and direction are implored how or by whom they are to be aided and relieved. The spirits, while reminding her grandiloquently that she is only a woman, full of infirmities, frail in soul, and not fit to enter the synagogue, yet favourably listen, and bid her be faithful and obedient as she is yoked, promising that she and her children shall be cared for. Meanwhile her husband is to gird himself together and hasten to see Laski and King Stephan.

This injunction seems not to have been obeyed for some time, for Dee was now very busy inditing letters to Queen Elizabeth and to other of his friends in England. He was reminded of it later when something went wrong, and another crisis arrived with Kelley. On March 27, a Wednesday, Dee was busy in his study, when the skryer burst in, demanding unceremoniously a copy of a certain magic circle of letters which he professed to have had revealed to him by spirits at Oxford. He wished to show it to a Jesuit priest with whom he had made friends. He protested he would quit the company of the spirits with whom they had recently dealt and return to his former associates—the evil set. Dee said he had no leisure to look for the paper now, he was writing letters of importance, and in a week's time or when able, he would see it was found. This of course was irritating. Kelley stormed and raged, said the old man should not stir his foot from the room till it had been produced, and was about to lock up the door when Dee caught him by the shoulders, "calling aloud to my folks. They came in all, and my wife, and so afterwards by degrees his fury assuaged, and my folks, my wife and his, went away, and after he had sitten two or three hours with me, he saw on my head, as I sat writing, Michael stand with a sword, who willed him to speak, which he did forbear to do above a quarter of an hour."

Kelley, like a spoilt child, demanded of Michael if he should have his circle of letters. The angel addressed him then in a passage of exceeding beauty, seeming to scorch and wither the promptings of the skryer's evil nature, while wrestling at the same time with all the powers of darkness for his soul:—

"O Jehovah, whose look is more terrible to thy angels than all the fires thou hast created, . . . wilt thou suffer one man to be carried away, to the dishonouring and treading under foot of thee and thy light, of thee and thy truth? Can one man be dearer unto thee than the whole world was? Shall the heavens be thrown headlong down, and he go uncorrected?"

He intimates to the partners that their work and calling is greater than honour, money, pride and jewels. As it is great, so must their temptations be great.

"Therefore God has framed one of you as a stiffe-made Ashe, to bind up the continuance of his work, and to be free from yielding unto Satan."

As for the other, Michael promises Kelley that no evil spirit shall visibly show himself unto him any more as long as he is in the flesh.

"Whosoever therefore appeareth hereafter is of good."

Thus begins to yawn before the pair the most dangerous pitfall of all. Pride and confidence in the perfect intuition and knowledge of God's will has led many a good and holy man astray. Soon even the stiff-made ash is to arrive at the pitch of believing that their teachers cannot err, and then comes a terrible downfall. Michael in an exquisite little parable bids them cleave fast together. And again it is clear why the elder man, the seeker after hidden knowledge, the pure-minded and gentle-hearted old mathematician and astrologer, though torn in pieces with his partner's wild outbursts, his notorious cupidity, impatience, and evil living, yearned over him and his rebellious youth as a mother over her child. Like Michael, he seems involved in a prolonged struggle for the rescue of his soul from the demons in whose power he devoutly believed.

"Parabola de Nobis Duobus.

"A wood grew up, and the trees were young, and lo! there arose a great Tempest from the North, and the Seas threw out the air that had subtilly stolen himself into them. And the winds were great. And behold there was one Tree which was older than the rest, and had grown longer than that which shot up by him. This Tree could not be moved with the wind, but the Tree that was young was moved to and fro with the wind, and strook himself oftentimes upon the stiff-set tree. The Forrester came and beheld, and said within himself, 'The force of this wind is great. See this young Tree beateth himself in pieces against the greater. I will go home, and will bring my ground instruments, and will eradicate him, and I will place him farther off. Then if the winds come, he shall have room to move.' But when he came home, the Lord of the Wood seeing him in a readiness with his Mattock and his spade, asked him of his goings, which told the thing in order unto his Master. But lo! his Master rebuked him, and he said thus: 'When the winds are not, they increase, they are not hurtful one to the other. Suffer them therefore. When the young Tree taketh roots, and shall look up unto some years, his roots shall link themselves with and under the roots of the greater. Then, though the winds come, they shall not be hurtful one to another, but shall stand so much the more fast, by how much the more they are wrapped together; yea, when the old tree withereth, he shall be a strength unto him, and shall add unto his age as much as he hath added unto his youth.'

"And he ceased to dig.

"Be not you therefore haled in sunder, neither be you offended one at another. Peradventure Reason would set you aside. But God will not. Behold, if you break the yoke that you are in and runne astray, he that erreth shall perish, even so shall he that standeth also be desolate. Love therefore one another, and comfort one another, for he that comforteth his brother comforteth himself. . . . Let youth yield to ripe years. . . . You have vowed that one of you do nothing without the other's counsel, but you shall not be two counsellors. Let the Doer occupie the superiority. The Seer, let him see and look after the doings of that he seeth, for you are but one body in this work."

In April, Dee and Kelley returned to Cracow. As they were nearing the city they saw a great whirlwind wreathing up the dust and shooting forward in a southerly direction. They found their house let under them to a "forced-in tenant," but as Dee had brought his keys, he effected an entrance, and secured at least a bedstead. By the aid of his lawyer, Mr. Tebaldo, "an ancient practitioner in Polish causes," he obtained a decree against his landlord that without six months' notice he could not be ejected. They took up their abode in the College of Nyepolonize. Laski now joined them in Cracow, and took Dee on May 23 to an audience of King Stephan. Stephan was seated by the south window of his principal audience and banqueting chamber, looking out upon the beautiful new gardens that he was then making. Polite speeches of greeting in Latin passed between the two, but there was scant time for more before the Vice-Chancellor and Chief Secretary, with others, came in, bringing Bills for the King to read and sign. Stephan had small time to spare for visionary alchemists. His very glorious reign was crowded with great achievements. Though a strong Catholic himself, he respected the liberties of his Protestant subjects, won back the Russian provinces for Poland, reformed the universities and established the Jesuits in educational seminaries, and protected the Jews. He died very suddenly about a year after Dee's third interview with him. Dee has the following very valuable note of his death, entered in the diary a few weeks after his arrival at Trebona Castle in 1586 : "December 11, Stephan Poloniensis obiit: natus anno 1530, die 13 Januarii, hora quarta mane min 26, in Transylvania. Obiit hora secunda post medium noctem, ut intellexi ex literis D^{ni} Lasky, receptis die 29 per Alexandrum."

Dee also visited Dr. Hannibal (Annibaldus), the famous divine, and discussed with him his commentaries on Latin authors—Hermes Trismegistus and Mandellus. He partook of the Communion at the Bernardine convent where the Doctor was a professor. Three times within Easter week did he communicate, "that in all manner of wayes I might have a clean and quiet conscience." On "Easter Monday, very devoutly, in St. Stephan's Church,[1] E. K. received the Communion, to my unspeakable gladness and content, being a thing so long and earnestly required and urged of him by our spiritual good friends." As Dee wrote to Walsingham, "Saul had become a Paul."

It was a very short interlude. For Laski had not yet paid him the "money long since due," and Kelley once more vows he will leave, for the "actions are unsuccessful and are to be cut off." Laski was again admitted to the sittings, and King Stephan granted them another interview. Laski urged the King to take the two alchemists into his service and give them "a yearly maintenance." In obedience to his instructors, Dee promises to make the philosopher's stone, if the King will bear the charge. He does not profess that he can, but he believes the angels will teach him the secret. Stephan was not so sanguine. In the King's private chamber, a sitting was held, with the crystal set before him, but he remained unconvinced. He gave no encouragement, and in August the pair, hopeless of patronage from Poland, returned to Prague, where Jane and Joan Kelley, the children and the servants, had been left under Edmond Hilton's care.

An anglicised Italian pervert, Francisco Pucci, now appeared upon the scenes and was admitted to the sittings at the shew-stone. Pucci had been a Lyons merchant, but had "laid aside his trade to study

[1] St. Stephan's Church, Cracow, in the Stephangasse, erected 1351, has still its beautiful late Gothic font of 1462.

TITLE-PAGE OF "GENERAL AND RARE MEMORIALS."

(See p. 39.)

"If I had knowne this and had done soe
I had avoyded mickle woe."

Thomas Norton *The Ordinall of Alchimy.*

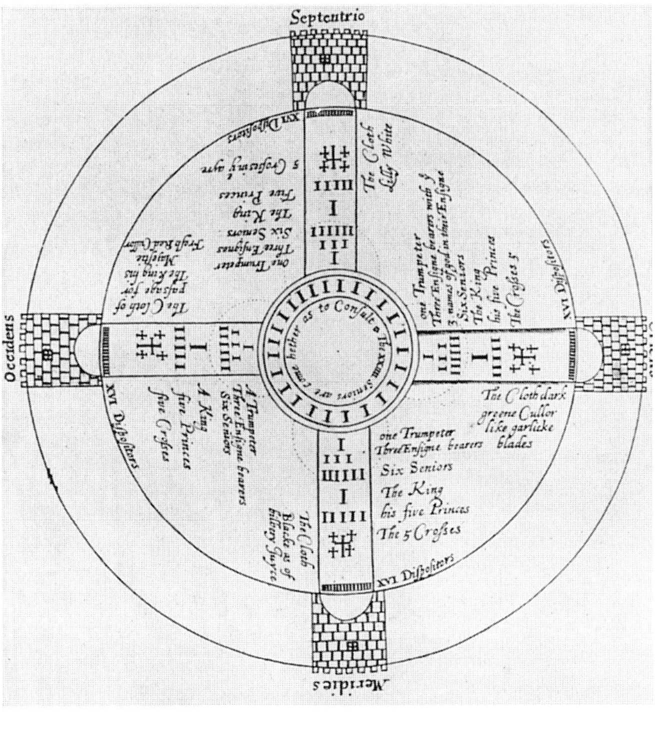

THE VISION OF THE FOUR CASTLES.

(See p. 141.)

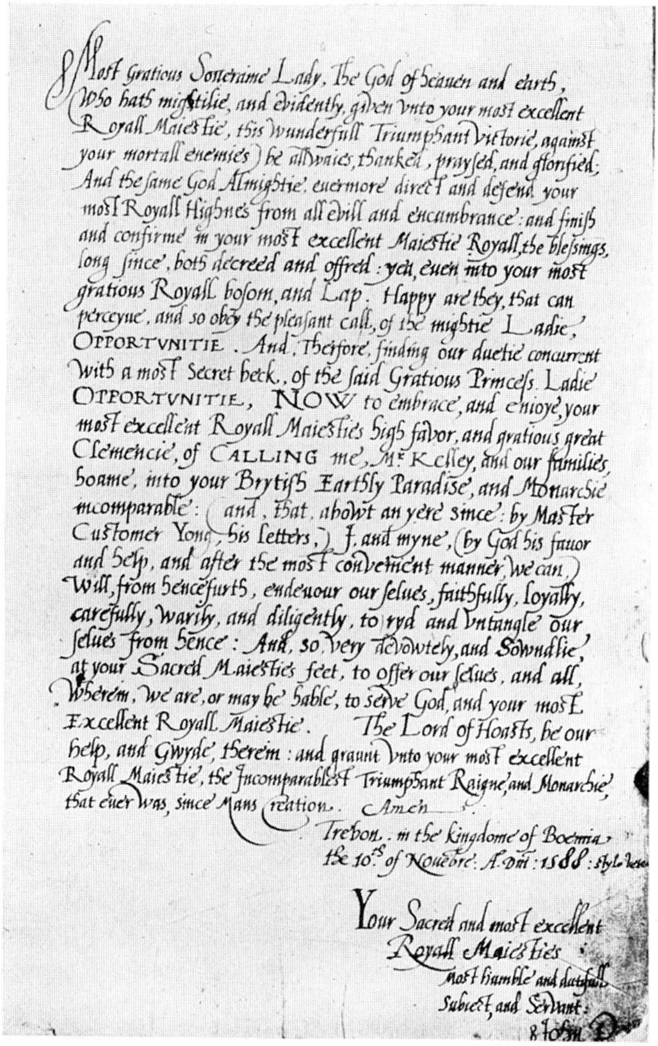

Most Gratious Soveraine Lady, The God of heauen and earth, (Who hath mightilie, and evidently, given unto your most excellent Royall Maiestie, this wunderfull Triumphant Victorie, against your mortall enemies) be allwaies thanked, praysed, and glorified: And the same God Almightie evermore direct and defend your most Royall Highnes from all evill and encumbrance: and finish and confirme in your most excellent Maiestie Royall, the blessings, long since, both decreed and offred: yea, even into your most gratious Royall bosom, and Lap. Happy are they, that can perceyve, and so obey the pleasant call, of the mightie Ladie, OPPORTUNITIE. And, therefore, finding our duetie concurrent with a most secret beck, of the said Gratious Princess Ladie OPPORTUNITIE, NOW to embrace, and enioye your most excellent Royall Maiesties high favor, and gratious great Clemencie, of CALLING me, Mr Kelley, and our families, hoame, into your Brytish Earthly Paradise, and Monarchie incomparable: (and, that, abowt an yere since: by Master Customer Yong, his letters,) I, and myne, (by God his fauor and help, and after the most convenient manner, we can,) Will, from hencefurth, endeuour our selues, faithfully, loyally, carefully, warily, and diligently, to ryd and untangle our selues from hence: And, so, very devowtely, and sowndlie, at your Sacred Maiesties feet, to offer our selues, and all, wherein, we are, or may be hable, to serve God, and your most Excellent Royall Maiestie. The Lord of Hoasts, be our help, and Gwyde, therein: and graunt unto your most excellent Royall Maiestie, the Incomparablest Triumphant Raigne, and Monarchie, that ever was, since Mans Creation. Amen.

Trebon, in the kingdome of Boemia the 10th of Novembr: A. Dni: 1588: stylo novo

Your Sacred and most excellent
Royall Maiesties
most humble and dutyfull
Subiect, and Servant:
John Dee

DEE TO QUEEN ELIZABETH ON THE DEFEAT OF THE SPANISH ARMADA.
(See p. 198.)

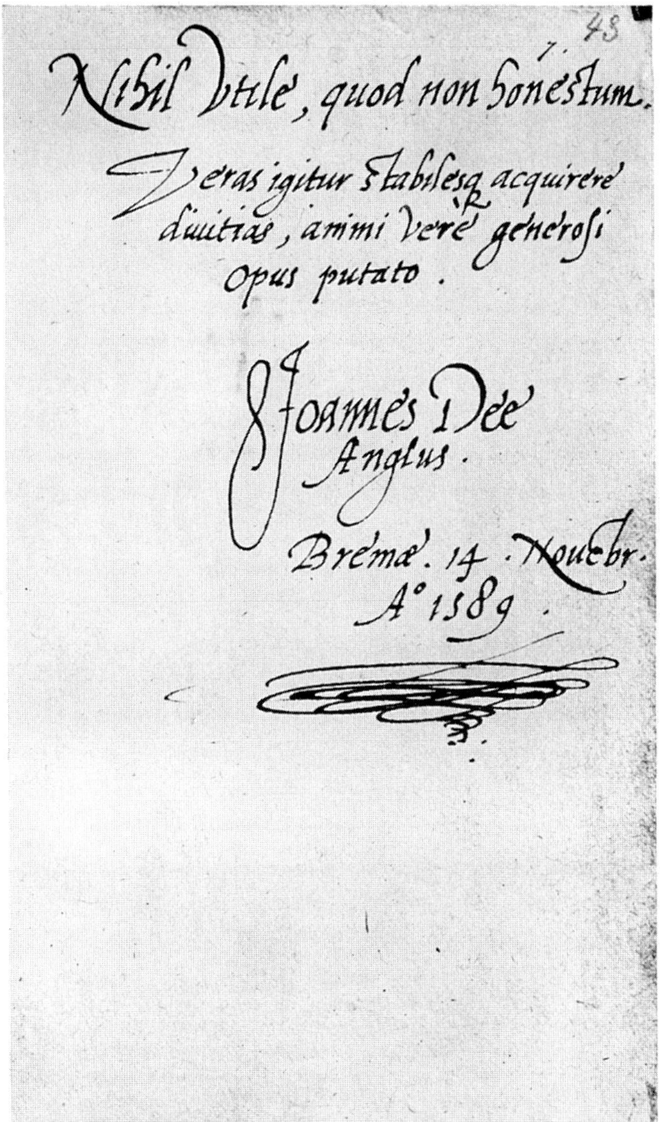

Nihil vtile, quod non honestum.

Veras igitur stabilesq acquirere diuitias, animi vere generosi opus putato.

Joannes Dee
Anglus.

Bremæ. 14. Nouebr.
A° 1589.

A page from the Thesaurus Amicorum of Timon Coccius.

"WHICH FIER MUST EVER BE COEQUALL
IN EVERY MINUTE, AND YET PERPETUALL;
FOR IT MAY NEVER ABATE NE INCREASE,
AND YET THE FIER MAIE NEVER CEASE."

THOMAS NORTON *The Ordinall of Alchimy.*

ARMS OF DEE AS SHOWN IN A CUT AT THE END OF HIS "LETTER APOLOGETICALL" (1599).

sacred letters," and become a theological disputant of the current type.[1] Professing himself a Protestant, he came to Oxford to study, graduated M.A. in 1574, and in London, Basle, Antwerp, and other places, became an open and notorious writer and champion against the Church which he had abjured. He had followed Socinus to Cracow, and had noisily opposed the Jesuits there. Soon after he recanted, became a Romish priest and secretary to a cardinal in Rome, where he died in 1606, and was buried in the Church of San Onofrio on the Janiculum.

On his information it appears that three copies of Dee's manuscripts were burned in Prague, April 10, 1586. These were the *Book of Enoch*, the *Forty-eight Keys of the Angels (Claves Angelicæ)* and the *Liber Scientiæ Auxilii et Victoriæ Terrestris*, works which had been written down from the spirit revelations since the partnership with Kelley had commenced. The books burned were not of course the originals, the two first of which still exist.[2] Of the *Book of Enoch* there are three copies, one made by Kelley, a remarkable tribute to the mechanical skill in draughtsmanship, the extraordinary application and ability, of this very versatile personage. It contains hundreds of diagrams of figures, round or rectangular in shape, composed of an infinite number of minute squares each containing a letter or figure. These letters occur in every possible combination and order, some reading straight across the page, others diagonally, and so on. Dee gives an extraordinary story of the

[1] Wood, *Athen. Oxon.*, vol. i., 587.

[2] *Sloane MSS.*, 3189 and 3191.

restoration on April 30 of the books said to have been burned, by a man like a gardener, invisible to himself, to Joan Kelley, and to all in the garden at the time, save Kelley. The gardener placed them under an almond tree in Carpio's vineyard, on a sloping bank between the banqueting house and the "cliff side." Trickery of Kelley's, no doubt.

The feeling against these foreign adventurers grew strong in the city. Sixtus V., who had succeeded as Pope, issued a Papal edict, dated May 29, 1586, banishing Dee and Kelley from Prague within six days. It seemed to trouble them very little, for Dee was already away on a visit to a new patron, William Ursinus, Count Rosenberg, at his country seat on the Moldau. From thence he went to see some glass-works at Volkanau, about twelve miles north of the city; then he proceeded to Leipsic in time for the fair on May 11. There he met Lawrence Overton, an English merchant to whom Jane Dee had given kind attention and hospitality when he had fallen ill in her house a year before. Overton had returned from England, where he had seen Edmond Hilton, sent in November with letters to the Queen, Sir Francis Walsingham and others. Hilton was expected back shortly. Overton was on the point of returning to England, and by him another letter to the Secretary was despatched.

Dee's letters to Walsingham, with their veiled allusions to secret affairs, form one of the grounds upon which the supposition has been based that he was employed by the Queen's minister as a secret spy and diplomatic agent abroad, and that his cabalistic diagrams contained a cipher. An elaborate theory was constructed to support this contention.[1]

From this letter it is evident that Dee wishes his friends in England to believe that he and his partner have already found the hidden secret, but he wraps his words in due mystery, and it is impossible to say exactly when Kelley first professed to have made, and when he induced his partner to believe that he actually had made, the gold on which his heart was set. That Dee's heart was equally fixed on the discovery is indisputable, but from what a different cause!

"To ye Rt. Honble. S^r.^ Fr. Walsingham Knt, her most excellent Maties. Principal Secretary my singular good Fr^d.^ and Patron with speed.[2]

"Right Honorable Sir,

"Albeit I have almost in vain come a hundred miles (from Prague to this Leipsic Mart) hoping either to meet my servant there with answer to my former letters, sent in November last to her Majesty (when also I wrote unto your honor and others). And so with speed from this Leipsick to have sent again most speedily, as occasion should have served. And now I find neither servant neither letter from him, neither word of mouth, yet all this notwithstanding; and whatsoever the hindrance or delay hereof may be (whether the keeping back of my letters from her Majesty, or the manifold and important most weighty affairs public hindring or delaying her Majesty's most gracious discreet and wise resolution herein. Or what other occasion else hath and doth cause this long and wonderful delay of answer receiving); all

[1] Robert Hooke, *Posthumous Works* (1705), pp. 206–7.

[2] Casaubon, *True and Faithful Relation*, p. 422.

this notwithstanding, I thought good before I set up my coach to write, and most humbly to salute your honour very faithfully, dutifully and sincerely, with great and the same good will that my Letter some years since written to your Honour (but then a stumbling block unto your Honour and others for the strangeness of the phrases therein) doth pretend. So it is, right Honorable, that the merciful providence of the Highest, declared in his great and abundant graces upon me, and mine, is so wonderful and mighty, that very few, unless they be present witnesses, can believe the same. Therefore how hard they are to be believed there, where all my life and doings were construed to a contrary sense, and processe of death contrived and decreed against the Innocent, who cannot easily judge?

"I am forced to be brief. That which England suspected, was also here, for these two years almost, secretly in doubt, in question, in consultation, Imperial and Royal, by Honourable Espies; fawning about me and by others discoursed upon, pryed and peered into. And at length both the chief Romish power and Imperial dignity are brought to that point resolutely that partly they are sorry of their so late reclaiming their erroneous judgment against us and of us, and seek means to deal with us so as we might favour both the one and the other; and partly to Rome is sent, for as great authority and power as can be devised; and likewise here all other means and wayes contrived, how by force or for feare they may make us glad to follow their humours. But all in vain, for force human we fear not, as plainly and often I have to the Princes declared. And otherwise than in pure verity and godlinesse we will not favour any (my words may seem very marvellous in your Honours ears, but mark the end, we have had, and shall have, to deal with no babes). I have full oft, and upon many of their requests and questions, referred myself to her Majesties answer thus in vain expected. Nuncius Apostolicus Germanicus Malaspina, after his year's suit to be acquainted with me, at length had such his answer that he is gone to Rome with a flea in his eare, that disquieteth him and terrifieth the whole state Romish and Jesuitical. Secretly they threaten us violent death, and openly they fawn upon us. We know the Sting of Envy and the fury of fear in tyrannical minds, what desperate attempts they have and do often undertake. But the God of Heaven and Earth is our Light, Leader and Defender. To the World's end, his mercies upon us will breed his praises Honour and glory. Thus much, very rhapsodically yet faithfully, *tanquam dictum sapienti*, I thought good to commit to the safe and speedy conveyance of a young merchant here called Lawrence Overton, which if it come to your Honours hand before my Servant have left his despatch, I may by your honor be advertised. Your Honour is sufficient from her Majesty to deal and proceed with me, if it be thought good. But if you make a Council Table Case of it, *Quot homines, tot sententiæ*. And my Commission from above is not so large: *Qui potest capere, capiat.*"

The almost apostolical flavour which Dee permits himself to impart to some of this letter, owing to the greatness of his believed mission, shows to what a height of "rhapsodical" fervours his spirit had now attained. It is still more emphasised in the concluding passage, which begins, however, very practically, with an anxious thought cast back to his English possessions. His desire that Thomas Digges, the eminent mathematician to whom his calculations for the reformed calendar had been submitted, should be sent over to inspect their doings, was curious, but it shows that he, at any rate, wished to deal openly and conceal nothing. He ends thus :—

"Sir, I trust I shall have Justice for my house library, goods and Revenues, etc. Do not you disdain, neither fear to bear favour unto your poor innocent neighbour. If you send unto me Master Thomas Digges, in her Majestie's behalf, his faithfulness to her Majesty and my well liking of the man, shall bring forth some piece of good service. But her Majesty had been better to have spent or given away in alms, a Million of gold, than to have lost some opportunities past. No human reason can limit or determine God his marvellous means of proceeding with us. He hath made of Saul (E. K.) a Paul, but yet now and then visited with a pang of human frailty. The Almighty bless her Majestie both in this World and eternally; and inspire your heart with some conceiving of his merciful purposes, yet not utterly cut off from her Majesty to enjoy.

From Leipsic this 14 of May, 1586,
at Peter Hans Swarts house.

Your Honours faithful welwisher to use and command for the honour of God and her Majesties best service,

"JOHN DEE."

On being ejected from Prague, Dee removed his family and goods to Erfurt, but in spite of the influence of Dr. Curtius, and of a friend of Rosenberg, he was not allowed to hire a house there, for the Italian was before him. Pucci called on Dee after supper, and held out hopes that he might obtain permission for their return to Prague, for the new Nuncio, the

Bishop of Piacenza, was inclined to a more favourable view than Malaspina. Pucci protested that they were only to be examined and if found heretical to be sent to Rome. He brought an invitation for their return, if they would promise not to exercise magical arts. Dee, who was starting early next morning to look at a house at Saalfeld, wherein to settle his exiled family, bade Kelley copy it and rode off. On the ride he thought it over. Pucci he had never liked, neither had Jane. "His household behaviour was not acceptable to our wives and family. He had blabbed our secrets without our leave. He was unquiet in disputation." Dee summed up the man as a spy, the letter as a bait, and set to work to devise a way of being rid of him "by quiet and honest meanes." He was absent two or three days, but the Italian was still there when he returned, urging them to go to Rome. Dee rebuked him for curiosity and interference, and accused him of conspiring against them; he, a mere probationer and not yet owned of the spirits (who in fact had said he was "leprous" and should be "cut off"), to presume an equal authority with them in their revelations!

Dee wrote a dignified letter to the Nuncio, and despatched it by the Italian, who was to receive from John Carpio, a wealthy neighbour and friend of theirs in Prague, a sum of fifty dollars for his expenses. The travellers went on to Cassel and to Gotha, but it was not long before a permanent asylum offered for the exiles. Their new patron, Count Rosenberg, was a friend worth having, for he was all-powerful with Rudolph; he was Viceroy of Bohemia and a Knight of the Golden Fleece.[1] His influence and protection were now to be at the Englishmen's disposal. On August 8, Rosenberg obtained from the Emperor a partial revocation of the decree against them, since they were permitted by it to reside freely in any of his lordship's towns, cities or castles. They settled on September 14, 1586, at Tribau or Trebona, in Southern Bohemia, and here for about two years their wanderings came to an end.

Dee resumed the writing of his private diary, in which he had made no entry for three years, the last event recorded there being the departure of the family from Mortlake just three years before, on September 21, 1583. He opened a new volume, an *Ephemerides Cœlestium,* calculated for the years 1581—1620, by Joh. Antonius Maginus, printed in Venice, 1582. The first entry made in it was Michael's birth at Prague on February 12, 1586; the next was their arrival at Trebona (for it will be more convenient to follow Dee's latinised version of the name).

[1] An interesting account of the two brothers, Counts William and Peter Rosenberg, their life at Trebona, their influence on the literature, music, and politics of Bohemia, is given by Count Lutzow in his *History of Bohemian Literature* (1899), pp. 314—321, but he says there that it was Count Peter who visited Elizabeth, and not William. Their famous library is now in Stockholm.

CHAPTER XIV

THE CASTLE OF TREBONA

"Welcome the sour cup of prosperity!
Affliction may one day smile again: and until then,
Sit down, sorrow."

—SHAKESPEARE, *Love's Labour Lost.*

TRIBAU, or Wittingau, the Trebona of our story, is a small village lying in the beautiful undulating scenery of the Ludnitz, a small tributary of the river Moldau. It is a few miles from Neuhaus and Weseli, not many from the town of Budweis, on the Upper Moldau, in Southern Bohemia.

In 1586 it consisted of little beside the castle, a Rathhaus, quarters for a small garrison, and a cluster of dwellings where Dee tells a fire broke out on Whit Sunday, 1585, and destroyed several houses. The castle was one of Rosenberg's many residences in Bohemia, and apparently a favourite one. The Viceroy was now just over fifty (he was born on March 10, 1535); he married about this time,[1] and his wife constantly accompanied him on his visits to Trebona. They had also another castle at Neuhaus, beside a residence with beautiful gardens bordering the Moldau opposite Prague. They were frequently

[1] His marriage was approved by the spirits and seems to have been considered a sign of conversion. He told Dee he wished his master, Rudolph, would amend his loose life and do the same. The Emperor had no lawful wife or child.

on the wing, flitting from Krumau to Vienna and from Vienna back to Prague. He welcomed the English travellers himself at Trebona, assigned them their rooms, and promised them all that heart could desire.

The actions, which had long been interrupted, were now resumed in "a goodly chapel next my chamber," where all the "appurtenances" were set up, with the "angelicall stone" in its frame of gold upon the table. Rosenberg had been already admitted to the sittings, in obedience to directions received on October 14. When the communications were made in English, Dee translated them into Latin for his benefit. But experiments with Kelley's powder were now all-engrossing, and even the spirits pass for a time into the background. Kelley went off to Prague for three weeks and was followed by Rosenberg. Dee remained with his wife and children; after their hardships, poverty, dangerous and wandering life, poor Jane must have been thankful for so luxurious a shelter. Visitors for Dee constantly arrived. Among them was Dr. Victor Reinhold, of Saalfeldt, perhaps a son of Erasmus Reinhold, the astronomer. Pucci also came for a fortnight.

In December Dee received a very flattering invitation from the Emperor of Russia (Feodor Ivanowich) to go and take up his residence at Moscow in the Court. Dee's fame as a learned astrologer and mathematician had spread to Russia; still more was his reputation as an alchemist bruited abroad: perhaps he was already credited with having actually made gold by projection or transmutation.

The first intimation of the Emperor's wish was

conveyed by Thomas Simkinson, an Englishman, of Hull, commissioned by Edward Garland to go to Brunswick or Cassel, or wherever Dee might be found, and beg him to remain there until Garland could come from Russia.[1] He might tell Dee that the Emperor, having certain knowledge of his learning and wisdom, is marvellous desirous for him to come to his country, and had given Garland a sealed letter of invitation, promising a sum of £2,000 yearly and free diet from the royal kitchen if he will come. His charges of removing shall be paid, and he shall travel royally with 500 horses to convey him through the land. If he thinks the salary offered too little, Garland, when he arrives, will assure him that if he asks as much more, he shall have it. The "Lord Protector," too, Prince Boris, took Garland in his arms on his departure and promised 1,000 roubles from his own purse beside the Emperor's allowance.

Simkinson reached Trebona on September 18, and at once declared his flattering errand. "On December 8 at noon, Garland came to me from the Emperor of Moschovia, according to the articles before sent unto me by Thomas Simkinson."[2] On December 17, at Trebona, Edward Garland drew up a paper repeating all the former promises in the Emperor's name, and signed it, with Kelley, his brother Francis Garland, and others, as witnesses.

There is no doubt that the Emperor thought he was inviting to his Court the man who could fill his

[1] Hakluyt's *Principal Navigations*. Glasgow, 1903, vol. iii., pp. 445–8. *Cal. S. P. Dom.*, 1581—1590, p. 354.

[2] Halliwell has misread this as "Hankinson" in the Camd. Soc. Diary.

coffers and bring glory and prestige to his name. Hakluyt hints at it when he says the offer was made partly for his counsel about discoveries to the North-East, *partly for some other weighty occasions.* Dee was no self-seeker, or Court flatterer, although this was the fifth sovereign he says he might have served. The offer seems never to have tempted him from his loyalty to his own Queen. He bade Garland at once dismiss six out of the eight Russian servants he had brought to attend them on their journey, and turned to matters more important.

"On 19th December, to the great gratification of Master Edward Garland and Francis, his brother, which Edward had been sent to me with a message from the Emperor of Muschovia, that I should come to him, E. K. made projection with his powder in the proportion of one minim (upon an ounce and a quarter of mercury) and produced nearly an ounce of best gold; which gold we afterwards distributed from the crucible, and gave one to Edward."

It is quite significant that *Kelley* made the gold, *Kelley* showed it, and Dee is content to give him all the credit. The pangs and heart-burnings and jealousies have yet to come. Now he only felt that at last he was victorious in his long quest. He was on the crest of the wave. His hour had come.

How the wonderful trick was done, Kelley could best describe.

Kelley was now constantly riding to Prague, or making longer expeditions to Poland, for he still had hopes of getting more money from Laski. By March his hope seems to have been realised, for Dee notes that

Kelley paid him about 500 ducats in two or more sums (about £233). This plenitude of money of course encouraged the idea abroad that they were actually making it. When he returned from Prague on January 18, Kelley brought a handsome present from Rosenberg to Jane Dee, in the shape of a beautiful jewelled chain, the value of which was "esteemed at 300 duckettes," says Dee, "200 the juell stones and 100 the gold." In three days Kelley had posted off again to Prague, to join Rosenberg at his house in the city. This time he took with him his brother Thomas, Francis Garland, and a Bohemian servant, Ferdinand Hernyck. No doubt he was pursuing his experiments for the "multiplying" of gold in the city, away from Dee.

Kelley's letter to Dee announcing this arrival of his in Prague is the only communication between this strange pair of partners that seems to have survived. It shows that erratic and wayward creature in a gentle and even affectionate light, and although its pious protestations are obviously overdone, it pictures for us quite vividly the relations between the two, and partly accounts for the strength of the tie that bound Dee to his intractable pupil, soon to become his master. For while Dee laboured laboriously and scientifically with his alchemical compounds, Kelley at one bound overleaped the chasm and by some process best known to himself professed to have arrived at the goal.

To Dee's single-hearted nature such success was magnificent, wonderful. He began forthwith to treat his quondam skryer with added respect; the expression "Dominus Kelley" creeps once into the diary; and

Kelley grew arrogant and overbearing. For the moment, however, he is all for friendship and respect.

" Prage. 1587. 25 Januarii." [This in Dee's hand.] (addressed) "To the Right Worshipful and his assured friend Mr. John Dee Esquire, give these. Magnifico Domino, Domino Dee.

" Sir. My hearty commendations unto you, desiring your health as my own; my Lord was exceeding glad of your Letters, and said, 'Now I see he loveth me,' and truly as far as I perceive he loveth us heartily. This Sunday in the Name of the Blessed Trinity I begin my journey [to Poland], wherein I commend me unto your prayers, desiring the Almighty to send his fortitude with me. I commend me unto Mrs. Dee a thousand times, and unto your little babes: wishing myself rather amongst you than elsewhere. I will by God's grace about twenty days hence return, in the mean season all comfort and joy be amongst you.

" Your assured and immoveable friend

" E. KELLEY."

When this letter reached Trebona, Dee had gone riding with two horsemen of the city of Neuhaus, hoping to meet Rosenberg, who he thought would return that way from Vienna to Prague. Mrs. Dee at once despatched the servant Ludovic to meet his master. So Dee received Kelley's affectionate letter " in the highway, without Platz," a village about half-way to Neuhaus. Ludovic carried also a little note from Jane to her husband. It is the only letter of hers we have, but it confirms all that we suspect. We know her to have been a well-educated, well-read woman; the writing is strong and clear; and did not Francis Pucci describe her as a learned woman, " lectissima femina "? She must also have been an extraordinarily capable one to have controlled and managed her large household of children, assistants, apprentices, servants and miscellaneous visitors, often in the absence of her husband, and in a foreign land, constantly moving on from place to place in this nomadic life they led. Dee has a charming name for her. Somewhere in a letter he speaks of "my payneful Jane." Full of pains she must indeed have been, the model wife for an elderly, incomprehensible husband, using her intellectual powers to accommodate her family, while the learned man pursued his angelic visions and his alchemical experiments unhampered. Above all things she must have been a peacemaker, hot and hasty although she sometimes was. Here is the letter to the husband who had only left her that morning:—

"Swethart. I commend me unto you, hoping in God that you ar in good health as I, and my children, with all my household, am here, I prayse God for it. I have non other matter to write unto you at this time."

There is a capable and managing sound about "my" children and "my" household, which leads one to wonder what this practical housewife thought of all the angelic promises which were never kept or performed. At the outset of the mysterious Kelley doings she was, we know, in her impetuous way, annoyed, angry, probably contemptuous, but by this time she perhaps had grown either to believe in them or tolerantly to acquiesce. She was only thirty-two, yet she had lived through many strange experiences and was soon to be put to the strongest test possible to a woman.

By April Kelley was once more settled as part of the household, and on the 4th the crystal gazing was resumed. He professed to hear instructions to Rosenberg, who was present, to build a commonwealth, render tribute to Rudolph, and he shall be Duke of Brandenburg. To himself things are said he is not reluctant to hear. We have seen how almost immediately after his marriage he took a violent dislike to his wife. In the four years, it seems, he had reproached her for giving him no child. To him generation was the root principle of alchemy, and the phase of it in which he centred his attention. It is always the marriage of the red man, copper, and the white woman, mercury, that is to tinge the whole world with gold. Now a voice tells him why he is barren. Not because of his reckless, disordered life, but because she was of his own choosing—the wrong woman! Therefore he is to be seedless and fruitless for ever. Had it not been for the Dees' kindness to her, and especially Jane's, poor neglected Joan Kelley would have had but a sorry time. She was only twenty-four; lively and docile, she seemed to please everyone but her husband. Pucci, with perhaps a little flattery, calls her "rarum exemplum juvenilis sanctitatis, castitatis, atque omnium virtutem." If she had not all the virtues, she at least had several. Her brother, Edmund Cooper, and another friend so loved her that they came over from England a year later on purpose to see if she and her husband could not be more reconciled.

Kelley had been more unsettled than ever, discontented with his wife, with his calling, its results, and above all with his position and his poverty. What was a pittance of fifty pounds a year to a man in constant intercourse with princes and nobles, with credulous fools possessed with dreams of gold? The same qualities that attracted Dee were equally magnetic with others. Laski loved him; Edward Dyer deserted his old friend Dee for this newcomer, a nobody. He had made himself invaluable to Rosenberg, who seems to have had implicit faith in his powers. Rosenberg induces the Emperor to employ him. Had he not already found the secret of projection? Was he not the possessor of the magic powder which waited only for the opportunity to be transformed into countless heaps of ducats? Only money was wanting, and that he could certainly get. But he must first be released from this galling position of medium. He told Dee that all through this Lent he had prayed once a day at least that he might "no more have dealing to skry." At Easter-time he did receive a promise to be set free from the crystal gazing, as he desired, but his wish for freedom was not exactly approved by the angelic ministers.

"Is it a burthen unto thee to be comforted from above? O foolish man! By how much the heavens excel the earth, by so much doth the gift that is given thee excel all earthly treasure. Notwithstanding, thou shalt not at any time hereafter be constrained to see the judgment of the Highest, or to hear the voices of heaven, for thou art a stumbling block to many. . . . And the power which is given thee of seeing shall be diminished in thee, and shall dwell upon the first begotten son of him that sitteth by thee."

The selection of a child as Kelley's successor seems not to have been altogether unexpected. It had been hinted in Prague a year before that a boy would serve for the office; but that the choice would fall upon Dee's own son must have come as a dreadful surprise, at any rate to his mother. No doubt the old man regarded it as a mark of special heavenly honour.

It is more likely that Jane, with her practical mind, regarded the change of medium with anything but satisfaction. Arthur was now seven and three quarters of a year old, a clever child, already well grounded in Latin, but far too tender in years and disposition to be made the subject of any psychological experiments. Fortunately for him, his skrying was a dismal failure, although it seems to have bent his childish mind towards the occultism he followed in after-life. Distinguished physician as he afterwards became, both at home and in the service of the Emperor of Russia, he was a true son of his father, and maintained to the end of his life a belief in alchemy and transmutation which nothing could shake.

Kelley was desired to initiate the child.

"I thereupon thinking that E. K. would, should or best could, instruct and direct the childe in that exercise, did alwayes await that E. K. would of himself call the boy to that exercise with him; and so much the rather because he said that he was very glad now that he should have a Witness of the things shewed and declared by spiritual creatures: And that he would be more willing to do what should be so enjoyned to him to do, than if only he himself did see. But when E. K. said to me that I should exercise the child and not he, and that he would not, I thereupon appointed with myself to bring the childe to the place, and to offer him, and present him to the service of Seeing and Skrying from God and by God's assignment."

Then Dee drew up a petition to put in the child's mouth that he might be "a true and perfect seer, Hearer, Declarer and Witness of such things as might be revealed to him either immediately or mediately by the angels." Three times a day for three days he was to offer this prayer thrice over, while seated at the stone. The poor child happily beheld in the magic crystal nothing more than dots and pricks, letters and lines, and "a young man in a white leathern doublet and a grey cloke, like Hans of Gloats, his cloak,"[1] of all which even his father could make little. On the fourth day came Kelley, to see how Arthur and his skrying progressed. But still the child saw nothing. Then Kelley applied himself to skry as usual. Looking from the gallery window, he had already without any crystal seen Il and Madimi, also Uriel, who justifies their words. What they command he hesitates to say. Next day he is again the percipient; the result is the same. At length, with feigned reluctance, he tells Dee of a vision of strange and subversive portent. It is so repugnant to him that he can hardly impart it. Madimi, throwing aside all her garments, mysteriously bids them participate in all things one with another. Kelley affects not to understand, but after more hesitation expounds to Dee that the sharing is to be in

[1] This was one of the servants, afterwards several times mentioned.

everything, even of their wives. All things are to be in common between them.

Dee, to whom Madimi is invisible, though he hears her voice, fiercely rebukes her: "Such words are unmeet for any godly creature to use. Are the commandments of God to be broken?" This participation, he insists to Kelley, can be meant only in a Christian and godly sense. Kelley construes the injunction very differently, but he affects a chaste horror and swears for the hundredth time that he will deal no more with the spirits.

Then Madimi, with scathing irony, addresses them both as "fools, and of little understanding." Not content to be hearers, would they be "Lords, Gods, judgers of the heavens"? She turns away. "Your own reason riseth up against my wisdom. Behold, you are free. Do that which most pleaseth you."

It is a comfort to learn that the child Arthur had all this time fallen down "in a swound." He was indeed very ill for some time afterwards, and small wonder.

Dee protested and argued with Kelley and with Madimi. He was consumed with grief and amazement that good angels could propound "so hard and unpure a doctrine." Had he not offered his very soul "as a pawn to discharge E. K. his crediting of them to the good and faithful ministers of Almighty God"? Was it not his life's work to withdraw Kelley from any kind of association with the bad spirits who had frequented him before he came to Mortlake?

Until two in the morning of this April 18, 1587, the pair sat up arguing, talking, praying. Kelley held forth about a little spirit, Ben, who had that day appeared to him in his laboratory alone, and had shown him how to distil oil from spirit of wine "over a retort in two silver dishes whelmed one upon another, with a hole through the middle and a sponge between them, in which the oil would remain." Ben had foretold Elizabeth's death in July (she lived for sixteen years), the death of the King of Spain and the Pope; in fact, a general moribundity of sovereigns. Francis Garland was a spy sent by Burleigh to see what they were doing; Rosenberg would be shortly poisoned; famine and bloodshed would cover the land. Many other dire calamities would happen if they were not conformable to the voice; chief of all, the virtue should be taken from Kelley's precious powder; it would be rendered unprofitable, and he would become a beggar. It was Ben, he says, who had brought him his powder.

Dee replied that he had found so much halting and untruth in Kelley's reports of actions when he was not present, that he would believe nothing save what by better trial he found to be true. But at last his resistance seemed to be overridden, and in the chill of the early morning he went to bed, heavy at heart in spite of his delusion. His poor wife was lying awake, wondering what turn their ill-starred fortunes were next to take.

"'Jane,' I said, 'I can see that there is no other remedy, but as hath been said of our cross-matching, so it must needs be done.'"

Poor Mrs. Dee, shocked and horrified, fell a-weeping and trembling for a full quarter of an hour, then burst into a fury of anger. At last she implored her husband never to leave her. "I trust," said she, "that though I give myselfe thus to be used, that God will turn me into a stone before he would suffer me in my obedience to receive any shame or inconvenience." She would eat neither fish nor flesh, she vowed, until this action, so contrary to the wholesome law of God, and so different from former actions, which had often comforted her, was confirmed. Both the indignant women demanded a repetition of the action.

In obedience to Raphael's counsel, a solemn pact or covenant was humbly drawn up by Dee on the 21st, and signed by these four strange partners in delusion. It promised blind obedience, with secrecy upon pain of death to any of the four. It deprecated all intention of impurity and guilt. Its subscribers promise to captivate and tread under foot all human timorous doubting that the true original power and authority of sins releasing or discharging is from the Creator. True Christian charity spiritual, perfect friendship and matrimonial liberty between the four is vowed, and they beseech that this "last mystical admonishment" be not imputed to them for rashness, presumption, or wanton lust.

Dee's hand is unmistakable in the document. He regarded the new development apparently only as a symbol of further spiritual union, and a means of obtaining a closer entrance into the secrets of all knowledge. It was no matter to him, he says, if the women were imperfectly obedient. "If it offend not God, it offended not mee, and I pray God it did not offend him."

Kelley drew up a paper the day after Dee's, washing

his hands of the whole matter, protesting he did not believe so damnable a doctrine would be commanded, recounting his warnings to his worshipful Master Dee, and so on. On May 6 Dee spread his covenant, a document of the most truly devout character, before the holy south table in the chapel of the castle, with many prayers for divine guidance. The next day Kelley obtained the paper, cut it in pieces and destroyed it, made away with one of the crystals (which was found again under Mrs. Dee's pillow), and threatened to depart elsewhere with John Carpio. Coldness and jealousy fell between the pair.

So ended the whole extraordinary episode of the Talbot - Kelley spiritualistic revelations. Madimi appeared for the last time on May 23. Then the *Liber Mysteriorum* is closed. For twenty years there are no more records of angels' visits. And the few pages that remain are written in a halting hand in Dee's stricken old age, when he was seldom visited by his unseen friends, badly though he needed their comfort. No other medium like Kelley was ever found. One can only wonder whether, after so rude an awakening, even Dee would have implicitly trusted anyone again. These five years with the skryer had filled him to the brim with a consciousness of some power beyond his wit to control, a power amazing in its ingenuity to torture him. He had asked Madimi piteously if he should suffer any more of these pangs. He knew now that he would. Yet, in spite of all, these marvellous doings had brought him hours of exquisite happiness, moments when he had seemed lost in the unity of the combined wisdom of the ages, which to him meant—God.

CHAPTER XV

THE END OF THE PARTNERSHIP

> "If all you boast of your great art be true,
> Sure willing poverty lives most in you."
> —BEN JONSON, *Epigram to Alchymists.*

DEE now resumed diligently his writing in the other diary, which becomes a strange medley of daily affairs small and great. He sent Francis Garland to England with another letter to Walsingham, dated June 17, begging him to continue his opinion of Dee's fidelity towards Her Majesty and the realm.[1] It would be useless as yet to render any account of commodity to them or their country reaped by this peregrination, "but I trust more will be glad of our coming home than were sorry of our going abroad." He has not heard from Mr. Justice Young since May twelvemonth, but hopes his pitiful case of the books and other injuries endured have, by Walsingham's favour, had some redress. There is no news of importance but the Polish King's election, "the mysteries whereof, by the time this bearer reaches England, will be known to you." "Remember me to your good lady and to your daughter Lady Sidney." Money was now plentiful enough, and on September 1 Dee covenanted with John Basset (who had arrived at Trebona on August 20) "to teach the children

[1] *Cal. State Papers Dom.*, 1580—1625, p. 212.

the Latin tong, and I do give him seven ducats by the quarter, and the term to begyne this day; and so I gave him presently seven ducketts of Hungary in gold, before my wife. God spede his work." Arthur, who was just over eight, was getting on with his "grammar"; Katherine was six. Thus was another element introduced into the oddly assorted household, and on September 4 Dee writes: "Basset his hurly burly with T. Kelley." Payments to Basset were entered regularly each quarter until August following, when the tutor, whose real name seems to have been Edward Whitlock, went off to Budweis on pretence of buying "cullors"—perhaps for painting, and never returned.

Various visitors came to Trebona, among them Pucci, bringing Christian Francke, the author of some books written against the Jesuits.[1] Rosenberg returned to Trebona, and finding a constraint existing in the relations of the household, set himself to reconcile them. "July 19th. a certayn kind of recommendation between our wives. Next day som relenting of E. K., also by my Lord's entrety." Rosenberg came and went frequently, so did his wife. Lord Biberstein, a friend of theirs, came to make Dee's acquaintance.

Alchemical experiments were being prosecuted with vigour. It was Dee's turn to make something prized, even if it were not gold. "Sept. 28th. I delivered to Mr. Ed. Kelley (ernestly requiring it

[1] One of Francke's books was translated into English by Wm. Charke in 1580. Another Dee carried to Archbishop Whitgift in October, 1592, begging him to cause it to be confuted.

as his part) the half of all the animall which was made. It is to weigh 20 ounces; he wayed it himself in my chamber. He bought his weights purposely for it. My Lord had spoken to me before for some, but Mr. Kelley had not spoken." Secrecy being necessary, he is evidently using a word of hidden meaning.

Kelley was constantly riding to Prague, and in October, while he was away, "John Carpio [who had joined them at Trebona] did begyn to make furnaces over the gate. He used of my rownd bricks, and for the yern pot was contented now to use the lesser bricks, 60 to make a furnace." Experiments on a large scale were about to be begun, and when Kelley returned a week later, *terribilis expostulatio accusatio*, etc., is the entry under his name. Edmond Hilton returned from England, and a month later Francis Garland, bringing letters from Edward Dyer. He brought also letters from Court advising their return home. People in the neighbourhood were beginning to talk about the strange doings of the foreigners in the Castle, and the Captain Critzin of the Guard disdained to come to a wedding supper in the Rathhaus because Dee and Kelley were to be present. The household grew larger and larger. Thomas Kelley was married in June. In December, "Mr. John Carpio went towards Prague to marry the maiden he had trubbled; for the Emperor's Majestie, by my Lord Rosenberg's means, had so ordered the matter." He was absent till February 16, and in April brought his wife. Dee turned back to his books of tables, figures and symbols. "The 30 and 31 day I began to frame myself toward the practice of the Heptagonos of my 4th boke. God prosper my purpose." Kelley, on the other hand, was absorbed in alchemical studies. Perhaps the secret he had once professed to have captured had again eluded him.

"Dec. 12 afternone somewhat. Mr. Ed. Keley his lamp overthrow, the spirit of wyne being spent to[o] nere, and the glas being not stayed with buks abowt it, as it was wont to be; and the same glas so flitting on one side, the spirit was spilled out, and burnt all that was on the table where it stood, lynnen and written books—as the bok of Zacharius with the Alkanor that I translated out of French for som by spirituall could not [?]; Rowlaschy his third boke of waters philosophicall; the boke called *Angelicum opus*, all in pictures of the work from the beginning to the end; the copy of the man of Budwise Conclusions for the Transmution of metalls, and 40 leaves in 40, intitled, Extractiones Dunstani, which he himself extracted and noted out of Dunstan his boke, and the very bok of Dunstan was but cast on the bed hard by from the table."

The "very bok of Dunstan"[1] was no doubt a copy of the manuscript *Tractatus . . . de lapide philosophorum*, which was formerly ascribed to the Saint of Glastonbury. It was the constant companion of these two alchemists, held in awe and great esteem, as we see by Dee's words above.

In his new liberation from crystal gazing, Kelley became a changed and haughty being. He was established in his own apartments, and when he felt

[1] It was printed at Cassel in 1649. Stubbs, *Memorials of St. Dunstan*.

weary his former master was now summoned imperiously to come and amuse him! He sends the old man a message by his brother Thomas, saying, "You study too much, it is too late in the day to go to Cromlaw, as you intended, he wishes you to come to pass the tyme with him at play." Dee mildly consents: "I went after dynner and playd, he and I against Mr. F. Garland and Mr. Rob., tyll supper tyme in his dyning rome, and after supper he came and the others, and we played there two or three houres and frendely departed. This was then after the great and wonderful unkindness used toward me in taking my man." A week or two later Kelley sent for Dee late in the evening to come to his laboratory over the gate, to see how he distilled sericon, "according as in time past and of late he heard of me out of Riplay.[1] God lend his heart to all charity and vertue."

It is evident that Kelley was jealously and secretly working at his experiments apart from Dee. He had learned much alchemy from his master and his master's wonderful library in the four years, but there was still knowledge stored in chambers of Dee's brain of which he could not pick the lock. To enter these inner recesses had been doubtless Kelley's aim when he represented the spirits as bidding them share everything with each other. But he, on his part, had no intention of sharing anything that he discovered.

The year 1588 began badly, for the child Michael, on New Year's Day,

[1] George Ripley, Canon of Bridlington, *The Compound of Alchymie*, 1471, printed 1591.

"going childyshly with a sharp stick of eight inches long and a little wax candell light on the top of it [evidently the child was keeping Christmastide in good old German fashion], did fall uppon the playn bords in Marie's chamber, and the sharp point of the stik entred through the lid of his left ey toward the corner next the nose, and so persed through, insomuch that great abundance of blud came out under the lid, in the very corner of the sayd ey. The hole on the outside is not bygger than a pin's hed; it was anoynted with St. John's oyle. The boy slept well. God spede the rest of the cure. The next day after, it apperid that the first towch of the stikes point was at the very myddle of the apple of the ey, and so (by God's mercy and favor) glanced to the place where it entred; with the strength of his hed and the fire of his fulness. I may make some shew of it to the prayse of God for his mercies and protection."

Dee of course was as skilled in medicine as any doctor of the time. He rendered medical assistance when Thomas Kelley's wife, Lydia, miscarried with twin boys. He notes his own symptoms carefully: "June 19, I had a grudging of the ague. June 22, I did evidently receive the ague and layd down. Jan. 17. The humming in my ears began." Another time "I was very sik uppon two or three sage leaves eten in the morning; better suddenly at night. When I cast them up, I was well."

The coldness between the two became unbearable to Dee, the peacemaker, of whom Aubrey relates that if ever any of his neighbours fell out, "he would not let them alone until he had made them friends." In April, he wrote to Kelley and his wife "2 charitable letters, requiring at theyre hands mutual charity." The same day he made friends with Captain Critzin, and on Sunday, when Jane was churched after Theodore's birth, received the Communion with her. He hears of some fresh treachery of Pucci, and of Rosenberg's displeasure, but all is forgotten on May 10, when Kelley "did open the great secret to me, God be thanked!" A few days after, "Mistris Kelley received the sacrament, and to me and my wife gave her hand in charity, and we rushed not from her." The reconciliation does not seem to have been altogether complete. Every visitor throughout that summer, Edmund Cooper, Joan Kelley's brother; Mr. Thomas Southwell, his friend; Edward Dyer, Francis Garland, and Count Rosenberg, all seem to have tried to patch up the quarrel, but things only grew worse.

The "great secret" opened by Kelley was no doubt the professed secret of the gold. Dee must very soon have found out the true value of this "secret," but apparently he continued to believe that Kelley had honestly transmuted base metal, and was keeping the method to himself. Nothing was less likely than that he would share his knowledge, even with the master who had taught him all he knew. The first essential in alchemy was secrecy. It is characteristic of Dee that he seems to have been more pained at Kelley's want of confidence in him, than chagrined at not knowing the secret. Of jealousy that Kelley was, or seemed to be, the successful alchemist, there is no trace. But Kelley was gradually undermining all Dee's influence and friendship with Rosenberg, who was their one powerful friend. The Viceroy of Bohemia had much influence with the Emperor. He was constantly at the Castle or with Kelley in Prague. Kelley had stolen the old man's best workman, and was now turning all his friends against him. Rosenberg and Kelley were always working in secret, while he was left outside in the cold. "September 15th, the Lord Chancellor cam to Trebona and went away on the 17th. The rancor and dissimulation now evident to me, God deliver me! I was not sent for." The pathos of the situation is irresistible. The man of a Continental reputation, whom five emperors had honoured, must stand aside and see his upstart pupil made much of and set on the high-road to fortune. But Fate was more just than she seemed, and Dee, who clung to the honest and true way, had in the end the better lot. Not in ease or success, truly; but who would not rather leave behind him the reputation of a sincere man deluded than that of a deceiver, even though not unmasked? Till then Dee says he had been "chief governor of our philosophical proceedings, but little by little I became hindered and crossed by fine and subtle devices, laid first by the Bohemians, somewhat by Italians, and lastly by my own countrymen."

The strange partnership had now run its tempestuous course to the end, and the heterogeneous colony of English men and women at Trebona was about to break up, never all to meet again. The first to depart was Mistress Kelley, thankful, no doubt, to disentangle herself from the web of pretences, deception and bickerings. On October 17, "Mistress

Kelley and the rest rode towards Punchartz in the morning." She was on her way to England, and only once thereafter does this young woman's name enter into our story.

On November 23, Francis Garland and Mr. Dyer's servant, Edward Rowley, who had come back a week or two earlier, left for England. Dee sent by them a most important letter to the Queen, also letters to Dyer, Mr. Young, and to Edmond Hilton. News from England travelled slowly, and Dee had not long since heard of the glorious defeat of the Spanish Armada of the previous May. The victorious captains, Frobisher, Drake, Hawkins, were all well known to him, and with the Admiral in chief command, Lord Howard of Effingham, he was very familiar at Court, for his wife had been Jane's early patron and friend. Patriot that Dee was, yearning to get back to England, he now wrote to the Queen a letter of congratulation (dated November 10, 1588) upon the splendid victory of her navy. It was couched in the graceful and fantastic terms of homage of the day, and is a literary production well befitting a man of his reputation. The letter is reproduced from the original. It is printed by Ellis in *Letters of Eminent Men.*

He speaks in it of his proposed return, and begs for a safe conduct through all the domains of princes and potentates which lay between him and home. "Happy are they that can perceive and so obey the pleasant call of the mightie Lady Opportunitie." The answer, of course, took long to come, but he began to make his preparations slowly. He gave to Kelley the wonderful convex glass which the Queen had so often admired. A fortnight after, Kelley gave it to Rosenberg, and the Count presented it to the Emperor. Dee says the Emperor had long esteemed it, but he has not told us when he showed it to Rudolph. He had described the mirror in his Preface to Billingsley's Euclid (see *ante*, p. 25).

On February 4 he also made over to Kelley "the powder, the books, the glass, and the bone, for Rosenberg, and he thereuppon gave me discharge in writing of his own hand subscribed and sealed." Rosenberg was away, and did not trouble to return to bid him good-bye. Instead he wrote to Kelley to take his leave of Dee for him, and said that he would send instructions to his man Menschik to "dispatch him," perhaps with some settlement of a financial character.

On the afternoon of February 16, 1588, Kelley rode away to Prague, taking most of the assistants with him: John Carpio, F. Garland, Simkinson. Dee never saw him again.

Three new coaches had been ordered in Budweis, and when they were ready, Dee dispatched Edmond Hilton (who had returned from England in December) to Prague to buy a dozen coach and saddle horses. Money was plentiful at this time, the practice of economy was impossible to Dee, so he set off to travel homewards in state, as became a man to whom an emperor had offered a princely salary. It was very unnecessary, even absurd, but it was characteristic of Dee and his exalted ideas, not so much of himself, as of his peculiar mission. The journey cost, as he reckoned up afterwards, more than £600. The horses—twelve young Hungarian coach horses and three Wallachees for the saddle—cost £120, and cheap they were at that. The three new coaches, with harness, saddles and bridles, cost £60; and the hiring of two or three waggons for his goods, books, furniture, vessels, etc., ran into £110. Then he had an escort of twenty-four soldiers from Diepholt to Oldenburg, as permitted by the Emperor's passport; and from Oldenburg to Bremen, the Duke of that province sent six musqueteers to protect him. It was a dangerous time to ride abroad, as he says, not long before the outbreak of the Thirty Years' War. A party of eighteen horsemen had lain in wait for his caravan for five days, but a warning came through a Scot in the garrison of Oldenburg, and Robert, the Landgrave of Hesse, extended his powerful protection.

The train of coaches and waggons, with the travellers and their baggage, left Trebona on March 11. The Castle had been their home for a year and a half, and we can fancy Jane, at any rate, dreading to take up once more the old wandering life. For it was to be a year and three-quarters more before they set foot in England. On the 18th they were in Nuremberg, where they stayed two nights; on March 26 they reached Frankfurt-am-Main, and on April 19, five weeks after leaving Trebona, they were in Bremen, their present destination.

CHAPTER XVI

THE END OF KELLEY

" All you that faine philosophers would be,
  And day and night in Geber's kitchen broyle,
Wasting the chips of ancient Hermes' tree,
  Weening to turn them to a precious oyle,
  The more you worke the more you loose and spoile.
To you, I say, how learned soe'er you be,
Go burn your Bookes and come and learne of me."

—Sir Edward Kelley, *Metrical Treatise on Alchemy*.

Before continuing the story of Dee's life in Bremen and his return to England, the end of Kelley's extraordinary meteoric career, which six more years extinguished, must be briefly traced.

Dee expected Kelley to join him at Stade. He confidently thought they would return to England together, obedient to the Queen's summons. But Kelley was now a great man with Rudolph, who had given him an estate and a title, and established him at his Court in Prague as a citizen and councillor of state. Apparently he succeeded in keeping up the deception of making gold. The news of his promotion was conveyed by Dee to Walsingham, at Barn Elms, in a letter dated August 22, 1589,[1] to which we shall again return. He speaks of Kelley as "my great friend, yet in Boemia," and surmises that

[1] *Lansdowne MS*. lxi. f. 159.

Walsingham may have heard direct from him, who is "now in most favourable manner created a Baron of the Kingdom of Boemia."

The actual title conferred was *eques auratus*, a synonym for "miles" which took its origin in the fact that a knight's armour was gilded. In English it was of course "Sir." The title must have been conferred on Kelley very soon after Dee left Trebona in March; for by the end of June he is called Sir Edward by a couple of Englishmen, Robert Tatton and George Leycester,[1] who with Edmond Hilton were at Trebona then, and came on to Dee at Bremen. Kelley commissioned them to take down particulars of the treachery of one Parkins, a Jesuit in Prague, who was plotting with the King of Spain and the Pope against England.[2] He wished of course to score "his faithful discoverie of this treason." He also desired Burleigh and others in England to know what great honour had been done him, and he obtained in February, 1590, a confirmation of the grant of his title to send over, lest there should be any doubt in English minds. The document,[3] curiously enough, is countersigned by Dr. Jacob Curtius, the acquaintance of three years before.

Constant letters passed between the two former fellow-workers through the year 1590, the messenger being either Thomas Kelley or Francis Garland. All manner of wild stories were current in England, and

[1] These appear as "Rolous Tattin and George Losin" in the diary printed by Halliwell.

[2] *Lansdowne MS.* lxi. f. 64; cf. *ibid.* f. 186.

[3] *Lansdowne MS.* dccclxvi. f. 243.

have been gathered up and repeated by every writer upon Dee and Kelley. The sober Anthony Wood relates that gold was so plentiful in Trebona before Dee left that the young Arthur played with gold quoits made by projection, while a youthful Count Rosenberg (he seems a quite fictitious person) was throwing about silver playthings procured by the like means. Burleigh had written for a specimen of their wonderful art, and it is said that the Queen was actually the recipient of a warming-pan, from the copper or brass lid of which a piece had been cut, transmuted into gold, and replaced. Elias Ashmole goes further in the story to say that "without Sir Edward's touching or handling it, or melting the metal, onely warming it in the Fire, the Elixir being put thereon, it was transmuted into pure gold."[1] He adds that he has heard from a credible person (who has seen them) that Kelley made rings of gold wire twisted twice round the finger, which he gave away, to the value of £4,000: at the marriage of Rosenberg's servant before alluded to. Ashmole adds: "This was highly generous, but to say truth, openly Profuse beyond the modest limits of a sober philosopher." Sir Thomas Browne says he heard from Arthur Dee, his friend, conclusive evidence of the manufacture of gold. The reader may smile at these fairy tales, but what is to be said of a staid and sober minister like Burleigh being ready to credit the truth of Kelley's exploits, whether convinced by the warming-pan, or by other means? In a long letter[2] to Edward Dyer,

[1] *Theatrum Chemicum Britannicum,* 1652, p. 481.

[2] Strype's *Annals,* vol. iii., 270.

in 1591, who was then acting as the Queen's agent in Germany, he urges him to use every means in his power to induce "Sir Edward Kelley to come over to his native country and honour her Majesty with the fruits of such knowledge as God has given him." Dyer had been Dee's friend for a great many years, as we know, and was Arthur's godfather, but he transferred all his attentions to Kelley as soon as that clever trickster began making gold. Dee only says he "did injure me unkindelie." Kelley and Dyer became inseparable, and Dyer wrote home to Burleigh wonderful reports of Kelley's miracles. Ignoring all that had passed, Burleigh is ready to welcome the quondam coiner, forger, or what not, with open arms back to the service of his Queen. "If his knowledge is as certain as you make it, what would you have me think could stay him from flying to the service of his own sovereign?" If he is afraid of old reports, actions, disgrace, being brought up against him (and we know Kelley's record was none of the cleanest), let him be assured that he shall have his Queen's protection "against all impediments that shall arise." Burleigh becomes almost poetical as he speaks of the patronage of "such a Princess, who never yet was stained with any breach of Promise to them that deserved her favour. If I did not know to whom I write, who has had long experience of her rare vertues, . . . I could use many arguments to move any man never to mistrust her." He implores Dyer to induce Kelley to come. If he does not come, it can only be because by cunning or legerdemain he has deceived them and cannot do what he promises, or else he is an unnatural disloyal man and subject. In case Kelley will not come, he asks if Dyer cannot send a very small portion of his powder to make a demonstration to the Queen's own sight. What the Treasurer would like most of all is that Kelley should "send her Majesty as a token a good round sum of money, say enough to defray the charges of the navy for this summer," for the ships of Spain were gathering courage after their defeat. "But wishers and woulders were never good householders," he ends. The Queen is at his house at Theobalds, and will be some time longer. He would be content the time were tripled, so he "had but one corn of Sir Edward Kelley's powder." Burleigh and Kelley were also in direct correspondence. Beside urging his return, the Lord Treasurer, who seemed to consider Kelley as the storehouse of the elixir of life as well as of the philosopher's stone, begs for a prescription with the proof of manufactured gold. In a brief note of February 18, 1591,[1] Kelley says he will "shortly send the good thing desired for your health." He has received the salutations sent through Mr. Dyer, and "at his return you shall know how I thank you." This, the only original letter of Kelley's to be traced, characteristically promises what he never meant to do. Burleigh replied in May, again begging him to send "something of your operation to strengthen me afore next winter against my old enemy the gout." He once more strongly urges Kelley's return. How can he hesitate to bestow the gifts that God has

[1] *Lansdowne MS.* lxvi. f. 164.

given him rather upon his own Prince and Countrie than upon strangers?

Kelley of course did not return, but apparently wrote again, urging powerful reasons of excuse. Burleigh's faith in him began to shake. He sent a last imperative recall, some of which may be quoted from the rough draft written in his own hand.[1] It shows once more what sort of men the great Queen had to serve her, and what a Queen she was to serve.

Beginning "Good Sir Edward Kelley," Burleigh acknowledges Kelley's letters by Dyer. "Without particular knowledge of your impedimenta, I may not give any such censures as others soe unconsiderately, yea uncharitably, may doe. You confess a desire to return to your native countrie; your minde draws to your sovereign. This is commendable, yet many say if you come not, it is because you cannot perform what has been reported of you. Malicious persons say you are an impostor, like some in other countries have been proved. You fear severe punishment. Now, good knight, though I write thus plainly to you, yet such is my credit in Mr. Dyer, such my allowance of your loyal profession, such opinion do I firmly conceave of your wisdom and love expressed in your letters, such my perswasion of your habillitie to performe what Mr. Dyer has reported (by reason of the estimation, honor and credit I see that you have gotton by yr behaviour), that I rest only unsatisfied in your delaye of coming; and I am expressly commanded by Her Majestie to require you to have regard to her honour, and according to the tenor of her former letters, to assure yrself singularly favoured in respect of the benefit you may bring to Her Majestie. . . .

"Be assured of worldly reward. You can make yr

[1] *Lansdowne MS.* ciii. f. 210. There is no date.

Queen so happie for her, surely as no subject she hath can do the like. Good Knight, let me end my letter conjuring you, in God's holy name not to keep God's gift from yr natural countrie, but rather help make Her Majestie a glorious and victorious power against the mallyce of hers and God's enemies. Let honor and glory move yr naturall hart to become honorable in yr own countrie rather than in a strange one, and leave a monument of yr name with posterity. Let no other country bereave us of this felicitie: that only, yea only by you, I say, is to be expected. Let no time be lost; we are all mortall: you that should be author, this noble Queen yt should be receiver thereof."

Then he politely acknowledges some gift Kelley has sent. Instead of an ingot of gold, it seems more like a geological specimen for a museum, and certainly does not excite the Lord Treasurer's immense gratitude.

"All this in answer to yours by Dyer. I thank you for the montayn or rock sent safely from Staden. I will place it in my house, where I bestow other things of workmanship, and it shall be memoryall of yr kindness, wishing I might receive some small receipt from you yt might comfor my spyritts in myn age, rather than my coffers with any welth, for I esteeme helth above welth."

But Kelley knew better than to face the astute Englishmen at home. In Prague he felt secure, and all too bitterly he learned his mistake. A couple of independent letters from two English merchants to Burleigh and to Edward Wootton give the exciting story of his fall from favour.[1]

[1] Thomas Webbe to Burleigh. *Lansdowne MS.* lxviii. f. 210; and Strype, *Annals*, iii., 272.

He had been established in a house of his own close to the Palace; his wife and brother had rejoined him; Edward Dyer made it his headquarters. One day, the last of April, perhaps even before Burleigh's letter was dispatched, he was suddenly arrested by the fitful Rudolph's command, and thrown into prison. A large force of the imperial guard, accompanied by the City Provost and one of the Secretaries of State, burst uninvited into his house to take him whilst at dinner. But a friend at Court had whispered a word, and the evening before he had ridden off with one attendant towards Rosenberg. The intruders had to be content with haling off brother Thomas to prison, "pinacled like a thief." They searched the house thoroughly, broke open doors, and thrust their halberds into the beds or any place where "Sir Edward" might possibly lie hid. Satisfied he was not there, they sealed up certain of the rooms, laid some of the servants in chains—one was afterwards "racked"—and departed, leaving a guard over "Lady Kelley" and Mr. Dyer, forbidding them to stir from the house. Returning with their news to the Emperor, Rudolph "cursed in the Dutch manner," and gave orders to search the town and the highways.

Kelley had ridden off many miles towards his patron, the all-powerful Rosenberg, but being weary and fasting, halted at the inn at Sobislaus, fed, and threw himself on a couch to sleep. By three days after, May 2, the soldiers had tracked him down; and roughly seizing him, they cut open his doublet with a knife to search for concealed valuables or papers, vowing they cared not whether they took him dead or alive to the

Emperor. Kelley appealed to his all-powerful friend, Rosenberg. "In Bohemia," says the merchant in his letter, "it is a rule that his Majesty dares do nothing without the Earl's consent, he being Burgrave of Prague, the immediate person and officer under the Crown." Rudolph was already sinking into the melancholy and madness in which he ended his days. However, Rosenberg's protection did not avail. Kelley was taken to the Castle of Pürglitz, three miles from Prague, and there he was closely confined for more than two years.

And now for the cause of Rudolph's displeasure, and the reason of the arrest.

First, it is surmised to be debt, but the merchant adds that although Kelley is known to owe a large sum to two Cologne merchants who trade in jewels, he owes nothing to the Emperor, nor ever has put him to any charge, save for coals and house room.

Next it is thought he was in league with a professed gold-maker from Venice, executed by the Duke of Bavaria at Munich, on April 25. (Of him, too, Burleigh has written in his letter to Dyer.) Thirdly, the Emperor's fear that Kelley would depart for England is adduced. Dyer had brought autograph letters from the Queen recalling him. A doctor's son in the town, who had served Sir Philip Sidney in England, and knew her hand, had reported this. It was of course an invention; and the merchant opines Dyer is of too rare a discretion to permit secret letters to be seen or even heard of; it is more likely that Kelley has some time or other vaunted at table that the Queen had sent for him. "He is a man who taketh, as I hear, a pleasure that Princes desire him."

Fourthly, it is the doing of the powerful family of the Poppels, second family in the kingdom, and great enemies of the Rosenbergs, who have been "the setters up and principal maintainers of Sir Edward Kelley hitherto." The fifth report is that Kelley had distilled an oil or medicine for the Emperor's heart disease, which was poison. Lastly, the writer comes to what he takes for the true reason of Rudolph's anger.

An Italian, named Scoto, having cast imputations on Kelley's powers of projection, the Emperor sent for him to come and make proof of his art at Court. Kelley of course excused himself, saying he was sick. Three times he was summoned, and then the guard was despatched to bring him. The accusation was *Laesus Majestatis*, and the city wonders what will be the end. The Emperor dare not openly execute him, for fear of Rosenberg and the strong feeling in the State for a change of ruler. Yet he may easily be put to death secretly in that castle where he is confined, "and Rosenberg not know otherwise than that he liveth, or is dead by disease. Almost grown now to be a common Practice in the Empire, and in the Palatine especially, noted that way."

This dark hint is almost a prophecy of Kelley's fate; but the doom was not yet quite prepared. On December 5, 1593, Dee received news of his having been set at liberty on the previous October 4, just two and a half years after his arrest. Not a word of him in Dee's diary in the meantime, until March 12 of that year, when the old man records that he dreamt much of Kelley two nights running, "as if he wer in my house, familiar, with his wife and brother."

Kelley characteristically says he was "utterly incapable of remaining idle even in prison, and employed his time in writing alchemical treatises," from which it seems he was allowed books and papers, for his writings are mere compilations from ancient chief masters of the art. In *The Stone of the Philosophers*, dedicated to Rudolph, he speaks of two imprisonments, tells him grandiloquently that he has for two or three years (1588–91) used great labour and expense to discover for him that which might afford profit and pleasure; and adds, with great bombast, "If my teaching displeases you, you are still wandering astray from the true scope and aim of this matter, utterly wasting your money, time, labour and hope." Truth is more desirable than anything else, and posterity will discover that he is to be counted among those who have suffered for it. Kelley as a sufferer for truth is highly entertaining, but he goes on to make a still more distasteful allusion. "It always was, and always will be, the way of mankind to release Barabbas and crucify Christ."

Beside this treatise Kelley certainly produced an earlier writing of some sort on the subject, which Dee discussed with the Archbishop of Canterbury on July 13, 1590. It had apparently incurred his displeasure. Mr. Waite attributes two other short papers to Kelley, *The Humid Path* and *The Theatre of Terrestrial Astronomy*. A couple of rather quaint alchemical poems—one of thirty-nine stanzas, from which the heading of this chapter is taken—are doubtless by him, perhaps written also in captivity.

During the next year letters were two or three

times exchanged between Kelley and Dee, and in March, 1595, Francis Garland, who had then not long returned from Prague, "came to visit me and had much talk with me of E. K." Kelley was apparently then restored to the Emperor's favour, for on August 12, Dee says he "receyved Sir Edward Kelley's letters of the Emperor, inviting me to his servyce again." Did Kelley think there might be further hints to be got from his old alchemical master? Then under date of November 25, 1595, Dee enters this curt note: "the news that Sir Edward Kelley was slayne." Never thereafter does he mention this adventurer's name.

The prevalent story is that Kelley was again imprisoned in one of Rudolph's castles, and that, attempting to escape by a turret window, he fell from a great height and broke both legs, receiving other injuries, from which he shortly died. It is even said with some amount of credibility, that the Queen wrote imperatively to Dyer to secure his release, and that everything was prepared in readiness to convey him secretly to England, and that he was escaping for that purpose when the accident happened. This story has hardly been tracked home to its source. It may be true. On the other hand, the end may have come in the more swift and secret manner suggested by the English merchant. In either case, the spirit warning of eleven years before, that he should die a violent death, was fulfilled. Into his forty years as much adventure, folly, trickery and deceit, fortune, fame, favour, riches and poverty, had been crowded as could supply material for many a volume of romance.

Some of the incidents were indeed used a few years after his death by more than one dramatist. Dee had only quitted the world about a year and a half when Kelley's pretensions, Dee's learning, and the whole paraphernalia of alchemy, were severely satirised by Ben Jonson in *The Alchemist* (1610), a play which reflects all the crudest superstitions of the time. The credulous knight, Sir Epicure Mammon, describes Subtle, the alchemist, as

> " A divine instructor can extract
> The soul of all things by his art ; call all
> The virtues and the miracles of the sun
> Into a temperate furnace ; teach dull nature
> What her own forces are.
> A man the Emperor
> Has courted above Kelley; sent his medals
> And chains to invite him."

In Butler's *Hudibras*, first published in 1663, but written ten or fifteen years earlier, Dee and Kelley are again cited, though the satire is chiefly directed against Sidrophel, *i.e.* William Lilly. The devil is said to have appeared "in divers shapes to Kelley;" and in the description of Sidrophel, these lines occur:

> " He had been long toward mathematics,
> Optics, philosophy and statics,
> Magic, horoscopy, astrology,
> And was old dog at physiology; . . .
> He had read Dee's Prefaces before
> The Devil and Euclid, o'er and o'er;
> And all the intrigues 'twixt him and Kelley,
> Lescus, and the Emperor, would tell ye."

One may wonder how much these scurrilous references had to do with fixing Dee's reputation in the eyes of his immediate posterity.

CHAPTER XVII

RETURN TO ENGLAND

"If I have done my dutiful service any way to her Majesties well liking and gracious accepting, I am greatly bound to thank Allmighty God, and during my life to frame the best of my little skill to do my bounden duty to her most excellent Majestie."

—DEE, *Compendious Rehearsall.*

UPON Dee's arrival in Bremen on April 19, 1598, a house was at once hired, and the family moved in on May 13. He put out his three saddle horses to grass in the town meadow till Michaelmas, for nine ducats, and presented the twelve Hungarian coach horses to the Landgrave of Hesse, to whose kindness he had been indebted for protection as he passed through his territories. In June, Thomas Kelley, his wife Lydia; Francis Garland, and Dyer's man, Edward Rowley, left for England. At the same time Edmond Hilton returned to Prague. An agreement or bond had been entered into between the late partners that the proceeds of the wonderful discovery should be shared. Hilton was back on July 30, with news of Kelley: perhaps not good news, for three nights after, towards daybreak, Dee's sleep was disturbed by a "terrible" dream, which visited him not for the first time, that "Mr. Kelley would by force bereave me of my books." Hilton left almost immediately for England with a letter from Dee to Walsingham to disclose the treason of the Jesuit, Parkins. This letter[1] has been already referred to (p. 201), but it contains other interesting matter, all conveyed in Dee's beautiful neat hand. He has already written to acknowledge the Queen's gracious letter of safe conduct, received from Walsingham, but Hilton and the two English gentlemen, Tatton and Leycester, are still detained at Stade, waiting for a wind. After speaking of the designs of the Jesuit, he goes on to give the Secretary an important summary of the state of affairs in the Low Countries, where the struggle for independence was well advanced. "The Provinces all incline to a desire to endure one fortune and become one whole united. They acknowledge Her Majestie's Wars to be just but uncompassable. Their minds are getting alienated from us, only fayr means and great wisdom will win them over." He has taken counsel of "the one of all the inhabitants the most sharp-witted, the greatest understander of all occurrences generall of secret purposes; the best languaged one (as knowing Hebrew, Greek, Latin, French, Italian, Dutch, etc.); and one employed in the councils; one who was courageous in the first bickerings with Spaniards at Antwerp; who has observed all the beginnings and proceedings of errors, political and military, committed on all hands. Now and then he visiteth me, and I have asked him to pen his opinion on what can be done to recover and reform the States, but as yet he has not found leisure."[2]

[1] *Lansdowne MS.* lxi. f. 159.

[2] Strype, by some curious mistake (*Annals*, vol. iii., p. 600), has taken all this to refer to Kelley, who of course had never left the neighbourhood of Prague, even if the description could be made to fit.

Then he begs the Secretary's leniency if he has offended in writing of matters not pertaining to him, "and of which no doubt your honour has already had all necessary advertisement from properly authorised persons." He will write no more of public affairs, his coming thither was no public but his private cause, the beginning of his "nere return-making into my most derely beloved Native Country."

At the same time (August 20), Dee wrote to his friend, Mr. Justice Young, that the messengers had been delayed twenty-five days waiting for a wind; that he feared the Low Countries were bent on shaking off the Queen's authority if they could; and that he feared he should have "to endure this Breamish habitation this winter, as I do not hear a word of the approach of Sir Ed. Kelley, or of Mr. Dyer's return."[1]

In Bremen, Dee mingled with all the learned and distinguished men of the time. A memento of this period is to be found in an album, the *Thesaurus Amicorum*, of Timon Coccius (or Koch), a young Bremen student who died while at Leyden University three or four years after. The album of white vellum, faded and yellowed with age, with its edges still shining with the mellow lustre of old gold, was the receptacle of autographs, wise and pithy sayings, original or quoted, all inscribed after the beginning of July, 1589.[2] Sayings from Plautus and Seneca, Juvenal, Pythagoras and Homer, follow and press close upon the wisdom of Boethius, from *De Consolatione*, and the divine poetry of Dante. The first

[1] *Cal. S. P. D.*, 1580—1625, p. 277.

[2] *Add. MSS.* 19, 065.

to write in the book was Bruno, Count Mansfeldt, Helmstad, July 1. He is followed by Dr. Christoph Pezel, then Professor of Divinity and superintendent of the churches at Bremen, and on the seventh page is Dee's beautiful signature and his motto—in the light of posterity's unchallenged view of him, full of irony—"Nothing useful if not honest."

Mr. Hart, minister of the English colony at Stade, who had escaped from the Spanish service in Flanders with Sir William Stanley, and the Deputy Governor of Stade, both came from the port town near by to see Dee. Dr. Heinrich Khunrath, the learned doctor, alchemist and mystic of Hamburg, was another visitor. Khunrath was the chief writer of the advanced school of alchemists who passed from the pursuit of material gold to the discovery of incorruptible spiritual treasures hidden in the palaces of truth to which they provided a spiritual key; and it is a pregnant fact that all his books were published after this conference with Dee. Daniel Vander Muelen was another visitor, and from Mr. Southwell Dee had news that Edward Dyer was sent on a mission to Denmark. Two or three weeks later, he met Dyer unexpectedly in the town. News came of Rosenberg, and several of Dee's men left him to return to Kelley. He was warned to leave his house in Bremen.

By November, Dee resolved to wait no longer for Kelley, but to start for England. He still hoped, however, to meet that individual ere he embarked. On November 19, his whole party took ship by the *Vineyard*. A crowd of townspeople and students collected to bid him good speed, and to see the homeward bound travellers off; quite a little scene took place, which must have pleased and flattered Dee immensely, for there was no lack of a man's full share of vanity in him. Pezel had composed some verses on his departure, had got them printed the night before, and as the party were leaving Bremen for the seaport, a few miles away, the Professor distributed copies as a parting surprise. The travellers arrived in the Thames at Gravesend on December 2, and on landing the next day went straight to the house of Mr. Justice Thomas Young, at Stratford.[1] We may imagine Jane's relief at getting her children safely back to England, with the addition of Michael, born at Prague, nearly four years, and little Theodore, born at Trebona, nearly two years before.

Since Dee's departure from England six years ago, great events had happened. The "invincible" Armada of Philip had been beaten in a six days' running fight up the Channel. The Queen's hated rival, Mary of Scotland, had been put to death; Leicester's short dictatorship of the Netherlands had begun and come to an end. Leicester had been dead about a year. New favourites had arisen in the Queen's favour. But even more significant than these public affairs had been the upward movement in literature, the birth of dramatic art, a passionate outburst of poetic fervour, the growth of a taste for well-disciplined prose. Many splendid fruits of this movement had not yet seen the light, Sidney's

[1] Dee calls him my "brother," but he not infrequently uses the term. He *may* have married Jane's sister, Elizabeth.

Arcadia and the first part of Spenser's *Faerie Queen* were to be issued within a few months; the first play of Shakespeare was publicly performed within little more than a year of Dee's return. But Lyly and Marlowe had already, during his absence, given *Campaspe*, *Tamburlaine* and *Doctor Faustus*, to be performed by actors in the first stationary home of the earlier nomadic players, the theatres of Shoreditch, immediately to be followed by those of Bankside. Bacon was perhaps even then meditating his *Essays*, published some half a dozen years later; Hooker issued the first books of his monumental *Laws of Ecclesiastical Polity* within four years; and Nash, Peele, Green, and a horde of other writers, were contributing to establish the English literary renaissance. One can scarcely help wondering how much the fabulous stories of Dee and Kelley, which must have reached Marlowe's ears, contributed to his splendid dramatisation of the Faust legend (first printed in Frankfort in 1587). But after all, even the story of Dee's angels and Kelley's gold, pales before the lurid glow of the stories of the earlier alchemists, Agrippa and Paracelsus.

Dee landed in England a disappointed and a partly disillusioned man, clinging to a belief which was yet useless, unprofitable to him. He could prove nothing of Kelley's exploits. But he lost no time in repairing to Court, and on December 19 he was graciously received by the Queen at Richmond.

On Christmas Day he first slept in his own house at Mortlake, and beheld for himself his ruined and rifled library, with its precious books and instruments missing. He himself was in dire straits. He had little left him save his wife and children, and some still faithful friends. He took the house over as a tenant from his brother-in-law, Fromond, and settled down in the old quarters. Adrian Gilbert was the first visitor, generously offering "as much as I could require at his hands, both for my goods carried away, and for the mynes."[1] Very soon Thomas Kelley arrived and followed suit by offering the loan of ten pounds in gold; he afterwards "sent it me in Hungary new duckettes, by John Croker the same evening. He put me in good hope of Sir Edward Kelley his returning."

A second daughter was born, and christened at Mortlake, on March 5. The name given her was Madinia, suggested by the busy little spirit who had been so helpful at her first coming. The child was christened at Mortlake on the 5th, Sir George Carew as godfather, Lady Cobham and Lady Walsingham, godmothers. Letters came from Kelley by Garland in March, and replies were despatched by Thomas Kelley in April. Dee is careful to give his former skryer his full title:—"Sir Edward Kelley, Knight, at the Emperor's Court at Prague." "Francis Garland was by, and Mr. Thomas Kelley, his wife. God send them well thither and hither again."

On Lady Day, the children begin to go to school with Mr. Lee at Mortlake. "I gave him his house rent and forty shillings yerely for my three sons and my daughter. The house rent was allmost 4*s*. yerely,

[1] A grant of royalties on Devonshire mines had been made to them jointly.

of Mr. Fisher his new house." Arthur was now ten, Katherine nine, Rowland seven and Michael five. The youngest boy, Theodore, born at Trebona February 28, 1588, was rather more than two. Dee notes that he was "wened" on August 14, 1589. Katherine was not long under the Mortlake schoolmaster, for on May 21 "my dowghter was put to Mistress Brayce at Braynford [Brentford], hir mother and Arthur went with her after dynner." On April 16, he writes of his neighbour and friend, the Vice-Chancellor: "Good Sir Francis Walsingham died at night *hora undecima*." Burleigh was the only one of the old friends left. He records an interesting visit from "the two gentlemen, the unckle, Mr. Richard Candish, and his nephew, the most famous Mr. Thomas Candish, who had sayled round abowt the world." Cavendish was a Suffolk man. His wonderful voyage occupied two years and nearly two months. He died at sea within a couple of years from Dee's note. The uncle Cavendish interested himself with the Queen and the Archbishop to obtain for Dee the Provostship of Eton. This, too, fell to the ground, and Cavendish considerately sent him a hogshead of claret. He also lent or gave money to Dee and his wife, in all £302: in "ryalls and angels." Dee gave him in return one of his most valued treasures—an alchemical work:—

"A copy of Paracelsus, twelve lettres, written in French with my own hand, and he promised me before my wife never to disclose to any that he hath it; and that if he dye before me he will restore it agayn to me; but if I dy befor him that he shall deliver it to one of my sonnes, most fit among them to have it. Theoddor had a sore fall on his mowth at mid-day."

Dee's income was now almost a negligible quantity. The parsonages had paid him no rent since he left England. He went two or three times to Lambeth, and talked boldly to Archbishop Whitgift of his right to them.

He began to interest himself in his immediate neighbourhood with the idea of stopping the "Bacchus Feast," at Brentford, a rowdy celebration which had excited his indignation and of which he gave the Bishop of London a warning.

In August a domestic tragedy occurred: one of the women servants became melancholy and went out of her mind. Lunacy being a disease beyond even Dee's medical knowledge, and for 300 years after, being treated more or less as demoniacal possession, it is no wonder that the remedies he tried were ineffectual. It seems another instance of the false views of Dee's character that have been repeated over and over again, that the editor of his Manchester diary urges as a proof of Dee's magic and evil experiments that "some of the inmates of his house became suicides when in his service."[1]

"Aug. 2. Nurs her great affliction of mynde. Aug. 22. Ann my nurse had long byn tempted by a wycked spirit, but this day it was evident how she was possessed of him. God is, and hath byn, and shall be her protector and deliverer. Amen.

[1] *Manchester Diary,* ed. J. Eglington Bailey, 1880, priv. pr., p. 17.

"25th. Ann Frank was sorrowful, well comforted, and stayed in Gods mercyes acknowledging.

"26th. At night I anoynted (in the name of Jesus) Ann Frank, her brest, with the holy oyle.

"30th. In the morning she required to be anoynted, and I did very devoutly prepare myself and pray for vertue and powr, and Christ his blessing of the oyle to the expulsion of the wycked, an then twyse anoynted, the wycked one did resist a while.

"Sept. 8. Nurse Ann Frank wold have drowned hirself in my well, but by divine Providence I cam to take her up befor she was overcome of the water."

After this Dee had the woman carefully watched.

"Sept. 29. Nurse Ann Frank most miserably did cut her own throte, afternone abowt four of the clok, pretending to be in prayer before her keeper, and suddenly and very quickly rising from prayer, and going toward her chamber as the mayden her keper thought, but indede straight way down the stayrs into the hall of the other howse behind the doore did that horrible act. And the mayden who wayted on her at the stayr fote followed her and missed to fynde her in three or fowr places, tyll at length she hard her rattle in her owne blud."

In November the Queen came to Richmond and sent for Dee. She offered gaily to send him something to "kepe Christmas with." This promise was repeated to his friend, Richard Cavendish, a week or so later: "she told him she wold send me an hundred angells to kepe my Christmas withall. Next day, December 4, the Queen's Majestie called for me at my dore, circa 3½ a meridie, as she passed by, and I met her at the East Shene Gate, where she graciously putting down her mask did say with mery chere, 'I thank thee, Dee. There was never promise made but it was broken or kept.' "

The thanks were obviously ironical for the reminder of the promise; the rest of the speech was rather cruelly jocose, for, as Dee adds, she had promised to send the money that day. However, on the 6th, an earnest of the gift arrived, in the shape of £50. On the 14th, she again called for Dee as she rode by his door, "to take ayre," and he met her at the park gate as before. He does not indicate the subject of the conversation, but it was probably a request on his part for some kind of royal permission to continue his experiments in alchemy or transmutation, for on the 16th he tells of a visit from Richard Cavendish, who has received from the Queen, "warrant by word of mouth to assure me to do what I wold in philosophie and alchemie, and non shold chek, controll, or molest me." Coupled with this message, she sent another promise to make up the £100.

Dee's mind was now bent, he says, to deal with his "alchemical exercises," and the only distractions he appears to have had were the constant visitors and small disasters of the children. The boy Rowland fell into the Thames on August 5, over head and ears, about noon or soon after. Their favourite place of play seems to have been on the river bank, and accidents there were of no infrequent occurrence. Arthur, when a child, had fallen from the top of the Water-gate Stairs to the bottom, and had cut his forehead badly. Theodore also had a nasty fall.

CHAPTER XVIII

A ROYAL COMMISSION

"A wise man never goes the people's way:
But, as the planets still move contrary
To the world's motion, so doth he, to opinion.
He will examine, if those accidents
Which common fame calls injuries, happen to him
Deservedly or no? Come they deservedly,
They are no wrongs then, but his punishments:
If undeservedly and he not guilty,
The doer of them, first, should blush, not he."

JONSON, *The New Inn.*

DEE had now abandoned all hope of recovering the two Midland parsonages, the small income of which was all that lay between him and utter dependence upon charity. His thoughts were now set on the mastership of St. Cross, at Winchester, a benefice which he had already, some twenty years before, petitioned the Queen to grant. Dr. Bennett, the present master, who had then obtained it, might now, he thought, fitly be made a bishop. The Countess of Warwick secured from the Queen a promise that Dee should have it, "if it were a living fit for me." The Archbishop of Canterbury affirmed that it was most fit for Dee and Dee for it. The Lord Treasurer protested, "I will do what I can with her Majestie to pleasure you therein, Mr. Dee." Lady Warwick, faithful to his cause, repeated her request the following year, and still there was no news of Bennett attaining a mitre. Dee went to Court at Nonsuch in August, and a day or two after his return dined, at Burleigh's invitation, with the Lord Treasurer and his two sons, Sir Robert and Sir Thomas Cecil, at Mr. Maynard's, at Mortlake. Burleigh also sent him venison and invited him again to meet Lord Cobham.

All promised their influence in obtaining for him the coveted Mastership. But it was another castle in the air. His friends were extremely good to him. In May, 1591, he says:

"Sir Thomas Jones, Knight (unaxed) offered me his castell of Emlyn in Wales to dwell in so long as he had any interest in it, whose lease dureth yet twelve yeres, freely with commodities adjoining unto it; and also to have as much mow land for rent as myght pleasure me sufficiently. The 27th day he confirmed the same his offer agayn before Mr. John Harbert, Master of the Requestes, in his hall at Mortlake, which his offers I did accept of and he was glad thereof."

He could never have entertained the idea of going to live in Wales, but no doubt it was policy to accept all offers. Herbert was an old friend and neighbour. His daughter Mary and Arthur had played at a childish marriage years before. They seem to have been playfellows still, after the Dees' long absence, for in this June an accident happened to Arthur "at Mr. Herbert's, about sun setting." He was "wounded on his hed by his wanton throwing of a brik-bat upright, and not well avoyding the fall of it again. The half-brick weighed $2\frac{1}{2}$ lb." On May 3 of the following year, Arthur aged thirteen, became a Westminster scholar. "Wensday at ten of the clock

Arthur was put to Westminster Schole, under Mr. Grant and Mr. Camden."[1] He came back home in two or three weeks, perhaps only for a few days, and Dee in returning him to lessons wrote a characteristic letter to his friend, William Camden, the antiquary.[2] It shows how carefully the father had studied the child's health, abilities, and the quick temper, inherited from his mother. There is a tender touch in that mother's forethought to furnish the boy with means towards a special cleanliness which the provision for ablutions at Westminster did not contemplate. The "little chest with lock and key" for the firstborn son to take to school is always a family event of magnitude.

"22 May 1592.
"Worshipfull Sir. I have here returned your scholer unto your jurisdiction, beseching you to shew your charitable affection towards him: he had more and in better order then he will recover speedily. Of your great skyll and faithfull industrie in your function, it is most certayne to your great credit and merit. Of the wonderfull Diversitie of Childrens Dispositions, much you can say by experience: but of myne (this Arthure) I am to request you to conceyve at my hands, that he is of an exceding great and hauty mynd naturally, ready to revendge rashly. The naturall inclination is to me evydent: as who hath ☉ [Sol] in horoscopo, and ♂ [Mars] in corde Leonis. *Dictum sapienti sat esto:* for *vera curatura* you may alter this naturall courage to true fortitude and not to frayle rash fancyes: Socrates did overcome by grace Divine and his industrie, his untowardness, signified by the

[1] William Camden, second master, succeeded Dr. Edward Grant as head master in March, 1593.

[2] *Cotton MSS.*, Julius C., v., f. 45.

Art physiognomicall—you know the historie. This spirituall grammaticall concords of good manners I have great care that all my imps may be instructed in, to the more apt and skilfull serving of our Creator. Syr, my wife hath delivered unto him some more apparayle and furniture in a little chest with lock and key, yea, and with some towales to wype his face on after the morning and other washings of hands and face: willing him to buy him a stone basen and a pott, of a potter, to have allways clene and wholsom water in for his use.

"The boy liketh abundance of meate well: but very bashfully he sayd that there proportion of Drinke is somewhat to[o] little. I pray you by discretion listen to the voyce and opinion of the rest of the counsells within him, for now & in the summer seasons, the proportion of Drink naturally doth increase above winters appetite thereof.

"Thus I am bold to cumber your wurship with these my speedy ragged lynes. And therein I beseche you of one thing more, that his writing, both of roman and secretary hand decay not, but rather be amended: for a fayre writing is often tymes a good grace to matter very simple.

"Wherefore know that today they have at the right Wurshipfull Mr. Deans [Dr. Nowell's] very honourable guests, and that this night it is intended that they will sup and lodge all night at Fullham. God bless your wurship and prosper you in all & ever your true and faithful wellwisher

"John Dee.

"To the Worshipfull my singular friende Mr. Camden these be delivered."

On New Years' Day, 1592, "at the sunrising exactly," Dee's third daughter was born. She was christened Frances on the afternoon of the 9th, and sent off with her nurse to Barn Elms the same day. In August her father notes, "Remember that all things is payd to our nurse at Barnes for the girle Francys Dee from hir birth untyll the ende of her eighth month, lacking 12*s.*, and on Sunday the 27th of this August we gave the nurse ten shillings. The eighth month ended the twelfth of this month." The child stayed on with her nurse till February 14 of the next year, when she was fetched home, "the woman very unquiett and unthankfull."

Two entries: "March 9, the Pryvy Seale at night," and March 16, "the great Seale," refer to a promise given by the Queen to Dee's cousin, Dr. William Aubrey, of Kew, now Vicar General and one of the Masters of Requests, about five rectories in the Welsh diocese of St. Davids, which Dee was to have when they fell vacant. They were only worth £74 11*s.* 2*d.* in all, and Dee says he never received a penny from them.

Things were so desperate that at last, on November 9, 1592, he drew up a supplication which his friend, Lady Warwick presented the same day to the Queen at Hampton Court. This document, which Dee says Elizabeth took in her own hand to read herself, instead of handing it to a secretary, begged for a personal audit of, and investigation into, the state of his affairs. It is probably a unique petition, and in reading it we are scarcely astonished at the confidence with which the astrologer, now grown old in the Queen's service, claims her consideration and provision. He appears to regard it as little less than a national reproach that a man of science like himself should be left in beggary. And so indeed it was. For thirty-four years had the Queen, true to the Tudor motto—to use everyone as a servant, to owe no gratitude, only acceptance or approval—spent promises upon him, but she had never given him a chance of providing for himself.

"Forasmuch as the intolerable extremitie of the injuries and indignities which your most excellent Majestie's faithfull and dutifull servant, John Dee, hath for some years last past endured, and still endureth, is so great and manifold as cannot in briefe be unto your Majestie expressed, neither without good proofe and testimonie have credit with your Majestie, and because also without speedy and good redress therein performed, it is to be doubted that great and incredible inconveniences and griefs may ensue thereof in sundry sortes, (which yet may easily be prevented) your Majestie's foresaid most humble and most zealously faithfull servant beseecheth your Majestie to assign twoe or more meet and worthy persons, nobly and vertuously minded, who may and will charitably, indifferently, advisedly, and exactly, see, hear and perceive at the house of your Majestie's said servant in Mortlake, what just and needful occasion he hath thus to make most humble supplication unto your Majestie; and so of things there seen, heard, and perceived, to make true and full report and description unto your Majesty. And thus your Majestie's foresaid most dutiful servant beseecheth the Almighty God most mercifully, prosperously and alwayes to bless and preserve your most excellent Majesty royal. Amen.

"A. 1592. Nov. 9."

The result of this unusual request was that two commissioners were at once appointed by the Queen. Within a fortnight Sir John Wolley, Secretary for the Latin Tongue to Queen Elizabeth, and one of her Privy Council, and Sir Thomas Gorges, Knight, of the Queen's Wardrobe, were seated in Dee's "late library room" at Mortlake, prepared to listen to his manifesto.

We may be sure he had long been preparing for this day. He seated the two gentlemen at a table in the middle of the room, placing near them a couple of other tables spread, one with letters and records of his "studious life for the space of a halfe hundred years, now by God's favour fully spent," the other, with all his own books, printed and manuscript, a complete author's collection of original works. At the suggestion of the commissioners he had occupied the interval of thirteen days in preparing the autobiography which he called "The Compendious Rehearsall of John Dee, his dutiful declaration, etc.,"[1] so freely quoted in these pages. "It was in some order of method most briefly and speedily contrived against this day;" and in every respect, save that of chronological order, it is a pattern document. It gives the impression of having been written down in fragments, each incident or recital being complete in itself and most carefully dated, on a separate sheet of paper, and then the sheets shuffled and picked out by chance to follow each other for putting together. The story leaps from college days in 1547 to travels

[1] The autograph MS. is in *Cotton MS.*, Vitell. c. vii. ff. 1—14.

in 1571, on to Christmas gifts in 1590, back to the Queen's visit in 1575, thence to his imprisonment and appearance before the Star Chamber in 1555, and his reformation of the Calendar in 1582. He passes very lightly over his late travels abroad, merely adding that he "was very ungodly dealt withall, when I meant all truth sincerity, fidelity and piety towards God, my Queen and Country." The catalogue of his works is valuable, but it is unnecessary to print it in the present volume.[1] He concludes his list of eight printed and thirty-six manuscript works ("some perfectly finished and some unfinished yet") with the very latest, the *Compendious Rehearsall* itself, adding that there were many other books, pamphlets and discourses not set down. He explains that the list is given neither "as they were written nor by order of yeares," but hastily as they came next to hand "out of diverse chests and baggs wherein they lay." He ends the chapter with a remarkable proof of the fecundity of his still active brain, in spite of his sixty-five years.

"The most part of all these here specifyed lye here before you on the table on your left hand; but by other books and writings of another sort (if God grant me health and life thereto of some ten or twelve years),[2] I may hereafter make plain and without doubt this sentence to be true, *Plura latent, quam patent.*" What other works he did accomplish in the sixteen years yet to run of his long life, he

[1] See Mr. Thompson Cooper's bibliography, *Dict. Nat. Biog.*

[2] The spirits had once told him he would live to be seventy-three and a half.

described in an Appendix to the *Rehearsal*, written about two years afterwards, and printed by Hearne, and by the Chetham Society at the end of the autobiographical narrative, to which he had already added a short chapter giving an account of the result of the Commissioners' visit, calling it "The Sequel of the Premisses."

To return to the day of the visit, November 22, 1592. The Queen's Secretary and the Gentleman of her Wardrobe arrived at Mortlake probably in the morning, and stayed to dinner. Having seated them at the tables in the library, Dee read to them, or related with the manuscript at hand, the story of the "halfe hundred" years spent in the attainment of "good learning," which he reckoned from his leaving Chelmsford Grammar School for Cambridge. It was, of course, drawn up with the skill of a practised author, divided into fourteen chapters, each with an attractive and pithy title. "Her Majesties specially Gracious and very Bountifull favours towards me used etc.," is by far the longest; the shortest is the twelfth: "The Resolution for Generall, very easy, and speedy Remedy in this Rare and Lamentable Case." The remedy he suggests is to make him either Master of St. Cross; Warden of Manchester; Provost of Eton; or Master of Sherborne, one of which posts had been already promised him four times in three years. The tenth chapter is "The hard making of provision for some hundred pounds [? a year] for the maintenance of me, my wife, our children and family for these three last years, and that but with a meane dyet and simple apparel: I having not one Peny of certaine Fee, revenue, stipend or Pension, either left me, or restored unto me, or of any yet bestowed on me." He shows how at his return three years before, he found himself penniless; cut off for ever from his two parsonages; disappointed as yet of the large yearly allowance promised him for his life from Bohemia. Probably on parting from the then affluent Kelley, some bond was entered into by him or by Rosenberg to transmit to him a share of the enormous profits they expected from the multiplication of the gold. "To save us from hunger starving," he had had to appeal to friends, and he records gratefully that some who had been unfriendly before he left came to his aid on his return. They "put to" their helping hands in many ways, and already he had received from them a sum of £500 and more. Yet he has had to pawn his plate little by little until all was gone. "After the same manner went my wife's jewels of gold, rings, bracelets, chaines and other our rarities, under the thraldom of the usurer's grips, till *non plus* was written upon the boxes at home." He has borrowed upon sureties, upon his personal bill of hand, upon his word, upon his promise, and he has run up accounts, so that now he is in debt for £333, beyond the £500. "The true accounts of all these gifts, loans, and debts upon score, talley, or book, is here before your Honours;" how the usurer devoureth him and how he is "dayly put to shame, may be seen." Other necessary expenses amounted to £267, so that he has spent but "£566 in three years for housekeeping," and that with great parsimony, and with gifts from good friends of "wine, whole brawnes, sheep, wheat, pepper, nutmegg, ginger, sugar, etc., and other things for the apparel of me, my wife and our children." He has mortgaged his house for £400, and now will have to sell it for half it cost to pay his debts, he and his family to become wanderers and homeless vagabonds, furnished only with bottles and wallets. What shall he do, he pitifully begs, that he may prevent his name being handed down to posterity as a warning to lovers and students of truth not to follow in his steps and be given to such disgraceful shifts and indignities? He ends with a passage of true eloquence:

> "Therefore, seeing the blinded Lady, Fortune, doth not govern in this commonwealth, but *justitia* and *prudentia*, and that in better order than in Tully's *Republica*, or Books of Offices, they are laid forth to be followed and performed: most reverently and earnestly (yea, in manner with bloody teares of heart), I and my wife, our seaven children and our servants (seaventeene of us in all), doe this day make our petition unto your Honours that upon all godly, charitable and just respects had of all that you have this day seene, heard, and perceived, you will make such report unto her most excellent Majestie (with humble request for speedy reliefe), that we be not constrained to do or suffer otherwise than becometh Christian and true faithfull obedient subjects to do or suffer. And all for want of due mainteynance."

CHAPTER XIX

DEE'S LIBRARY

The commerce of books accosteth and secondeth all my course, and everywhere assisteth me. It comforts me in age, and solaces me in solitarinesse. It easeth me of the burden of a wearysome sloth, and at all times rids me of tedious companies. It abateth the edge of fretting sorrow and . . . is the best munition I have found in this human peregrination.—MONTAIGNE, *Essays* (Florio).

THE account of the library at Mortlake as it was when Dee left it in 1583, forms one of the most valuable portions of the *Compendious Rehearsall.* Comparing it with the catalogue which he made before leaving with Laski, we can see at a glance of what intrinsic value was this collection of precious books which so often haunted its owner in his dreams. Two original copies of the Catalogue of manuscripts remain,[1] one of which is dated September 6, 1583, a fortnight before he sailed from England, and there is a third, made by Ashmole from one of these.

The library contained, however, not only books and manuscripts, to the number of four thousand, bound and unbound, but scientific instruments collected from several parts of Europe. The books alone Dee valued at £2,000 in the current value of the day, for many of them were unique *autographia* of famous and rare authors. As a further proof of

[1] Trin. Coll. Camb. MSS. *Harleian MSS.*, No. 1879. Printed in the Diary, Camden Soc., pp. 65–89.

this estimate, he cited to the two Commissioners a great volume in Greek, two others in French, and a third in High Dutch, which together cost him, and his friends for him, £533, as the endorsements upon them will show.

The instruments included a valuable quadrant, used and he says made, by his friend, Richard Chancellor, the navigator to Russia and the White Seas. It measured five feet in semi-diameter, and Dee relates that Chancellor and he together made observations of the sun's height at meridian with it, before this exploring seaman sailed on his last voyage (in which he and his crew perished) in 1556. Many years after, the quadrant was repaired and re-engraved by Mr. Bromfield, the Lieutenant of Ordnance who had given it to Dee, at a cost of £20. On Dee's return to Mortlake, he found it barbarously hacked to pieces with hammers.

There was also a ten foot *radius Astronomicus*, (some early form of telescope), its staff and cross divided with equal markings, like Chancellor's quadrant. It swung in a frame, and could be easily directed to any point in the heavens, or used for mensuration on the earth.

A couple of globes of Gerard Mercator's best make were among the most valuable contents of the library, especially as upon the celestial globe Dee had marked his own observations of comets, their place and path in the heavens. There were other objects which Mercator had constructed specially for Dee, *viz.*, three theorics, two with horizon and meridian lines in copper. A number of compasses of many kinds were among the objects, for Dee had invented, as we have seen, what he calls a "Paradoxall Cumpass." There was also a great piece of load-stone, or "magnes-stone," of extraordinary virtue. It had been sold for five shillings, but "being divided up and parted with piece-meal it made more than £20."

"There was also an excellent watch-clock, made by one Dibbley, a noteable workman, long since dead, by which clock the tyme might sensibly be measured in the seconds of an houre, that is, not to faile the 360th. part of an houre. The use of this clock was very great, more than vulgar."

Then in the three laboratories, the chambers and garrets, were stores of "chemical stuff," which he had been twenty years getting together. Also a great cart-load of special vessels for chemical use, some earthen, some of glass, metal and mixed stuff, which he had brought from Lorraine when Mr. Powell and he had gone over in 1571. Of these, only a few broken bits remained. He describes other things left in his outer or "open" library, and in particular a "great bladder with about four pounds weight of a very sweetish thing, like a brownish gum in it, artificially prepared by thirty tymes purifying it; whosoever came by it hath more than I could well affoord him for one hundred crownes, as may be proved by witnesses yet living."

As regards the manuscript treasures of the library, he mentions specially a great case or frame of boxes, full of rare evidences of lands in Ireland which had been in the hands of some of the ancient Irish Princes. Agreements for submission and tributes, with seals appended, and many other valuable records of the descent of these manors to such families as the Mortimers, the de Burghs, the Clares, etc. How he came by these, save in the way of a collector, does not appear. His interest in Welsh ancestry would account for his amassing Welsh records, of which he says there were many deeds of gift from Welsh princes and nobles, of land devoted by them to the foundation and enriching of religious houses. Norman deeds also dating back to the Conquest. These were all methodically stored away in separate boxes, each marked on the front—"the fore part of the boxes"—with chalk, explaining its contents. When he returned from his six years wandering abroad, and looked in the poor boxes, he found the name outside was all that was left. The deeds had been "imbezzled away, every one of them, which is a loss of great value in sundry respects, as antiquaries can testifie for their part, and noble heralds can tell for their skill, and as her Majesties officers, for her interest and titles Royall, may think in their consideration."

Near this great chest of boxes stood another box, very much less in size, measuring only two feet by one and a half, which was filled with nothing but seals of coats of arms; many of these were named, and had already proved invaluable to students of heraldry and genealogy, as well as to the Queen's Heralds who had carefully examined them, also a number of other antiquaries as Camden, Stow and others. The Clerks of the Records in the Tower had sat whole days in the library at Mortlake, "gathering rareties to their liking out of them." Dee was no blind collector, hoarding things because they were of value to himself. He was a true altruist, gaining his knowledge to share with others.

"Unto the Tower I had vowed these my hardly gotten muniments (gotten as in manner out of a dunghill, in the corner of a church, wherein very many were utterly spoyled by rotting, through the raine continually, for many yeares before, falling on them through the decayed roof of that church, lying desolate and waste at this houre).

"But truly well deserve they the imprisonment of the Tower, that will now still keepe them, if any publique warning by her Majestie or her right honorable Councill were given for restitution of them to the Office in the Tower."

Dee's own works were of course in the library although not included in his catalogue. He drew up a list of them for his *Apology* to the Archbishop in 1595, by which it appears that before he left England eight had been published. The unprinted books and treatises, some, he owns, not perfectly finished, numbered forty-six. To these others were added before he died; two that may be especially named were upon the Three Oracular Sentences of the Ancients: *Nosce te ipsum*, *Homo Homini Deus*, and *Homo Homini Lupus*, (1592); and a "Treatise upon the Queen's Sovereignty over the Seas," a fitting subject indeed for an author who had personally known most of the great navigators, and who had already written so intelligently upon the navy and the coast fisheries of "Albion." This book was undertaken at the request of "an honorable friend in Court." It had, of course, a long Latin title—*Thalattocratia Brytannica*, etc. It was finished at Manchester and dated September 20, 1597. Another work projected, and perhaps partly finished, was to be called *De Horizonte Æternitatis*, to consist of three treatises in answer to Andreas Libavius, who had published a book written in misapprehension of something in Dee's *Monas*.

We spare the reader the long list of titles of Dee's own books, poured out in an almost continuous stream since *The Art of Logicke, in English*, printed 1547, during his college days. The only idle years as regards literary output, from then up to his departure for life abroad in 1583, seem to have been 1563, 1564, and 1566—9.

The most important of his printed contributions to knowledge are mentioned in these pages. One more may be alluded to here—his edition, in 1582, of Robert Recorde's arithmetical work, *The Ground of Artes*, etc. Dee had probably known this accomplished physician, antiquary and mathematician at Cambridge, where Recorde was a tutor before 1545. Recorde was afterwards Comptroller of the Mint at Bristol, and Surveyor of Mines and Money to King Henry VIII., but he died a youngish and impoverished man, in the King's Bench Prison, Southwark, in 1558. He introduced algebra into this country; was something of an astrologer and a good mathematician. His choice of titles for his books was ingenious. In *The Whetstone of Witte* (1557), the signs for *plus*, *minus* and equality were first used in this country. In his *Castle of Knowledge*, a beautiful and dignified hymn of his own composition appears. *The Ground of Artes*, his first work (1540), went through eleven editions before Dee augmented it and added some of his apologetic doggerel rhymes.

That which my friend hath well begun
For very love to common weale
Need not all whole to be new done
But new increase I do reveale.

Something herein I once redrest,
And now again for thy behoofe
Of zeale, I doe, and at request,
Both mend and add, fit for all proofe.

Of numbers use, the endlesse might
No wit nor language can expresse,
Apply and try, both day and night,
And then this truth thou wilt confesse.

I. Dee.

From original and autograph works we may now turn to the miscellaneous contents of Dee's library—a truly vast and precious collection for one private gentleman of precarious fortune to own in the sixteenth century. Printed books were by no means easy to obtain, and manuscript copies entailed a great expenditure of skill, industry, time and cost. The text was often ignorantly or corruptly rendered by an imperfect scribe or copyist, and the scholar and collector could not rest satisfied without several versions of one work.

The cataloguer of the 200 most important manuscripts—Dee himself—enters with exactitude the size and substance of each volume. The bulk of course were in quarto, although a few folios and octavos are mentioned. Most of them were written upon parchment, but a certain number were on paper. Bindings were not noticed, chiefly because as yet few were bound. Two of Roger Bacon's tracts, however, on the multiplication of species, and on perspective, the owner describes as together "in paste-bords with strings." These identical tracts, in Dee's own hand, are now being edited by Mr. Robert Steele, from the originals in the Mazarine Library, Bibliothèque Nationale, Paris. From Dee they passed to Sir Richard Eden, afterwards to the Kenelm Digby Library. Treatises on kindred subjects often followed straight upon each other on the same parchment, and sometimes as many as twenty composed a single manuscript, included under a list of titles numbered as one. In some cases the treatise is described as a fragment. Once he writes "the second tract is cut out and to be answered for."

The owner's tastes and pursuits point, of course, to a large representation among his books, of works in philosophy, alchemy, astrology and medicine, with a substantial proportion dealing with metallurgy, geometry, optics, physics, Ptolomaic and Copernican astronomy, and every branch of science already known in a crude form to Dee's famous predecessors. There are also historical chronicles; works of devotion and ethics; with a fair sprinkling of authors upon poetry, music, and the gentler arts.

Taking first the classics: Dee names the Meno, Phædo and Timæus of Plato; writings of Aristotle, Socrates and Hippocrates, of Cicero, Cato and Archimedes. A copy of Pliny's *Mundi Historia*, Lib. ii., printed Frankfort, 1543, now in the British

Museum, bears Dee's signature, Louvain, January, 1550, and many of his notes. Of Euclid he had many copies, and Augustine was his guide and confessor. A vast number of Arabic and Persian writers were comprehended in the list. He was particularly rich in manuscripts of the early and mediæval writers upon alchemy and the philosopher's stone: Hermes Trismegistus, Geber, Albertus Magnus, John Sacrobosco, Raymond Lully, Philip Alstade, and Arnold de Villa Nova. Other sciences are represented by Guido Bonatus, Anselmus de Boot (Boetius), Alhazen, John of Saxony, Jacob Alkind, and Petrus Peregrinus and a score of learned writers. Dee's own perfect and clean copy of the rare printed Epistle of Peregrinus, upon the Magnet (Augsburg, 1558), is now in the British Museum. It bears his name, "Joannes Dee, 1564," in faded ink, with many and copious notes written by its owner mostly in his large copy-book hand, with a few in the scribbling writing which he used for speed, and some marginal sketches.

Several of the manuscripts named in Dee's list are to be found among the Cotton MSS. at the Museum; in Trinity College, Dublin; and at Oxford and Cambridge.[1]

Of English authors, who are very numerous in the list, the most eagerly sought after, judging by the number of works included by one author, were Roger Bacon and Robert Grosseteste, Bishop of Lincoln. Bacon's writings were owned by Dee in fragments. Some had been already collected and

[1] See Halliwell's notes to the printed catalogue, *Diary*, ed. Camden Soc., pp. 65–87.

printed in Nüremberg and Paris. The only other writer as often repeated in the catalogue is Boethius, whose *Consolation of Philosophy* had tempted King Alfred into literary translation some seven hundred years before. Dee notes that he gave a manuscript of it in Greek to the Library of Cracow, on July 28, 1584. Some of the ethical and philosophical works of St. Isidore, the canonised Bishop of Seville, were duplicated. Thomas Aquinas; Duns Scotus; Richard of Wallingford, Abbot of St. Albans; Robert of Holcot, the Bible Commentator; Robert of Gloucester; William of Woodford, the Franciscan opponent of Wycliffe; Richard Rolle (de Hampole), the hermit and ethical writer, are among his other English authors. A finely illuminated history of the last years of King Richard II., by a French gentleman who was in his suite, once the property of Dee, is now in the Lambeth Library.[1] His manuscript Life of Edward the Confessor, by Ethelred, Abbot of Rievaulx, is another treasure that has survived the wreck of time. It is now among the Harleian MSS. at the British Museum, with his name and the date 1575 inscribed.

Of the three or four thousand printed volumes even Dee's industry has left no catalogue. Many of them he mentions in his diaries, as Holinshed's and Stow's *Chronicles;* the Arabic book that was lost; the collection of writings upon demonology and witchcraft, which were to be so useful to his Lancashire neighbours in after life. The books of the alchemist of Louvain, Cornelius Agrippa, he once

[1] *Archæologia*, xx., 1–242.

speaks of as lying open in the window of his study, and therefore in constant use in the "actions," whether theurgic or alchemistic.

He refers no doubt to Agrippa's *de Occulta Philosophia* (Cologne? 1533), a work enormously read in all countries in the sixteenth and seventeenth centuries, and translated into many languages. Another book by the alchemist of Queen Margaret of the Netherlands had an even greater popularity in England, France, Germany and Italy. This was *On the Nobility and Excellence of the Female Sex* (*de nobilitate et præcellentia fœminei sexus*) which in the translation by Henry Care in 1670 becomes magnified into *Female Pre-eminence; or, the Dignity and Excellency of that Sex above the Male.* It is dedicated to Queen Catharine of Braganza.

These are a very few of the authors and writings contained in the manuscript catalogue. Such as they are, however, they give us a faint glimpse into that realm of learning and romance wherein Dee, shut into his library at Mortlake, roamed a free citizen of the world and dwelled where he would.

CHAPTER XX

ADIEU TO COURTS AND COURTING

Let me weep
My youth and its brave hopes, all dead and gone,
In tears which burn! Would I were sure to win
Some startling secret in their stead, a tincture
Of force to flush old age with youth, or breed
Gold, or imprison moonbeams till they change
To opal shafts!—only that hurling it
Indignant back, I might convince myself
My aims remained supreme and pure as ever.

—BROWNING, *Paracelsus*.

THE immediate result of the Commissioners' visit to Mortlake was a gift of a hundred marks from the Queen. The Countess of Warwick sent off "her gentleman, Mr. Jones, very speedily," to tell Dee that Sir Thomas Gorges "had very honorably dealt for" him in the matter, and that the gift was granted. The money was brought next day (December 2) by Sir Thomas himself. He brought also a letter "full of courtesie and kindness and a token of six old angells of gold," from Lady Howard to Jane. Dee seems to have become intimate with Lady Warwick[1] through his early friendship with John Dudley, Earl of Warwick, who died, aged twenty-four, in 1554. In his Preface to Euclid, Dee has left an etched portrait of this friend of his own age. "No two besides himself," says Dee, "can

[1] A daughter of the house of Russell, she married as 3rd wife (1565) Ambrose Dudley, Leicester's brother.

so well say what roots vertue had fastened in his breast, what rules of godly and honorable life he had framed to himself, what vices noteable he took great care to eschew, what prowesses he purposed and meant to achieve."

Dee's "few lynes of thankfulness" to the Queen for her gift were probably written at once, but only delivered by Lady Warwick on February 15, at Hampton Court, on the eve of a move to Somerset House.

On the strength of this dole, Dee was able to settle some pressing debts, and to hire a coach and go off with his wife and Arthur and Kate, to spend Christmas and New Year's Day at Tooting, "at Mr. R. Luresey his howse." The Lord Treasurer, he reports, lay dangerously sick at the time. On the 2nd they returned. On the 7th, welcome letters, perhaps containing money, arrived from Count Laski in Livonia, to which Dee replied on the 20th, sending his letter by a Danish ship called the *John of Dansk.*

His reputation as an astronomer and mathematician now procured for Dee a pupil, from whom he was to receive in exchange a considerable gift or loan.

"March 17, 1593. At six after none received from Mr. Francis Nicholls £15, part of one hundred pounds, the rest whereof, £85, is to be receyved from Mr. Nicholls within a fortnight after the annunciation of Our Lady next; and after that in the beginning of June £100, and in Julie the third hundred pounds, and I am to teach him the conclusion of fixing and teyming of the moon."

A rather unwise purchase seems to have been made this May; Dee bought the "next mansion house, with the plat and all the appertenances abowt it," of Mr. Mark Pierpoint, of Mortlake. It is true the whole mansion only cost £32, but it entailed other purchases and soon had to be mortgaged. Possession was not obtained till the autumn. A "hovel" in the yard was bought from Goodman Welder in July for a new angel and five new shillings. The bargain with Pierpoint was concluded in the street, when "before Jane my wife, I gave him a saffron noble in ernest for a drink penney."

Crowds of visitors came to Mortlake to dine. Mr. Beale (who was a borrower of books from Dee—his own *Famous and Rich Discoveries*, and the *Chronica Hollandiae Magnæ*), and his wife; Francis Blount, uncle of Sir Charles, who had been in Constantinople; Mistress Banister; Mr. Redhead, one of the Queen's gentlemen ushers, and his wife; the mother of John Pontoys, about whom we shall hear more; Mr. Gubbens, book-binder, and Mrs. Gubbens, and many others. Hospitable as ever, Dee had offered shelter for two months to Antony Ashley, Clerk of the Council, his wife and family, "who used me worshipfully and bountifully for our friendship. They had my mother's chamber, the mayde's chamber, and all the other house."

Not only books were lent, but instruments also. "On Thursday, Mr. Saunders of Ewell, sent home my great sea cumpass, but without a needle. It came in the night by water."

In August he is much in train with the Lord Keeper, Sir John Eckford, at Kew. On the 8th he dined there, again on the 17th, this time taking Mrs. Dee and Katherine, who at twelve was sufficiently grown up to dine out. On the 28th he was all day with the Lord Keeper. The entries we have here, "Mr. Web and the philosopher came as I was with the Lord Keeper," and "Mr. Web and the philosopher cam again," pique one's curiosity.

At the end of the month, Dee notes the departure from his service "uppon no due cause known to me," of Elizabeth Kyrton, a servant who had been with him twelve years, had passed through the vicissitudes of travel-life in Bohemia, as Rowland's nurse; left in charge of him, as we have seen, in Cracow when the others went on to Prague. She had served five years on apprenticeship and seven for wages: five at four and two at five nobles a year. Of her wages there was now four pounds four shillings due. Dee in paying her, presented a new half-angel; Jane Dee gave her another; Arthur half-a-crown for him and his brother (Rowland), and Katherine the like sum for herself and Madinia. Elizabeth's going seems to have upset the domestic arrangements, for a month or so later Dee makes an unusual entry about his wife: "Jane most desperately angry in respect of her maydes." Margery Thornton, Elizabeth's successor, left next day, and Dorothy Legg came for 30*s*. yearly.

A messenger from Laski arrived, Mr. Cornelio Camaiere, and stayed a week. These constant communications do not by any means support the contention that Laski parted with Dee in anger, ruined by his costly experiments. It is more probable that Laski was urging him to return and continue Kelley's work.

The Countess of Cumberland, Lord Willoughby and his sister, the Countess of Kent, came to visit Dee. Willoughby dined and next day sent him £20. Dee was annoyed by "Mr. Gray, the Lady Cumberland's preacher, his wrangling and denying and despising alchemichall philosophers." A New Year's gift of 20 angels, in a new red velvet purse, came to Jane Dee from the Lord Keeper.

Michael Peiser, doctor to the Duke of Brandenburg, visited Dee, also Walter Van der Laen, "an astronomer of great promise." Mr. John Aske sent as a present two little double gilt bowls, weighing thirteen ounces and a half. "Sir Thomas Willes offer philosophical cam to my hands, by Mr. Morrice Kiffen." The children, Madinia and Theodore, were not very well. Several visits were paid to Mr. Webbe, who had been in the Marshalsea prison since the days before Christmas. His chests and boxes were sealed up. It is possible he was the Mr. Webbe who was employed by the Queen to visit and report on Dyer and Kelley at Prague. He may even have been suspected of bringing some of Kelley's manufactured gold to Dee. Bartholomew Hickman and his brother were a good deal to and fro; Bartholomew was first brought to Dee as a lad by his uncle, in 1578, with an introduction from Sir Christopher Hatton. Now, his daughter Jane was taken into service. Dee gave him a nag that the Lord Keeper had presented, and he rode frequently "homeward," to Shugborough in Warwickshire. In December, 1594, Dee "preferred" him to Lord Willoughby's service at the Barbican, and there is a whole history about his livery, which was ordered from a Fleet Street tailor, Mr. Jonson.

Dee's health was now often affected in one way or another. The first mention of trouble in the kidneys was in 1592, when, at Court at Greenwich, a midnight seizure was eased by a glyster,[1] applied by Dr. Giffard. There were other slight attacks, and in March, 1594, he had a

> "Great fit of stone in my left kidney: but I drunk a draught of white wyne and salet oyle, and after that, crabs' eyes in powder with the bone in the carp's head, and about four of the clock I did eat tosted cake buttered, and with sugar and nutmeg on it, and drunk two great draughts of ale with it; and I voyded within an hour much water and a stone as big as an Alexander seed. God be thanked! Five shillings to Robert Web part of his wages."

This servant was discharged on June 23 with forty shillings for a full satisfaction of all things. "On July 1, I gave Robert yet more, a French crown for a far well."

A year and a half passed after the visit of the Commissioners, and beside the immediate result of a donation of a hundred marks, nothing had accrued to better Dee's position. He determined then to redouble his efforts and bring something to pass. He certainly had enlisted the aid of powerful friends, although no doubt there were still many suspicious enemies.

On May 3, 1594, the Queen sent for him to come to her in the privy garden at Greenwich, between six

[1] An early form of enema, made from the bladder of a sheep.

and seven o'clock in the evening. She received him alone save for the presence of her two ladies, Lady Warwick, Dee's very good friend, and Lady Cecil. Dee presented her with a writing which he calls "the heavenly admonition," which he says she took with grateful thanks. On the 18th, he writes "Her Majestie sent me agayn the copy of the letter of E. K. with thanks by the Lady Warwick." He had received letters from Kelley four or five weeks earlier, on March 28, and he probably had copied out for her certain passages, doubtless referring to the fabulous transmutation of metals. Did he still hold out hopes that he might be able to achieve a like success? On the 21st, "Sir John Wolley moved my sute to her Majesty. She granted after a sort, but referred all to the Lord of Canterbury." "On the 25th. Dr. Aubrey moved my sute to her Majesty, and answere as before." His suit was promotion to the Mastership of St. Cross, the post which had so long been the goal of his hopes, but which he was never destined to attain. He had set out at length in his *Rehearsall* for the Commissioners, sundry good reasons why he desired it, "rather than any other living, see, or dignity of like value in any other place." First, he gave as a reason his longing to retire to a quiet spot away from the multitude and hoards of friends and acquaintances, chance visitors, and distinguished strangers, who positively "haunted" his house at Mortlake. There, he could deny himself to no one without offence or breach of friendship. It was fatally easy and cheap for every curious person from London, or from the Court, to find his way down to that big rambling place by the riverside, with whose stills and furnaces, and wonderful doings, rumour was so rife. So much for privacy, next for economy. Fuel, coals, bricks, and all things necessary for his purpose, will be cheaper at Winchester than near London; the glass-houses of Sussex are not far away, and he will be able to give personal supervision to the making of special vessels. At Mortlake there are too many eyes and tongues. The south coast is within easy reach, and it will be possible to communicate with his friends abroad, to get over things and workers necessary, and "have the more commodious place for the secret arrival of special men to come unto me there at St. Crosses; some of which men would be loath to be seen or heard of publickly in Court or City." Is it possible that he is still thinking of Kelley, who, though then (1592) an Emperor's favourite and the bearer of a title, could easily in England be identified with Talbot the coiner, forger, and necromancer of former days?

Then Dee sets out in his *Rehearsall* the capacity of the dwelling at St. Cross, which is roomy enough to entertain rare and excellent men from all parts of the world, as well as any of his fellow-countrymen. This will be for the honour and credit of England. There is room also for lodging his staff of mechanical assistants; for a printing house to be set up for "reproducing good, rare, and antient bookes in Greek and Latin," and "some of my own, to be printed with my own ordering and oversight." Then he lays stress upon the desirable surroundings, a chapel where divine service is held every day, for bringing up his children and family devoutly. He ends with the advantages of Winchester School, close at hand, not only for his four sons "to become Grammarians in," but for his obtaining help from the "good Greek and Latin Grammarians and fair writers in that school, for copying out books for Her Majesty."

He is teeming with all these projects and activities in spite of his sixty-five years. He was a born librarian; and still had a national library of books and manuscripts at heart as much as when, nearly forty years before, he had tried in vain to induce Queen Mary to found one.

Dee's eloquent persuasions so far prevailed with the Queen that a draft was prepared before the end of May, granting to Lord Cobham the next advowson of "Holyrood," or St. Cross, at Winchester, in the Queen's gift, to present to John Dee, M.A., on the death or resignation of Dr. Robert Bennett, the present incumbent.[1]

Having drawn up this very full account of his doings and writings, to present to the Commissioners, Dee was naturally anxious that the appeal should be as widespread and far-reaching as possible. Archbishop Whitgift had shown himself favourably inclined, and Dee determined to approach him with a copy of that part of the *Rehearsall* in which he recited the titles of the books he had written. He prepared à *Letter containing a brief Discourse apologeticall with a plaine Demonstration and fervent*

[1] *Cal. State Pap. Dom.*, 1594, p. 513. The day of the month in May is left blank.

protestation for the lawful sincere and very faithful and christian course of the philosophicall studies and exercises of a certaine studious gentleman, an ancient servant to her most excellent Majesty Royall, addressed to the Archbishop; he probably presented it himself during this summer of 1595. It is a protest and an appeal, and emphatically states that from his youth up he has used good honest lawful and Christian means to attain such knowledge as shall honour God, his country and his Queen. It ends with a prayer that he may be found of the Archbishop, and undoubtedly acknowledged by the wise and just, to have been a zealous and faithful student in the school of Verity and an ancient Graduate in the school of Charity.

On June 3, Dee and Jane, accompanied by all their seven children, four boys and three girls, their ages ranging from Arthur, the Westminster boy of fifteen, to Frances, the baby of two and a half, presented themselves before the Queen at Sion House, Isleworth. Jane was permitted to kiss her hand. Evidently this was an expression of thanks for the official preliminaries of the grant of St. Cross. The Archbishop was present, and Dee humbly requested him to come to his "cottage." The invitation was repeated on the 6th, when Dee supped with the Primate. Things were not, however, settled so quickly. Dr. Robert Bennett had to be provided with a better position before he would resign; some hitch occurred, and on June 29, after a visit to the Archbishop, at Croydon, the poor man writes distractedly of his broken hopes:—

"After I had hard the Archbishop his answers and discourses, and after that he had byn the last Sonday at Tybalds with the Quene and Lord Threasorer, I take myself confounded for all suing or hoping for anything that ever was. And so adiew to court and courting tyll God direct me otherwise! The Archbishop gave me a payre of sufferings [*sic*] to drinke. God be my help as he is my refuge. Amen."

Everything fell through, and things began to look darker than ever. Michael, who had been a delicate child, fell ill in July. On the 6th, he "becam distempered in his head and bak and arms." Dee himself was unwell, complaining of headache and internal pains, but he does not forget to note that he paid "Letice my servant 5*s*., part of her wages, with part whereof she is to buy a smok and nekercher." Michael's illness was short: "July 13th, *in ortu solis*, Michael Dee did give up the ghost, after he sayed 'O Lord, have mercy upon me!'" His father omits any reference to the child's burial.

The summer passed with very little to record in the diary beyond a visit on Aug. 26, from Gerard, the herbalist of quaint and fragrant memory; another on the 30th, from "Monsieur Walter Mallet, who toke his leave to go to Tholose. He had the fix oyle of saltpetre." Dee sends letters in September to Kelley, and in October determines on another appeal to royal favour. But Elizabeth was getting old and hard to move; Burleigh also was failing. Dee wrote in his wife's name to Lady Scudamore, her old friend and Katherine's godmother, begging her to intercede with the Queen that either he might appear and declare his case before the Council, or else have a licence under the Great Seal to go where he would. St. Cross was farther off than ever; England cold and inhospitable; and he prepared to say a final good-bye to courts and courting at home, and betake himself to Germany, or Austria, or some other land. Francis Garland arrived on December 2 from Prague, "just as I came five years ago to a day from Bremen to England." Little profit indeed had he reaped in that five years.

On the 7th, "Jane delivered her supplication with her own hand to the Queen, as she passed out of the privy garden at Somerset House, to go to dinner with Sir Thomas Heneage at the Savoy." Elizabeth handed the letter to the Lord Admiral, but took it again from him, and kept it on her cushion. The next day, the Lord Admiral and Lord Buckhurst reminded her of the matter; presently she told the Archbishop that she wished Dee to have Dr. Day's place of Chancellor at St. Paul's. "8th Dec. The Chancellorship presented. The Archbishop of Canterbury willing," he writes; but this was apparently another castle in the air, for Dr. William Day was not appointed Bishop of Winchester till a year later, November 23, 1595, and although Dee's name appears as Chancellor under the date of December 8, 1594,[1] he seems never to have held office.

His friends, however, were not idle. In a month's time, January 3, Archbishop Whitgift was recommending Elizabeth to grant him the Wardenship of

[1] Le Neve, *Fasti*, vol. ii., 361.

Christ's College, Manchester, in her own gift. Dr. William Chadderton, who was then Warden and Bishop of Chester, was to be promoted to the see of Lincoln, and here was an opening for Dee. On February 5, Sir John Wolley endeavoured to get her to sign the patent for his appointment, "but she deferred it." Dee was up and down to London from Mortlake, and on February 10, at two in the afternoon, he "toke a cut-purse taking his purse out of his pocket in the Temple." On April 18, the Queen did sign the bill, when it was offered her by Dee's friend and neighbour at Mortlake, John Herbert, Master of the Requests. On May 25, 26, 27, it passed the Signet, the Privy Seal, and the Great Seal[1]; and, as a climax to this entry in the diary, Dee adds, "£3 12*s.* borrowed of my brother Arnold,"[2] doubtless to pay the fees.

The Earl of Derby gave him letters of introduction, and he was soon in correspondence with Oliver Carter, one of the Fellows; with Thomas Williams, another; and with Mr. Goodier, lessee of the tithes belonging to the Warden and Fellows. Carter and Williams were already at law with each other, and soon were both to be at loggerheads with Dee and his laudable desires to set the tangled affairs of the college straight. Carter was one of the moderators

[1] *Cal. State Papers*, 1595–7, p. 45. The patent, dated May 26 in the Queen's name, gives her beloved and faithful servant John Dee, M.A., Clerk, the place of Warden with all rights, whether present or absent.

[2] Perhaps Arnold was Jane Dee's brother, but, as before noticed, Dee frequently uses the term.

of the monthly lecture in Manchester, had great influence, and seems to have been unprepared to welcome a Warden of Dee's reputation.

"July 31st. The Countess of Warwick did this evening thank her Majestie in my name, and for me, for her gift of the Wardenship of Manchester. She toke it gratiously and was sorry that it was so far from hense, but that some better thing neer hand shall be fownd for me; if opportunitie of time would serve, her Majestie wold speak with me herself. I had a bill made by Mr. Wood, one of the clerks of the signet, for the first frutes forgiving by her Majestie."

So at length there was something tangible in prospect. Things had to be settled up at Mortlake and preparations made for the journey northward. We may be sure that Dee's gratification at receiving a post of some sort, after a lifetime of waiting, was mixed with regret at quitting the place that had been his home for so long. His "yong coosen, John Aubrey, came in May to recreate himself for a while," and stayed nearly a month.

On August 14, Jane's youngest child, a girl, was born. She was baptised at Mortlake as Margaret Dee on the afternoon of August 27; godfather, the Lord Keeper; godmothers, the Countesses of Cumberland and Essex, all three represented by deputy. The Countess of Essex was Walsingham's only daughter and heir. She had been Sidney's widow, and was now married to Essex.

Dee was now entertained often by Lord Derby at Russell House, once to meet some German guests.

On October 9 he dined with Sir Walter Raleigh at Durham Place. This palace in the Strand had seen many vicissitudes before it had been given to Raleigh by the Queen. Originally the residence of the northern bishops, it had been seized by an earlier king. Lady Jane Grey had been wedded there. Her too ambitious father-in-law had gone thence to the Tower and the scaffold. Catholic plots against Elizabeth had been hatched by Spaniards in this, her own house, and now the great seaman, fresh from far Guiana, was housed in a little turret, overlooking the river and the ships.

Dee was anxious to reclaim, before going to his new home, an Arabic book lent to some friend in Oxford. He had written to Mr. Harding and Mr. Abbott several times for its return about a year and a half before. Now, on October 20, he sent his man Richard Walkden to Oxford to find and bring it. The man returned from a fruitless errand, but on November 19 "my Arabic book was restored by God's favour." His gratitude expressed itself in a practical manner to the trusted Richard:

"I delivered unto Richard Walkedyne my man, Mr. Robert Thomas his fustian dubblet, for 10 shillings of his wages. I gave him more when he was to ride down with my wife: 10*s.*, whereof 6*s.* 4*d.* was due to him that he had layd out for me. The other 3*s.* 6*d.* was of his wages."

A portion of goods and furniture had already been despatched towards Manchester by a carrier named Percivall, and on the 26th Jane and her children all set off by coach towards Coventry, a usual half-way halting place on the high-road to Lancashire. A last piece of business was transacted on December 23 with John Norton, stationer, to whom Dee owed money, perhaps for printing: "I payd him ten pownds in hand and was bound in a recognisance before Doctor Hone for the payment of the rest, £10 yearly, at Christmas, and Midsummer £5, tyll £53 14*s*. 8*d*. more were paid." The same day he received £30 in part payment of £100 for the house at Mortlake, which he had lent to Mr. Paget.

CHAPTER XXI

MANCHESTER

" He hath, my lord, wrung from me my slow leave,
By laboursome petition ; and, at last,
Upon his will I sealed my hard consent."
—SHAKESPEARE, *Hamlet*.

THE Collegiate Church, now the Cathedral of Manchester, was founded about 1420 in this already ancient town by Thomas de la Warre, baron and priest, rector or parson of St. Mary's, Manchester, and lord of the manor. The flourishing town of woollen industries, introduced by the Flemings a hundred or more years earlier, demanded a new and more capacious church ; and De la Warre, the last of his noble house, determined to provide buildings in which a Warden, priests or Fellows, and choristers, should be continually resident, as well as to found a new church. He gained the consent of his parishioners to the appropriation of estates belonging to the existing rectory, as an income for the college, and supplemented it from his own lands in the district. He also obtained a charter of foundation from Henry V., dated May 9.[1] The college was dissolved by Edward VI. and refounded by Henry VIII. ; but by the time of Elizabeth its lands had been

[1] Hibbert Ware, *History of Foundations in Manchester* (1834), vol. i., p. 38.

plundered, sold or leased, she herself becoming a sharer in the profits of spoliation until there was hardly any clear property left. At the instance of Dean Nowell, an inquiry was instituted, with the result that the college was granted a new charter in 1578, as Christ's College, to consist of a Warden, four Fellows, and two chaplains, with choristers. Nowell and Oliver Carter were two of the first Fellows. The second Warden was Dr. Chadderton, who had been Leicester's chaplain, and was Bishop of Chester. Under him the Catholics were relentlessly persecuted, Manchester prisons were filled, and the famous Marprelate printing press was discovered and seized. Chadderton's promotion to the see of Lincoln in 1595 made an opening for our persistent place-beggar to be disposed of at last.

Dee arrived in Manchester on Monday afternoon, February 15, 1596, and took up his abode in the college. On the following Saturday he was installed in the Wardenship, between nine and eleven o'clock, as he tells us. He has unfortunately left no account of the ceremony. His first business was to become acquainted with the tenants of the college lands, and the owners of tithes which constituted its revenue. On April 2, he says Sir John Byron and his son, Mr. John Byron, dined with him at the college. This family, although Newstead had been acquired some forty or fifty years previously, were still often resident on their Lancashire estates. Clayton, near Manchester, was in fact then their chief residence. A little later in the month, Dee records the courts kept for the manor of Newton, in Manchester parish, of which the Warden and Fellows were lords. The Dean and Canons, the present representatives of Warden and Fellows, still hold a court leet twice a year for this manor.

There is an interesting letter from Dee to Robert Bruce Cotton, the antiquary, dated in May this year, throwing light on his relations with the people in his employ—copyists, assistants or apprentices.[1] He had brought with him from Mortlake Antony Cowley, who had formerly been in Cotton's service. Dee was anxious to know if he had departed from the employ of his late master with his good will.

"Truely, for my part, I will receyve none to my simple service (man or woman) unleast they come from theyr Masters or Mistresses with theyr well liking of suche their departure from them. Therfore, I wold, by this bearer, gladly receyve your answer herein, by word of mouth or by your letter. And so shall I be free from all offence giving to your worship, or any els in this cause: as I am most free from coveting, desyring or longing after my neighbour's wife or any servant of his. If I might have a thousand pounds to sollicite or procure any mans servant to forsake his master or mistress, and to come to me or any other, I wold not do it, God knowes."

In about three weeks Dee received a reply to this considerate letter, evidently not entirely satisfactory, for on June 3 he paid Antony Cowley 20*s.* and discharged him. Next day "Antony went forth early from my house, I know not whither."

Dee now began to direct his whole attention to

[1] *Cotton MS.*, Jul. C. iii., f. 136; Ellis, *Letters*, p. 87.

his charge: the college and the college lands. A royal commission was appointed to sit and examine its internal affairs. On June 18 "the commission for the college was sent to London to be engrossed in the Duchy office." Dee was a layman; he had always stipulated he should have no cure of souls attached to whatever benefice he might hold. For the daily services at Manchester he employed a succession of curates (mostly unsatisfactory), to whom he paid "wages 50*s*. for three months." He was far more interested in the temporal than the spiritual welfare of his college, and indeed his desire for such an appointment seems rather to have been solely prompted by the selfish, if necessary, wish for an income and means to pursue his own studies in peace. He was to find neither in Manchester.

In June he received a visit from Mr. Harry Savile, the antiquary, of the Bank, Halifax, and by him he sent a request to Christopher Saxton, of Dunningley, near Halifax, to come and arrange a survey of the town of Manchester, and consult about the parish boundaries. Saxton was a well-known character of the time, the holder of a patent from the Queen, whose arms appear upon the maps he made of the three counties of Chester, York and Lancaster. They were the first maps of Britain made from actual survey, and had been issued as an atlas in 1579, most of the maps having been engraved in 1577. His visits to Dee lasted over three weeks; notes are entered of his measuring the township and visiting Hough Hall, the seat of Nicholas Mosely, the Lancashire clothier who, two or three years later, became Lord Mayor of London, and was knighted by Queen Elizabeth. The boys, Arthur and Rowland; the two faithful assistants, Crocker and Walkden accompanied Dee and Mr. Saxton on the peregrination. Harry Savile seems to have made one of the party also. Unfortunately, Saxton's Manchester survey is not now known to be in existence.

A surprise visit was paid to the Warden on June 26 by his landlord, the Earl of Derby, and a large party of ladies and gentlemen, including Lady Gerard, wife of the Master of the Rolls; her daughter Frances, and her husband, Sir Richard Molyneux, of Sefton, a former member for the county of Lancaster. Their son-in-law, Mr. Richard Hoghton, of Hoghton Towers, and others, also accompanied the Earl. The Warden says: "They came suddenly upon me after three of the clock. I made them a skoler's collation, and it was taken in good part. I browght his honor and the ladyes to Ardwick Green toward Lyme, to Mr. Legh his howse, 12 myles off." Mrs. Legh was Lady Gerard's second daughter, so it was altogether a family party that descended so unexpectedly on the Warden, and no doubt ate merrily of his "scholar's collation." The only absence from Manchester recorded by the Warden (except the two years in London) was on August 13 this year, when he says that he "rid toward York and Halifax, returning from York on the 20th."

On September 1, Mary Goodwyn came "to govern and teach" the two younger children, Madinia, aged six, and Margaret, one year old. There was a field or two let with the College House, and the Warden now turned farmer, getting a small drove of seventeen head of cattle up from his kinsfolk in Wales to graze the pasture. They were brought up by the "courteous Griffith David, nephew to Mr. Thomas Griffith, and were a present." Dee had to visit Sir John Byron about the college tenants

"Who pretended that we have part of Faylesworth Common within our Newton Heath, which cannot be proved, I am sure. We wer agreed that James Traves (being his bayly) and Francis Nutthall, his servant for him, shold with me understand all circumstances, and so duly to proceed."

The close of the year was marked by an episode which might have gone far towards clearing Dee's character from the aspersions still being cast upon him. Nowhere was superstition and belief in witchcraft more prevalent than in Lancashire, and in November and December of this year he seems to have been applied to for advice as regards a woman and seven children, said to have become demoniacally possessed through the influence of one Hartley, a "conjurer." Dee's curate, Matthew Palmer, happened to go in as Hartley was praying over the woman in a fit. He demanded what he was doing.

"'Praying.'

"'Thou pray! thou canst not pray,' quoth he. 'What prayer canst thou say?'

"'None,' saith he, 'but the Lord's Prayer.'

"'Say it,' quoth he, the which as I remember, he could not say."

Dee "utterly refused to meddle with the affair,

and advised the father to consult with godlye preachers and appoint a private fast." Perhaps he remembered that when he asked, long before, if he had done well concerning Isabel Lister, vexed of a wicked spirit, the angel's reply had been "Friend, it is not of thy charge." He sent for Hartley, and "so sharply rebuked him that the children had more ease for three weeks after." The devils were finally exorcised by a godly preacher, John Darrell, or, as we suspect, by the children's release from Hartley's attentions, who was hanged soon after. Dee's library, a good part of which he must have moved to Manchester, was constantly in request at this time. It was rich in books on demonology and possession, and Lancashire justices of the peace who had to deal with these cases of witchcraft brought before them seem to have resorted to such works, for and against the persecution and annihilation of witches, as the *De Praestigiis Daemonum* (Basle, 1566) of John Wier, the *Fustis Daemonum* and the *Flagellum Daemonum* of the monk Hierom Menghi (Frankfort 1582, Boulogne 1586). All these Dee records lending to Mr. Edmund Hopwood, of Hopwood, a deputy-lieutenant and ecclesiastical commissioner, as well as a J.P. Wier or Weier was very likely known to Dee at Louvain. He was one of the earliest apologists for these unfortunate folk, and pleaded that, their brains being disordered by melancholy, they merited pity, not punishment. His book contains the first account of "The Pied Piper of Hamelin," from the archives of the town of Hameln. A Spanish grammar was lent to

Mr. Barlow for his son. Mr. Matthew Heton was the borrower of theological works, including the *Concordantiae Bibliorum* (1555) of Robert Stephens, the illustrious printer of the New Testament; and a Calvinistic treatise, *De Coena Domini*, written by Dr. Pezel, who had, we remember, commemorated Dee's departure from Bremen in 1589 by verses. Dee lent Heton books, but Heton lent Dee ten pounds on a bill of hand. To John Cholmeley " I lent my Latyn boke in 8vo, *De Morbis Infantum*."[1]

The disputes and difficulties over tithes and lands belonging to the college naturally affected the Warden's income, and Dee found himself compelled to borrow small sums as before. Finally he was reduced to raise money on his plate, and especially on the handsome double gilt tankard, with a cover, which was the christening gift of the Countess of Hertford to her god-daughter Frances. It weighed 22 ounces, and Dee tells how he delivered it to Charles Leigh, one of the college "singing men," to lay in pawn in his own name with Robert Welsham, the goldsmith, " till within two days after May-day next. My daughter Katherine and John Crocker [the old servant], and I myself [John Dee], were at the delivery of it and waying of it, in my dyning chamber. It was wrapped in a new handkercher cloth." All that was obtained on the tankard was £4 of the current value.

In the spring of 1597, Dee records, on May 4, the last of the Rogation days of the year, a very

[1] Perhaps *De Morbis Puerorum*, by Hieronymus Mercurialis, Venice, 1583.

interesting topographical event, viz., the perambulation of the bounds of old Manchester by himself, the curate, and the clerk.

Away in the south-eastern corner of England, in the little village of Bourne, near Canterbury, about this very time, Richard Hooker, the saintly scholar, was performing a similar perambulation, of which Izaak Walton has left us the immortal picture. A homily was prepared for the service, a psalm sung, and the malediction pronounced, "Cursed be he that removes his neighbour's landmark." Izaak Walton tells us that Hooker, to look at, was an

> "Obscure harmless man in poor clothes, his loins girt in a coarse gown or canonical coat; of a mean stature and stooping, yet more lowly in the thoughts of his soul; his body worn out, not with age, but study and holy mortification. Yet he would by no means omit the customary procession; persuading all, both rich and poor: if they desired the preservation of love and their parish rights and liberties, to accompany him in his perambulation; and most did so. In which perambulation, he would express more pleasant discourse than at other times, and would then always drop some loving and facetious observations, to be remembered against the next year, especially by the boys and young people; still inclining them, and all his present parishioners, to meekness and mutual kindnesses and love, because love thinks no evil, but covers a multitude of sins."

The Warden of Manchester has not left us such an impression of the ancient antiquarian custom performed as a holy rite of devotion, but as an exact topographer and mathematician he has given a highly valuable record :—

1597. "May 4. I with Sir Robert Barber, curate, and Robert Tilsley, clerk of Manchester parish church, with diverse of the town of diverse ages, went in Perambulation to the bownds of Manchester parish : began at the Leeless Birche against Prestwicke parish, and so had vew of the thre corner stake, and then down tyll Mr. Standysh new enclosure on Thelmore, wher we stayed, and vewed the stake yet standing in the back of the dich ; [it] being from the corner eleven measures of Mr. Standley's stik, then in his hand, and 2 fote more ; which stik I did measure afterward, and it did conteyn in length : feet 6, ynch 3. The total mesure : fete 69, ynches 9. At which place Teblow, servant to Mr. Ashton of Chaderton, did meet us. The survey geometricall of the very circuits of Manchester parish wer ended in this, being the sixth day of my work folks doings."[1]

In the Chetham Library is a holograph letter from Dee to the rector of Prestwich, William Langley, dated two days before this perambulation, informing him of the project for making a chart of the parish bounds, and inviting him,

"As one side of our parish in Thielmore doth border uppon some parts of your parish of Prestwiche, to request some one or two of the auncient of your parish to be allso beholders of our bounds, notifying

[1] In the diary as edited by the Camden Society this passage is misread, and the most ridiculous nonsense about "Kentish feet" and "corne stacks" is printed. These local landmarks are "leeless bench," and "the Low." Both are doubtless long since swallowed up in streets, but the "Leeless Birch" probably existed many years after Dee's death. Thelmore is now the White Moss.

toward your parish in that place. My neighbours do intend to come on Wensday next, in the morning about 9 or 10 of the clok, to that part that is by Goodman Smehearst's house, and so toward the birche tree that is called the *Leeless Byrche*, and thereabouts, for a little space ; to beggyn the vew of the bownds and meres of Manchester parish: by the order of an enjoyned work by the higher powres, for avoyding of undue encroaching of any neighbourly parish one on the other. You understand me sufficiently well, I dowt not. Pardon my boldness so bluntly to borde you with so homely a sute.

"Your wurships sincere
"Wellwisher in Christe,
"JOHN DEE, Warden."

John Crocker and several other men were occupied for some weeks in marking the boundaries of the manor ; they met with extraordinary opposition from the landowners, and on June 14 Dee alludes to a riot that took place at Newton, Captain Bradley and others endeavouring to hinder the college employees in their labour. What with opposition abroad and difficulties with his curate at home, Dee was finding the coveted appointment no bed of roses. He records another of his characteristic dreams—the dreams of a bibliophile, to whom his books are treasures as dear almost as his children :—

"This night I had the vision and shew of many bokes in my dreame, and among the rest was one great volume, thik, in large quarto, new printed, on the first page whereof as a title in great letters was printed *Notus in Judœa Deus.*[1] Many other books

[1] The title of the 75th Psalm.

methought I saw, new printed, of very strange arguments. I lent Mr. Edmund Hopwood of Hopwood my *Malleus Maleficarum* to use till New Year's tyde next, a short thik old boke, with two clasps, printed anno 1517."

It was now early August. So Hopwood, who was bent on mastering the subject of witchcraft, was to have about four months to study *The Hammer for Witches*, a book first issued in 1489, after the Bull against sorcery of Pope Innocent VIII., by the three sorcery inquisitors. It was translated into German, *Hexenhammer*, and formed the text-book of procedure against witches in Germany. Its authors give emphasis to their learned observation that witchcraft is more natural to women than men, because of the inherent wickedness of their hearts! In mediæval times there appeared, alas! no safe and inconspicuous path for ordinary women. The entire sex consisted apparently of either angels or devils.

On a Sunday in August, Dee entertained the Earl and Countess of Derby at a "banket at my lodging at the College, hora 4½." They had newly taken up their residence at Alport Park, which had been the college property before the dissolution of the monasteries. It is now in the heart of the city, somewhere near the Midland Railway works.

There was scant time for literary labours amid so much entertaining topographical work and litigation; but in September Dee sent to his former friend, now Sir Edward Dyer, a treatise he had some time written on "The Queen's Title Royal and Sea Sovereignty in St. Georges Channel and all the

Ocean next adjoining to England, Scotland and Ireland." He quotes in it so freely from his *British Monarchy* (see *ante*, p. 39) that he encloses a copy of that work, written twenty years before, in case his correspondent does not possess one handy. The letter gives such a graphic picture of the state into which the college affairs had fallen, and of the characteristic energy with which Dee set about to try and reform them, that it must be quoted at some length. When the accompanying volume and manuscript have been fully discussed, the writer passes on to the

"intricate, cumbersome, and lamentable affairs of estate of this defaced and disordered college, whereunto not only I am assigned for my portion of maytenance, for me and all myne, but allso, by college oath, bownde to see unto the right and dignitie thereof. Which hath bred unto me already, both wonderfull care of mynde and no little payne taking, ever since my entrance, and daylie doth and will brede me more and more. And hath browght me likewise in great debt, by reason of the pore Revenue of my stipend (of only iiij*s*. a day for me and all myne), and that in these tymes of very great dearth here, yea, so great, that unleast (in his most fatherly Providence) the Almighty God had stirred up some mens hartes to send me, this present yere, from Dantzig, some barrells of kye; from Wales some cattall, and from Hull some fish for Lent: God knoweth that it passed all our wittes and habilitie to devise or use any other meanes, sufficient to the preserving of the lives of me and my familie togither, being now but of eightene persons, most nedefull: I my wife and our children, being the one half of them. So hard and thynne a dyet, never, in all my life, did I, nay was I forced, so long to use: Neyther did ever any household servants of myne have so slender allowance at their Table. And yet all that hath not so much pynched me inwardly as the cares and cumbers for the college affaires have done, for they have altered, yea barred and stayed my whole course of life, and bereaved me of my so many yeres contynued Joyes, taken in my most esteemed studies and exercises.

"But as it pleaseth the king of heven and earthe thus to deale with me: So I beseche him to give me grace to like best of this his long leading of me *per multas tribulationes.* And Beside all the rest, This encreaseth my grief: that I know no one as yet of her Ma[ties] most honorable Privy Counsaile, who willingly and comfortably will listen unto my pitifull complainte and Declaration: How this Colledg of Manchester is almost become No College, in any respect; I say in any respect, for I can verifie my wordes to[o] manifestly. But why do I cumber yr wurship (thus abruptlie) with such my colledg cumbers? Pardon me, I pray you, the pang of my mynde, half amazed, when the multitude of these cumbers and of the confused and intricate causes of this Colledge, do russh at once into my fantazie. But, undowtedly, either God will give me grace sufficient and send me mighty help (*tempore opportune*) to end them, or else they will help to hasten my deliverance from these and all other vayne and earthly Actions humayne.

"Sir, how well (and that hartily) not onely I, but my paynfull Jane, and my children of discretion, allso do, at God's handes, wish unto yr wurship, you my easyly gesse, for it is our duetie.

"And so, I beseche your wurship undowtedly to

perswade your selfe of us. Manchester, September 8, A°. 1597.

"Yor wurships in fidelitie and sinceritie,

"JOHN DEE."[1]

A new steward of the college was appointed: Humphrey Davenport, who afterwards became Chief Baron of the Exchequer, and as such delivered judgment upon ship money in Hampden's case. Very few allusions to domestic and family matters occur in the diary for these Manchester years, but in November, 1597, an accident is recorded to Arthur, who was at home for a time. He was amusing himself by fencing with Edward Arnold, one of Dee's men and his usual messenger to London, when the foyne or thrust of the rapier of his opponent damaged his left eye. The lad was now about seventeen, probably already entered at Christ Church, Oxford.

Correspondence with friends in London, as Dr. Julio, a well-known physician of the time, and Dr. Cæsar (afterwards Sir Julius Cæsar and Master of the Rolls), both of Italian origin, sometimes relieved the Warden's tedious and tiresome disputes with the Fellows, the tenants and the tithe owners of the college.

To Cæsar, as Master of the Requests, Dee wrote on October 2, 1596, on behalf of William Nicholson, about an action he had brought against two persons for enclosing moor and mine land at Reddish. Some idea of the lawless proceedings of the time may be

[1] *General and Rare Memorials*, Brit. Museum, C. 21, c. 12.

gathered from Dee's description of the injuries the plaintiff had received in having his barns pulled down and his corn and hay, "to the quantitie of a great number of loads, cast out of doors, which some of my family beheld." Dee adds pointedly: "I shall be forced ere it be long to fly to your direction and help in causes Judiciall"; and ends by a reference to Cæsar's recent marriage, six months earlier, to a Manchester lady (Alice, daughter of Christopher Green): "God bless you and your new Joye."[1]

Oliver Carter was more troublesome than ever, and lawsuits were instituted by the Warden both against him and George Birch, another of the Fellows. On Sunday, September 25, Dee writes: "Mr. Oliver Carter, his impudent and evident disobedience in the church." There was evidently a scene, though not, as Mr. Halliwell has it, caused by Carter's "dissoluteness in the church." There was no house for the Warden, but the fines of the Fellows for absence were by the last charter to be devoted to its provision. If they did not pay, Dee had to meet the rent himself.[2] At the beginning of 1598 there were four lawsuits on the Warden's hands, but he records that he "stayed" them all, for one cause or another, one until Sir John Byron returned. In January the college gate and a large piece of the wall fell down at midnight, so there were repairs to be made. He had a letter from John

[1] *Lansdowne MSS.*, clviii., f. 16; *Manchester Diary,* ed. Bailey, p. 93.

[2] The house was not provided for a century, when the college was taken for a hospital.

Pontoys, the friend who had sent him twenty-one loads of Dantzic rye, very useful for consumption. Another welcome contribution for domestic use arrived at this time, viz., "two lings and two haberdines from Mr. Harry Savill, from Lichefield." Haberdines are dried and salted cod. He records an eclipse of the sun on February 25, with the comment that although it was a cloudy day there was great darkness about half-past nine.

In March, the entries in the diary end abruptly, and are not resumed again till June, 1600, a period of more than two years, of which there appears no record. The time was apparently spent in London or at Mortlake; the purpose of the journey was no doubt to represent to the Privy Council or other authorities the terribly involved state of affairs in Manchester, where the college had become almost "no college."

CHAPTER XXII

COLLEGE AFFAIRS

"I came among a people who relied much on dreams. And I told them except they could distinguish between dream and dream they would mash or confound all together. For there were three sorts of dreams. For multitude of business sometimes caused dreams; and there were whisperings of Satan in man in the night season; and there were speakings of God to man in dreams."—George Fox, *Journal.*

The Warden was apparently absent from his charge at Manchester for two years and a quarter, between March, 1598, and June, 1600. When he resumed his diary to chronicle his return, it appeared that he had been very busy in London, arranging for a special commission to sit in the college chapter house, to inquire into encroachments made upon the manor of Newton. His wife and two elder sons, Arthur and Rowland; Mary Nicholls, daughter of his old friend and pupil, Francis Nicholls; all travelled with him from London. What became of the younger children we can only guess. The party set out on the 10th and arrived in Manchester on June 18. Rowland was then seventeen, a Grammar School boy on Bishop Oldham's foundation in Manchester. Early in the following December, he obtained an exhibition at Oxford from the school. Dee, as Warden, was charged with certain official visits of inspection of the Grammar School, and was by no means always pleased with the result. He says, for instance, on August 5 of this year, "I visited the Grammar Schole, and fownd great imperfections in all and every of the scholers, to my great grief." Of an earlier visit he says it was "to see to the ower, &c., for Mr. Heton," *i.e.*, to see the clock.

Dee had almost completed his seventy-third year, and had maintained his bodily strength on the whole remarkably well. This summer he observed that for the first time in his life his pulse assumed the well-known symptom of intermittent beating, or pulsation. With all his usual exactitude, he records that his pulse kept on missing a pulsation after the fifth, or the seventh, or eleventh beat, although it was for the rest strong and equal. He mentions a great many sleepless nights. "Nocte Amaritudo mea," "Circa mediam noctem Amaritudo mea," are entries that occur with some frequency. On July 7, he says, "This morning, as I lay in my bed, it came into my fantasy to write a boke: *De differentiis quibusdam corporum et spirituum.*" His views on this subject would have been profoundly interesting, but the book remained a fantasy. His dreams are again sometimes noted. If they are not about books, they concerned that long-frustrated hope of his life, that he might actually one day, and by no fraud or trickery, stumble on the secret which Kelley had professed to know. By this time, Dee must have been assured of Kelley's knavery, and yet his faith in the possibilities of alchemy remained unshaken to the end. "I had a dream after midnight," he says, "of my enjoying and working of the philosopher's stone, with other. My dream was after midnight, toward day." Alas! this pleasure he was never to enjoy in the flesh. Next night: "I dreamed that along betwene Aldgate and the postern on Tower Hill did men stand in a lane, with pikes in theyr hands, as though more should come to them, or that they wayted for somebody. But theyr regard and looking was directly to Y^e Towre, where certeyn great personages dyd stand; and one of them as upon a stage did declare with a loud voice to the pikemen, matter of importance, very loud."

The description of the topography of his dream, given by this Londoner born, is very exact. The gate of Aldgate, taken down in 1606, was the eastern postern of the City, not far from St. Botolph's Church. So the lane of pikemen was a very long one, or seems so to us, who know the distance covered with hundreds of buildings and a network of streets.

There was little time now for him to devote to alchemy by day. His work lay in a more practical direction:—

"July 17. I willed the Fellows to com to me by nine the next day. July 18. They cam. It is to be noted of the great pacifications, unexpected of man, which happened this Friday; for in the fore-noone (betwene nine and ten) when the Fellows were greatly in doubt of my heavy displeasure, by reason of their manifold misusing of themselves against me, I did with all lenity interteyn them, and shewed the most part of the things that I had brought to pass at London for the Colleg good; and told Mr. Carter going away) that I must speak with him alone. Robert Leghe and Charles Legh [the singing men] were by. Secondly, the great sute between Redich men and me was stayed, and by Mr. Richard Holland, his wisdom. Thirdly, the organs, uppon conditions, wer admitted. And fourthly, Mr. Williamson's resignation granted, for a preacher to be gotten from Cambridge."

Richard Holland, of Reddish and Heaton House, was a man of some note in Manchester, a feoffee of the Grammar School, and three or four times sheriff of the county. The "preacher gotten from Cambridge" to succeed the last unsatisfactory curate was William Bourne, a Fellow of St. John's. "July 31. We held our audit, I and the Fellows, for the two yeres last past in my absence: Olyver Carter, Thomas Williams and Robert Birch, Charles Legh, the elder, being receyver." This entry in the diary seems to make it plain that Dee was absent from Manchester during the whole of the two years of which we have no account. In July, too, Dee records the loan of his second part of Holinshed's *Chronicle* to Mr. Randall Kemp.

In September, the commissioners appointed by the Bishop of Chester again met, and called Dee before them in the church, "about thre of the clok after none, and did deliver to me certain petitions put up by the Fellows against me to answer before the 18th of this month. I answered them all *eodem tempore;* Yet they gave me leave to write at leisure." The commissioners were Richard Holland and William Langley, both of whom we have met before, with the rector of Stockport, Richard Gerard. Things perhaps were set on a little better foundation for a time. Points of dispute were referred to the steward, Humphrey Davenport, "Counsayler, of Grays Inn," and Oliver Carter, the contentious Fellow, died within three or four years.

The last troublous years in Manchester must be briefly passed over, and indeed the material for them is scanty. Dee had to borrow money on more plate, "double gilt potts with cover and handells," "bowles and cupps with handles," from Edmund Chetham, the high master of the Grammar School; and he had not been able to redeem them when Chetham's father and executor made his will in March, 1603. He says in it that Dee delivered to his son "six severall parcells of Plate to be kept as a payne or pledge for the same [loan], which by reason of my said executorshippe are now come into my possession," and he wills the ten pounds lent upon them to his other sons Humfrey and Ralphe.[1] When, if ever, the pieces were redeemed, does not appear. Another valuable article—"a silver salt, dubble gilt, with a cover, waying 14 oz.," had to be deposited with Adam Holland in January, 1601, for a loan of five pounds for one year. Dee's store of plate, though large, was being heavily drained and irrevocably scattered in this way. The old man doubtless saw his treasures, the gifts of friends and patrons of half a century, disappear with feelings of deep chagrin and disappointment, mingled with memories of past

[1] The standard rate of silver, 43 Eliz., was *5s. 2d.* per ounce, so the value of the six parcels was £12 *8s.*

triumphs, and little light upon the future. A piece of the plate came to light at the Tudor Exhibition in the New Gallery in 1890, when a silver cup, the property of Mrs. John Hookham Frere (said to be Dee's great-great-niece), was exhibited. Writing of this cup to her son Bartle Frere, about the end of the eighteenth century, Mrs. Frere says, "My great thrice-great uncle, John Dee, because he was a wise man, was taken for a conjurer. I have his silver cup now here with me, and you may drink of it, but I know no story in the family that he ever divined by it. It serves me here for a sugar basan." Evidently Mrs. Frere took an entirely rational view of the powers attributed to her famous ancestor.[1]

Perhaps in these sad days he looked back regretfully to the glorious visions and promises made him by those angelic visitors in the years when he and his skryer lived in the Courts of kings and emperors, and were consulted and deferred to as seers and wise men. Even the thoughts of suspicions harboured; of secret and open foes, at home and abroad; the recollection of heart burnings and passionate scenes with the incalculable Kelley, must have seemed dazzlingly brilliant as compared with these grey hopeless years. It is little wonder that he began to seek among his assistants and friends another skryer, through whom he might renew some glimmer of the former days. Mr. Francis Nicholls, who had come to Mortlake in 1593 to learn astrology, seems to have been tried.

[1] Miss Festing, the author of *Frere and his Friends* (1899), says Mrs. Frere's mother was Mary Dee, a great-niece of our John, but no brother of Dee has hitherto been discovered (see Appendix I.).

He was frequently with the Warden, and his daughter Mary stayed for two or three months with the Dees in Manchester on their return from London. She would be a companion in age for Katherine, and the Warden tells how the two girls, his wife and himself, partook of the sacrament together on August 10, 1600. Bartholomew Hickman was more successful as a medium than Mr. Nicholls, and yet at first not always to be trusted. Dee had learned by now to be very discriminating, and he found many of the "reports of sight and hering spirituall," obtained through this skryer, so untrue that he made a bonfire of all the writings on Michaelmas Day, before his wife; Mr. Nicholls; his brother, William Nicholls, and a Mr. Wortley. "A copy of the first part, which was afterward fownd, was burnt before me and my wife." The revelations afterwards transmitted through Bartholomew were not so treated, and were evidently considered by Dee to be genuine messages from the unseen. His visitors left the next day after the Michaelmas bonfire, the Warden accompanying them on foot as far as Deansgate, where they parted. On his return home a surprise awaited the old man.

Dee's servants, many of them, attached themselves to him for life, as we have seen. They, at least, regarded him without suspicion. He was no invoker of devils or conjurer of evil spirits to them. No master could be kinder, more gentle, considerate or more strictly honourable. In whatever straits he found himself, he always contrived to pay, and faithfully record in his diary the payment of, their wages. We have seen how he writes to Sir Edward Dyer of their diet. It will be remembered that one of his early apprentices, Roger Cook, left him after fourteen years, jealous that another man should be admitted to processes from which he was excluded. This was over twenty years ago, nor had his name ever been mentioned in the diary since. Now, Roger Cook reappeared in Manchester, quite unsought, offering and promising

"his faithful and diligent care and help, to the best of his skill and powre, in the processes chymicall, and that he will rather do so than be with any in England; which his promise the Lord blesse and confirm! He told me that Mr. Anthony (his late master) considered him very liberally and frendely, but he told him that he had promised me. Then he liked in him the fidelity of regarding such his promise."

A week or two later, on November 1, Dee writes that R. C. began to distil. Afterwards there seems to have been cause for suspicion that Roger had spread false reports about his former employer, but the mistake was generously acknowledged; matters were cleared up, and peace once more reigned:—

"Feb. 2. Roger Cook, his supposed plat laying to my discredit was by Arthur, my sone, fownd by chaunce in a box of his papers, in his own handwriting, *circa meridiem,* and afternone about 1½ browght to my knowledg face to face. All was mistaken and we reconcyled godly. Feb. 5. *O libera nos a malo.* Feb. 10. Reconciliation between us, and I did declare to my wife, Katharine my dowghter, Arthur and Rowland, how things were mistaken."

In October, Sir George Booth, High Sheriff of

Cheshire, came to Manchester to see the steward of the college, Humphrey Davenport, of Gray's Inn, about some of the college property in Cheshire, which he held. Booth had been knighted since his last visit. After all parties had been interviewed, they came to a mutual agreement that the Warden and Fellows would accept the arbitrament of the steward on the point in question, his decision to be delivered after the lawyer had paid his next visit to London. Davenport's clerk, John Radclyffe, and Mr. Dumbell were at the college at the time, but Dee says "they hard not our agreement, we were in my dining room."

He received a kind letter from the Bishop of Chester (Richard Vaughan), recommending Mr. Thomas Billings to him for a curacy. He does not say if the spiritual ministrations of Mr. Billings were accepted. The commissioners were still sitting, and in November they made an award against Mr. James Ashton, of Chadderton, for holding the manor or property of Nuthurst while its title belonged to the college. There was a final scene with Oliver Carter in the college, before Mr. Birch, Robert and Charles Leigh. At the college audit on December 2, Dee was allowed his portion of £7 yearly for house rent up to the Michaelmas before. A grant was now made to Arthur of the chapter clerkship, but the holder, Owen Hodges, was only going to relinquish it on condition of £6 being paid for his patent. So more silver had to be pledged to meet a loan.

The last entry made by Dee in his diary is on April 6, 1601, when he made "Mr. Holcroft, of

Vale Royall,[1] his first acquaintance, at Manchester, by reason of Mr. William Herbert, his servant. He used me and reported of me very freely and worshiply."

For the concluding seven years of the old man's life there are only a few scanty outside records on which to rely, beside two or three fragmentary entries printed in the end of the *Book of Mysteries*. In such a practised and ready writer as our aged mathematician and astrologer, the failure to set down records seems to betoken failing strength of both intellect and body.

[1] Sir Thomas Holcroft, knighted 1603, a gentleman of the Privy Chamber and High Sheriff of Cheshire.

CHAPTER XXIII

LAST DAYS

"If I read aught in Heaven,
Or Heaven write aught of fate, by what the stars,
Voluminous or single characters
In their conjunction met, give me to spell,
Sorrows and labours, opposition, hate
Attends thee; scorns, reproaches, injuries."
—MILTON, *Paradise Regained.*

A FEW days after the diary closes, Dee's fourth son, Theodore, died. The boy was just over thirteen, perhaps at the Grammar School. Michael, we remember, had died at Mortlake seven years before, so the only sons left were Arthur and Rowland, both now grown almost to man's estate. Within about a year, Arthur married, and soon embarked on his successful career as a physician in London, Manchester, Moscow and Norwich, to which we can return later.

Arthur's wife was Isabella, daughter of Edmund Prestwich, Justice of the Peace, of Manchester, a member of a family whose name is perpetuated by a large district of the town. The marriage took place in 1602, when Arthur was twenty-four, his bride just under twenty. The young couple settled with or near his parents at first, and Dee had the joy of seeing grandchildren grow up around him. Four of Arthur's twelve children were born during the old man's life, and he pleased himself by drawing a horoscope for two of these, Margarita 1603, and Jane

1605, on the vellum leaves of a small square manuscript volume which still fills us with wonder at his boundless industry.[1] It contains an anatomical drawing of the human body and tables of astrological signs for its different parts, aphorisms, studies of medicine, the actions of metals, and other hermetic notes. Arthur's horoscope, drawn and expounded by his father in the same book, is sufficiently remarkable, with its prophecy that he should have good fortune from a prince, and die abroad, a violent death. In the centre of the figure, Arthur himself has added the words "*sententia patris mei de mea nativitate erat. Magna bona cum multis malis.*" Arthur only added one horoscope, that of his seventh child, Isabel, born 1614; otherwise, as they appeared almost annually (twelve in eighteen years), he contented himself with simply writing names and dates on leaves of coarse paper, added to the beginning and end of his father's little commonplace book, which has been rebound roughly in cheap modern cloth.

Beyond these events, there is nothing to tell of the next three years, which are without a single jotting of his own in any of his diaries; but the old prejudices and suspicions must have revived in a very active and bitter form. The aged student could endure them less patiently than before. He had lost hope of outliving them; he had lost his Queen, who, though she had held out to him promises of preferment as unsubstantial as a mirage of the desert, had ever been friendly and kind; had constantly welcomed, nay, invited, him to her presence; and had apparently

[1] *Sloane MS.*, 1902.

maintained her faith in him to the last. Burleigh's death in 1598, and now the Queen's, left him without patron and protector. Elizabeth died at Richmond on March 23, 1603, but Dee, presumably, was far away in Manchester, and not near at hand at Mortlake, even had he been required. The course of the magnificent life was run, and no prognostications of her astrologer could put hope into the physicians and courtiers watching around that royal deathbed. The Queen was seventy, and had reigned for fifty-three years.

From King James there was nothing to be hoped for Dee, the man familiar with occult sciences. The Scotsman felt himself a special expert on the subject of witches, demons and magic. Had he not attended the infamous trials of 1590 and 1591? And was he not the author of a book intended to shatter the doubts of those who were still unconvinced of the infamy? He was aghast at the new and unorthodox views of apologists like Wier and Reginald Scot, and upon his accession promptly ordered *The Discoverie of Witchcraft* (1584), by the last-named, to be publicly burned. James's *Demonologie* is a strange piece of reasoning, a plea, in fact, for the devil, with whom he seems to be on peculiarly intimate terms. "God's hangman"—that is the title awarded him—is, according to King James, able to return and reanimate any dead body. He announces his faith in the power of conjurers to invoke the devil when they choose, and to invest others with his spirit. He adjures all pious people to unite in exterminating and utterly destroying all persons so possessed: a somewhat unkind request, since he has previously allowed that such objects of reprobation are permitted to exist in order that the godly may be warned!

The first Parliament of James met on March 19, 1604. On the 27th a new and more stringent Act against Witchcraft was brought into the House of Lords. It was referred to the bishops, who discovered it was imperfect, and had a fresh one drawn. On June 9 the execrable Act that disfigured our statute book for 150 years became law. This haste, it was supposed, was used to meet offences exposed by the Scottish trials, now again evidently revived and much talked of in England. It is significant to remember that Shakespeare finished writing *Macbeth* in 1606. In what way Dee felt himself specially involved, unless by the publication, in 1603, of Harsnet's tirade against impostures and exorcists,[1] it is hard to conjecture, but the times were ripe for him to make, at this identical moment, a passionate appeal to the King and Parliament. On June 5 he presented to James, in the Palace at Greenwich, a petition couched in the strongest and most piteous terms that any man could devise.

He urged upon the King

"to cause your Highnesse said servant to be tryed and cleared of that horrible and damnable, and to him most grievous and dammageable sclaunder, generally, and for these many yeares last past, in this kingdom raysed and continued, by report and Print against him, namely that he is or hath bin a conjurer or caller or invocator of divels."

[1] *Declaration of Egregious Popish Impostures.*

He went on to relate how he had published many times his "earnest apologies against the slander [one we remember in his preface to Billingsley's Euclid in 1570, and another, the letter to the Archbishop in 1595, he had republished in 1599 and 1603], and yet this ungodly and false report, so boldly, constantly and impudently avouched," has been uncontrolled and unpunished for so many years; and, moreover, in spite of all, some writer, either a "malicious forraine enemy or an English traytor to the flourishing State and Honor of the Kingdom," on January 7, 1592, had called him, John Dee, in print, "the conjuror of the Queen's Privy Council." It seems, therefore, very needful that the suppliant shall be brought to trial, for the credit of the Lords of the Privy Council as well as for his own. "Therefore he offereth himself willingly to the punishment of Death, yea eyther to be stoned to death, or to be buried quicke, or to be burned unmercifully, if by any due, true, and just meanes, the name of conjurer, or caller, or invocator of Divels or damned Spirites, can be proved to have beene or to be duely or justly reported of him," or "if any one of all the great number of the very strange and frivolous fables or histories reported and told of him (as to have been of his doing) were true, as they have been told or reasonably caused any wondering among or to the many-headed multitude, or to any other whosoever else."

Dee's sympathies were so strongly with the unfortunate, persecuted, so-called witches, that he was willing to throw in his lot with them and share the same fate. He ends this extraordinary petition with "a great and undoubted hope" that the King will "soon redress his farder griefs and hindrances, no longer of him possibly to be endured, so long hath his utter undoing, by little and little, beene most unjustly compassed."

Following up this petition, the poor man, grown desperate, three days later (June 8) presented an address in verse to Parliament, begging them to pass "an Act Generall against slander, with a special penal order for John Dee, his case." He was far too much in earnest to be suspected of any humorous intention, but a thought of the needful reformation such an Act might have wrought in the country by this time cannot be suppressed. Certainly it would have been a more creditable piece of legislation than the Act which afforded such wicked and cruel pretext for espionage and terrorism, and for putting unfortunate lunatics—called witches—to death by hanging, burning and stoning by a mob.

It seems as if Dee's ruined and beggared condition, the long procession of disappointments he had patiently borne, had entirely destroyed the sense of proportion in his mind between personal and public affairs. Continual brooding over the thought of the neglect, the suspicion, that his undeniable talents had undergone, the obstinate slander, ignorant incredulity, or flat denial of things in which he most truly put his faith, all distorted by his natural vanity and good opinion, seems to have convinced him that his crushed and melancholy fate was little short of a national disaster. This feeling had become an obsession.

There was unfortunately nothing in his halting

verses to induce Parliament to pay any heed to a tiresome old petitioner, a survival from the last century and the last reign, who had outlived every contemporary inclined to believe in him, and whose course was now nearly run.

Nor did James respond in any way to his heart-broken petition. Robert Cecil, and all who wished to stand well with him, took their cue from the King, and Dee in his old age was left forsaken and alone.

The following is the address to Parliament:—

"TO THE HONORABLE ASSEMBLIE
OF THE COMMONS IN THE PRESENT PARLIAMENT.

"The Honor due unto you all,
And reverence to you each one,
I do first yeeld most speciall;
Grant me this time to heare my mone.

"Now (if you write) full well you may,
Fowle sclandrous tongues and divelish hate,
And help the truth to beare some sway
In just defence of a good Name.

"In sundry sorts, this sclander great
(Of *conjurer*) I have sore blamde:
But wilfull, rash, and spiteful heat,
Doth nothing cease to be enflamde.

"Your helpe, therefore, by Wisdom's lore,
And by your Powre, so great and sure,
I humbly crave, that never more
This hellish wound I shall endure.

"And so your Act,[1] with Honour great
All Ages will hereafter prayse;
And Truth, that sitts in Heavenly seat,
Will in like case your comforts rayse.

Most dutifully in all humilitie at your commandment, John Dee, servant and Mathematician to his most royall Majestie.

An. 1604. Junij 8."

[1] The Act for Suppressing Slander.

Dee's good name was one of his dearest possessions, but he had long seen it shadowed and dimmed. Another treasure—his "painful" Jane—the wife who had loyally cleaved to him through good and ill report, was to be the next of which he was to be bereft. She was so much his junior that he might reasonably have expected her to tend his declining years and to survive him. But it was thoroughly in keeping with her unselfish character and devoted life that her death came as a sacrifice to duty. In the spring of 1605, a terrible scourge of plague visited Manchester. She nursed her children safely through the epidemic, but fell a victim to it herself. She died and was buried on March 23 in the collegiate church of St. Mary. The old man had no heart to take up his pen and record her death. The bare fact is all we know, from another source ; and the fate of all Jane's children, save Arthur, is wrapped in a like mystery. At her death, Jane was a month under fifty years old; the twenty-seven years of her married life had been crowded years, the one thought in them all to watch over and ward her great childlike, learned, marvellous husband and her children. Now she passed the task on to her daughter Kate, who faithfully fulfilled it.

A few fragments of angelic visions, which after nearly twenty years were once again vouchsafed, are all that remain to tell of the last two years of the old man's life.

Bartholomew Hickman was the skryer, and Dee was in London, "at Mrs. Goodman her house," very ill. On March 20 and 29, Raphael appeared, to comfort him as regards his alarming symptoms of hæmorrhage, and bade him use the medical skill that God had given him. Dee, in utter dejection, owned that he was beaten in his "great attempt to make the Council privy of my beggary, and to offer to the Earl of Salisbury[1] such my duties as I may perfect to his account." He was right to hope nothing from the great Burleigh's little-minded son. Robert Cecil lacked almost everything that had made William Cecil great, even a great sovereign to serve.

In July Dee was again in London, this time staying in Westminster, at the "Three Kings" in King Street. Katherine was with him, his devoted daughter, now a woman of twenty-six, apparently unmarried. Two companions or servants, Patrick Saunders and Thomas Turner, were in attendance. On the 9th, the angel Raphael came to the sad and broken old man of eighty, holding out promises and hopes that seem cruelly delusive. But Dee was still wrapped in that inviolable armour of faith or credulity that had already withstood so many severe shocks. Whether he now actually beheld Raphael, whether he still with his ears heard the angel's voice, or whether only within his spiritual consciousness he felt the impulse and the message, is quite immaterial. But it is noticeable that there are now no descriptions of Raphael as an apparition. The message is all he heeds. As he is sinking slowly down into his grave from natural decay, there is a double and figurative meaning to be read into the angel's words. Raphael

[1] Robert Cecil had been created Earl of Salisbury, 1605.

bade him first believe that his perishing bodily frame shall be restored and made sound, for, however reluctant he at his great age may feel, he is to go shortly on a long journey to friends beyond the sea, where the secrets of wisdom, the philosopher's stone, the book of St. Dunstan, and "that Jewel that was delivered," shall be made known to him. He is not to go alone, for his good friend, John Pontoys, will come from Dantzic to be his stay and helper. "Therefore set thy things in order for thy Wardenship, and all other thy worldly affairs, as shortly as thou canst, by all means possible." He is not to mistrust because of his physical weakness, for he shall have long life like Hezekiah, and instead of living in want or beholden to those who love him not, he shall be provided for where he shall be able to do God service. He shall enjoy fame and memory to the end, and Raphael will accompany him, as he did the young Tobias, on his journey. Perhaps Dee remembered the mystical words of Gabriel, used to him at Cracow in April of 1584,—

> "Happy is he that hath his skirts tied up and is prepared for a journey, for the way shall be open unto him, and in his joynts shall there dwell no wearinesse. His meat shall be as the tender dew, as the sweetness of a bullock's cud. For unto them that have shall be given, and from them that have not shall be taken away. For why? The burr cleaveth to the willow stem, but on the sands it is tossed as a feather without dwelling. Happy are they that cleave unto the Lord, for they shall be brought unto the storehouse, and be accounted and accepted as the ornaments of his beauty."

The old man penned on a slip of paper some notes to aid his failing memory when next he should see his instructor. In two days, on July 11, he was able to put the questions.

What country shall he go to?

The answer is, where he will. "Thou hast been a great traveller, and it is referred to thy own choice," subject to divine approval. Dee suggests Germany, and receives consent.

Whom shall he take with him besides John Pontoys? What about his daughter Katherine, and the young man, Patrick Saunders?

The answer is very emphatic. It shows how dependent the old man had become upon this elder daughter of his old age. "John Dee, thou of thyself dost best know that without thy daughter, thou canst not be without her."

Certainly he could not part from Katherine, even with Pontoys as his "speciall comfort and aid," and the "honest and well-disposed young man," Saunders, who had been sent on purpose to go with him.

What about books and appurtenances? Is Mr. Bardolf to go? What shall Arthur do in his intended travel? "Shall I ever return to England, and shall I keep a title to enjoy my house when I do return?" Will the King grant a licence, or will it not be another disappointment, like so many that have gone before?

It is all a vain and illusory and impossible chimera. The only journey left for the old man to take was the one to "that undiscovered bourne from whence no traveller returns." Still, the wonderful visions perhaps brought him ecstatic hours. His brain was yet strong and clear, less worn out than his body, but like all old people, he lived over again and loved to dwell upon the past. A few days later he sat talking after dinner to Bartholomew "of divers my doings with Mr. Kelley." He had forgotten little of these dazzling experiences, and perhaps to while away the time he read his precious diaries over and over again. But of later events his memory was failing: "I asked Bartholomew if he had ever seen my jewel that was brought since it was set in gold [this had been done more than twenty years before], and he thought that he had not seen it." Surely tactful politeness on Bartholomew's part. "Whereupon I went speedily to my chest, unlocked it, and took it out, and undid the case and set the stone in his due manner."

Soon Raphael appeared in the stone, and Dee heard his voice, promising that the powder (*i.e.*, Kelley's powder) which he was keeping—"the which thou dost make account of as no better but dust"—should be turned to its right use.

Is it possible that the old belief in the golden secret had at last been killed? The powder was now but dust, as the old man would soon become, and as all his fixed dreams of projection had ever been.

The last entry in the spiritualistic diary was made on September 7, 1607, but whether Dee was at Mortlake or in London cannot be said. Pontoys had arrived. He was anxious to know if he would be thought fit to serve Dee in Bartholomew's absence. Also he earnestly desired to know his guardian angel, and he would fain hear also "the end of the Polish troubles."

Captain Langham, it is hoped, is going to lend £100 ; if not, Pontoys will set to work "to win some help for money by distillations and alchemical conclusions." Poverty is again stretching her gaunt fingers over this fond dreamer of gold. He had missed his "silver double gilt bell salt" and many other things from his house. He is "bereaved of his own goods." The truth was that Arthur had secretly taken them away to sell or pawn, in order to provide necessities for the family. Dee has been expecting a sum of money from the Emperor Rudolph, how much he does not know. But Raphael tells him to "let it go and speak no further of it. The Emperor of all emperors will be thy comfort. Thou hast no more need of him [Rudolph], only to keep good will and friendship betwixt him and thee."

Then Raphael fades into the eternal invisible, and the last word of the angelic visions is written.

In the private diary, kept in the almanack from Venice throughout this last year, there is little beside the bare stroke marking the months off into weeks, as was Dee's usual habit. The strokes are continued beyond the month of his death—December, 1608. The last written entry is on December 19, and is almost illegible. It is in the old man's hand and appears to read "tonitrum a Corrfe."

On which day at the death of the old year, Dee's spirit joined those others that had always been so near to him, we do not know, or on what precise date he was buried in the chancel of the church standing so close to the house at Mortlake which had been his home for thirty years. The parish registers for five years are missing, and the stone which Aubrey says[1] marked his grave has long since disappeared.

Fifty years later, John Aubrey talked to Goodwife Faldo, an old woman of eighty who had known him, and was shown a slab from which the brass had disappeared. She said that her mother had tended him in his sickness before he died in his own house in Mortlake, "next the house where the tapestry hangings are made." Evidently his last days were passed in the cottage which he had purchased many years before to add to the larger house, inherited from his mother. The old woman's gossip was interesting to Aubrey, for he was a grandson of Dee's cousin and neighbour, Dr. William Aubrey, the Master of Requests who had helped Dee to the Manchester post. She was full of marvellous stories, of course, for Dee's reputation for "magic" was impelled to survive him. But they were harmless stories enough: he had "layed a storm for Sir Everard Digby"; he had recovered a basket of clothes which she as a girl, and one of his younger daughters of her own age,[2] had negligently lost together; he had bidden a butler who had lost his master's plate on a boat coming down from London by water to go back on a certain day, and he would see the man who had taken the wrong

[1] *Lives*, ed. Clark, 1898, vol. i., pp. 210—215.

[2] Frances was fifteen, Margaret thirteen, when the old man died, if indeed both survived the epidemic that carried off their mother.

basket by exchange: the butler had done so and had found his plate; he had told a woman that she laboured under the evil tongue of an ill neighbour; he would not recover some lost horses, though he was offered several angels. He used to distil egg-shells, and kept a great many stills going. He had given and built the gallery to the church at Mortlake, and Goody Faldo's father was the carpenter that worked on it. "He was a great peacemaker, and if any of the neighbours fell out, he would never let them alone till he had made them friends." "A mighty good man he was."

The old woman remembered that he entertained the Polish ambassador not long before he died, and showed to him the eclipse of the sun, in a dark room. She could call to mind the stone upon his grave: it was between the tombstones of two other servants of Queen Elizabeth, Mr. Holt and Mr. Miles, upon both of which were brasses. The children, she said, dreaded him because he was accounted a conjurer, and yet whenever they strayed into the church, they would run straight to play upon his gravestone. There were steps at the upper end of the chancel when he was buried, but the minister laid them plain in Oliver's days, and then the stone that covered Dr. Dee was removed. She could recall his appearance: a man tall and slender, clad in a gown like an artist's gown, with hanging sleeves and a slit.

These garrulous reminiscences give us a picture of the old philosopher's end more valuable than any mere formal entry of the date. Some day, however, it may be possible to recover that.

Meanwhile, Dee's memory may be entrusted to the kinder judges of to-day, who will be more charitable because more enlightened and less impregnated with superstition. They may see in him a vain, presumptuous and much deluded person, but at any rate they must acknowledge his sincere and good intentions; his personal piety; his uncommon purity of thought and mind. If, in his thirst for knowledge of the infinite unknowable, he pushed back the curtain farther than was wise or justifiable, did he harm any one's reputation beside his own? Did he not suffer all the penalty in his own miserable failure, so far as comfort and prosperity in material things were concerned? In all the vague hopes held out by him to Queen, Princes and Emperors, of enriching them through his alchemical skill, he was no conscious charlatan, playing a part to lure them on, but a devout believer in man's power and purpose to wrest scientific secrets from the womb of the future. Can we look back upon the discoveries of three hundred years and feel his certainty was vain? The powers of electricity, the training to our uses that marvellous and long concealed agency and light; the healing virtues of radium, should be worth more to us than much manufactured gold.

APPENDIX I

THE DESCENDANTS OF JOHN DEE

WHEN the aged mathematician died at Mortlake in 1608 he left to survive him five or six out of his eight children. Michael, born at Prague, had died on his father's birthday in 1594. Theodore, born at Trebona, died at Manchester 1601. Arthur and Rowland were left. Katherine was his companion to the end. The three younger girls, Madinia, Frances and Margaret, had, for anything we know, survived the plague which was so fatal to their mother, but there is no trace of either of them after that event in March, 1606. Aubrey, indeed, did hear from Goody Faldo of a daughter, whose name he thinks was Sarah, married to a flax dresser of Bermondsey. Dee had no daughter Sarah, and Aubrey does not suggest a name for the problematic husband.[1]

Arthur, the eldest son, we have followed through a childhood of accidents to his selection and setting apart with a solemn rite to be his father's "skryer" in the magic crystal, in the eighth year of his age. We have traced the failure of that ill-advised choice, and have seen the lad of thirteen sent off to Westminster School with a little trunk and his mother's blessing. The next events in his life recorded by his father are his being wounded by a foyne while fencing with Edward Arnold, and the grant of the chapter clerkship of Manchester, in 1600.

[1] Mr. Thompson Cooper has included other Dees among the Doctor's children, whom he gives as eleven in number.

He married in 1602, lived for a while in Manchester, and began practising medicine. Wood says he spent some time at Oxford, but his name has so far not been found in any college admissions. In his will he is described as " Doctor of Physic." Probably he took a degree abroad. His marriage to Isabella Prestwich, daughter of a well-known Manchester justice of the peace, took place when he was twenty-two, and it is to be presumed that he continued living on in Manchester until his father left that city some time in 1605 or 1606, after the sad death of his wife. Arthur set up a practice in London some time about that year, although precise dates are not obtainable. He seems to have followed the common usage of hanging outside his door a list or " table " of medicines, and their excellent therapeutic properties, which were said to effect certain cures of several diseases. This attracted the attention of the censors appointed by the Royal College of Physicians, who proceeded against him forthwith, under the powers granted them against empiricks, which they had exercised since the foundation College in the early years of Henry VIII. The learned members of the college esteemed this " crime " such an " intolerable cheat and imposture," that they summoned Arthur Dee to appear before them with his remedies that they might impose a due penalty upon his presumption. The rest of the story is unrelated, and we cannot say what fine or order was his reward.

He seems, either through influence or talent, to have made his mark as a doctor. In July, 1614, he was recommended by the Archbishop of Canterbury and the Lord Chancellor to be elected physician of Thomas Sutton's newly founded hospital, the Charterhouse,[1] and we may presume the appointment was

[1] *Cal. State Pap. Dom.*, 1611—18, p. 246.

made. In May, 1627, Charles I. recommended him as physician to the Emperor of Russia, and in June it was agreed to send letters out by him or his agent, the stipulation being made that he must sail at once, "or not have passage this year."[1]

He took up his abode at Moscow, if not in the splendour and riches offered to his father, at least sufficiently provided for to maintain his huge family in comfort. Four or five of his twelve children died in infancy; the complete list of them, as given in his father's book of horoscopes in the British Museum,[2] is as under:—

Margaret	*born*	April 4, 1603.
Jane	,,	March 31, 1605.
John	,,	July 24, 1606 (*died*).
Arthur	,,	March 16, 1608.
Maria	,,	February 24, 1612.
Rowland	,,	September 8, 1613.
Isabel	,,	September 5, 1614.
Frances	,,	October 25, 1615.
William	,,	August 27, 1617.
John	,,	March 30, 1619.
Edmund	*baptised*	August 27, 1620.
	buried	September 23, 1621.
Anna	*born*	January 15, 1622.

Arthur's wife, Isabella Dee, died July 24, 1634. About this time he returned to England and settled in Norwich, near his friend, Sir Thomas Browne, who was then busily engaged in writing down the ethical and theological conclusions which he called the *Religio Medici*. Browne was, of course, the younger man. Writing in 1658, a few years after Arthur's death, to Elias Ashmole, Sir Thomas tells of the many talks about the doings of Dee and Kelley that he had with "my familiar friend, sonne unto old

[1] *Cal. State Pap. Dom.*, 1627, pp. 197, 211.

[2] *Sloane MSS.*, 1902.

Doctor Dee, the mathematician," who had "lived many years and died in Norwich." Browne sent to Ashmole "the scheme of Arthur's nativity, erected by his father, Dr. John Dee," a copy from the original, made by Arthur himself, with comments added by a Moscow astrologer, Franciscus Murrerus.

Dr. Arthur, in spite, or perhaps because, of his early environment, retained until his dying day a devout belief in the possibilities of alchemy to make projection or transmutation. He had grown up in the fixed idea that the ever-elusive secret would soon be found out. In fact, he was persuaded that divers workers had indeed discovered the art. The child of seven or eight, who had played with quoits or playthings, which he understood had been turned into gold upon the premises, was likely to retain this conviction. To doubt it would be to cast a slur upon his father's memory. Of Kelley his recollections—the recollections of a boy under nine—could be but dim and hazy, untouched with any possible scepticism or critical judgment. After the February day when Kelley rode off to Prague in 1588, neither Arthur or his father had ever set eyes on this adventurer again.

He had succeeded in convincing his old friend of the truth of these recollections, for Browne writes of him as "a persevering student in hermeticall philosophy, who had no small encouragement, having seen projection made, and with the highest asseverations he confirmed unto his death that he had ocularly, undeceivably and frequently beheld it in Bohemia. And to my knowledge, had not an accident prevented, he had, not many years before his death, retired beyond sea and fallen upon the solemn process of the great work."

Continuing the correspondence six months later, when additional matter rises to his mind, Sir Thomas writes again to Ashmole, in 1675, with more particulars of the "solemn process."

"I was very well acquainted with Dr. Arthur Dee, and at one time or other he has given me some account of the whole course of his life. I have heard the doctor say that he lived in Bohemia with his father, both at Prague and in other parts. That Prince or Count Rosenberg was their great patron, who delighted much in alchemie. I have often heard him affirme, and sometimes with oaths, that he had seen projection made, and transmutation of pewter dishes and flaggons into silver, which the goldsmiths at Prague bought of them. And that Count Rosenberg played at quoits with silver quoits, made by projection as before. That this transmutation was made by a powder they had, which was found in some old place, and a book lying by it containing nothing but hieroglyphicks; which book his father bestowed much time upon, but I could not hear that he could make it out. He said also that Kelley dealt not justly by his father, and that he went away with the greatest part of the powder, and was afterwards imprisoned by the Emperor in a castle, from whence attempting to escape down the wall, he fell and broke his leg, and was imprisoned again. That his father, Dr. John Dee, presented Queen Elizabeth with a little of the powder, who having made trial thereof, attempted to get Kelley out of prison, and sent some [persons] to that purpose, who, giving opium in drink unto the keepers, laid them so fast asleep that Kelley found opportunity to attempt an escape; and there were horses readie to carry him away; but the business unhappily succeeded as is before declared. Dr. Arthur Dee was a young man [he was a boy of eight] when he saw this projection made in Bohemia, but he was so inflamed therewith that he fell early upon that study, and read not much all his life but books of that subject; and two years before his death, contracted with one Hunniades, or Hans Hanyar, in London, to be his operator. This Hans Hanyar having lived long in London and growing in years, resolved to return into Hungary. He went first to Amsterdam, where he was to remain ten weeks, till Dr. Arthur came to him. The Dr. to my knowledge was serious in this businesse and had provided all in readiness to go, but suddenly he heard that Hans Hanyar was dead."

During his residence in Moscow, Arthur compiled a book of alchemical notes and extracts, which was published at Paris in 1631 under the title of *Fasciculas Chemicus,* etc. Ashmole, among his early enthusiastic labours upon alchemical authors prosecuted under the name of "James Hasolle," translated this into English in 1650. While the book was at press in the beginning of the year, he wrote to Arthur, apparently as a stranger, informing him of his occupation, and putting at the same time a question or two upon his father's books.

Arthur's reply, dated Norwich, January 31, 1649 [50], now in the Bodleian Library, begins by expressing regret that "you or any man should take pains to translate any book of that nature into English, for the art is vilified so much already by scholars that daily do deride it, in regard they are ignorant of the principles. How then can it any way be advanced by the vulgar? But to satisfie your question, you may be resolved that he who wrote Euclid's Preface was my father. The *Fasciculus,* I must confess, was my labour and work." He ends by saying that he will be in London that day week, and if Ashmole wants to see him, he may hear of him in Butler's Court at the end of Lombard Street, at his son Rowland Dee's warehouse. The writing, and especially the signature of this letter, are good testimonies to the care bestowed by William Camden of Westminster School on the boy's handwriting. His father, as we remember, had asked for special supervision of the roman hand, since matter, poor in itself, but set down in a good style, did, in his opinion, often receive more attention than good material badly written and expressed.

Browne had received from Arthur a complete catalogue of all his father's writings, both finished and intended. But there was one not included, viz., the *Book of Mysteries.* Sir Thomas, writing in 1675, says he never heard him say one word of "the Book of Spiritts sett out by Dr. Casaubone, which if hee had knowne I make no doubt butt hee would have spoake of it unto mee, for he was very inquisitive after any manuscripts of his father's, and desirous to print as many as he could possibly obtain." He goes on to say that Arthur understood that Sir William Boswell, the English Resident in Holland, owned a number of Dee's MSS., which he had collected and kept in a trunk in his Dutch home. Boswell refused many applications from Arthur for leave to print some of these, which the famous mathematician's son considered should not be locked up from the world. Boswell announced his intention of printing them himself, which of course he never did.

Nor did the Book of Spirits see the light of day during Arthur's lifetime. Perhaps had Casaubon appealed to him as Ashmole had done, it would never have been issued at all. A son would certainly have remonstrated against this revelation, this tearing down the veil from the inner tabernacle of his father's soul.

Arthur died in the autumn of 1651, eight years before Casaubon published his book. He made his will on September 17, describing himself as Doctor of Physick, of the city of Norwich, and leaving a small legacy of twenty shillings to the poor of the parish of St. George Tombland, in which he had lived.

Only three sons out of his seven, and three daughters of the six are named in the will, all the others being dead, unless it was Arthur, the eldest, who had been a merchant in Amsterdam. There is a legacy of twenty pounds to his wife.

The second son, Rowland, was established, as we have seen, in Lombard Street as a merchant. To him Arthur had already given his father's portrait, now in the Ashmolean Museum and reproduced as the Frontispiece to this book; and a painted coat of arms. Sir Thomas Browne, who had often seen it, speaks of an addition made to the coat by grant of the Emperor Rudolph in the shape of a mathematical figure; probably the delta which Dee always used for his name in the spiritual diary. To Rowland's wife there is a legacy of twenty pounds.

"To John Dee, my youngest son," Arthur left one hundred pounds and his gold seal ring with the coat of arms cut in a sapphire. John was a Russia merchant.

There is no mention of his eldest child and daughter, Margaret, who is said to have married another Russia merchant named Abraham Ashe.

To three sons-in-law, "my son Grymes;" "my son Anguish" (this was the husband of his youngest child, Anne); and "my son Fowell," he leaves respectively a plush coat; a saddle and pistol; and a black gown and plush suit.

To each of his three daughters, their wives (none of them mentioned by name), he gives £20; and to the two elder, his two iron-barred sealskin trunks with long cushions and foot carpets, feather bed, blankets, bolsters and coverlets. He appoints his friend John Toley, of Norwich, his executor, and gives him his watch and silver chain, with a square box of cypress wood, double-leafed, with drawers. His servant, John Sergeant, is to have all the contents of his extensive wardrobe, consisting of his coloured cloth suit and cloak; black suit and cloak lined with rough bayes (Norwich was the seat of the bay and say industry); his winter pair of boots, and two pairs of summer boots; his "hatts;" his "stockins whatsoever;" his black satin doublet; shirts; six of his "worst-falling bands and ruffs;" and forty shillings due for wages at the Michaelmas following.

Arthur Dee died before October 16 of the same year, 1650, when the will was proved by John Toley.

Rowland, Arthur's fourth son, married, and died in 1687, when his wife was executrix of his will. Rowland's sons by this wife Jane (d. 1698) were Rowland, born March 25, 1646, married October, 1675; Elizabeth Gardiner of Aldersgate (d. September, 1698); and Duncan, born November 3, 1657. Both were educated at Merchant Taylors' School on the Bishop of Peterborough's foundation (see below). Duncan went on to St. John's College, Oxford, and entered the legal profession. He was chosen Common Serjeant of London in 1700. He defended Dr. Sacheverell for four days of his trial in the House of Lords in 1710; died in 1720, and was buried in St. Mary Aldermanbury. By his wife Mary (d. Stoke Newington, March 24, 1728) he left a son Henry (d. 1725), others having died young.

David Dee, born in Shropshire, of St. Mary's Hall, Oxford, rector of St. Bartholomew the Great, Smithfield, 1587—1605, is said to have been a grandson of Bedo Dee. If so, he must have been either brother or cousin of John Dee of Mortlake, who, strange to say, alludes nowhere in his diary to any relation of the name of Dee, although he speaks often of his Welsh kinsfolk, and of his cousin Aubrey. As he died at Mortlake in 1608, aged eighty and a half, David, who survived him twelve years, must have been his junior. David Dee was deprived of St. Bartholomew, "for what," says Newcourt, "I know not"; but he was brought back there to be buried on February 3, 1620. By his wife Martia, daughter of John Rogers, David Dee had three sons, of whom Francis, the eldest, was educated at Merchant Taylors' School and St. John's College, Cambridge. He entered the Church, held various livings in London and elsewhere, and four years before his death was consecrated Bishop of Peterborough. By his will (dated May 28, 1638), he gave his rectory of Pagham, Sussex, to found two fellowships and two scholarships in St. John's College, one of which was to be held for ever by "one of my kindred or of my name, from either Merchant Taylors' School, London, or from Peterborough School." We have seen that two of John Dee's great grandchildren were sent to Merchant Taylors', and one, Duncan, proceeded to St. John's, probably on this foundation. The Bishop's eldest son, Adrian Dee, Canon of Chichester, died unmarried, but his younger sons, John and Daniel, left descendants.

APPENDIX II

BIBLIOGRAPHY

THE principal authorities for Dee's Life are his own Diaries, already frequently cited in the foregoing pages, viz. :—

(1) *The Private Diary.* The original notes comprising this are in two 4to almanacks in the Bodleian Library, Oxford, numbered Ashmolean MSS. 487, 488. They were transcribed and printed for the Camden Society (1842), with numerous omissions, by Mr. J. O. Halliwell [-Phillipps]. The Manchester portion of this Diary, covering the years 1595—1601, was edited with much local knowledge and care by Mr. J. Eglington Bailey, and privately printed ; only twenty copies (1880). Mr. Bailey also reprinted from *Notes and Queries* (May, 1879) his paper on Dee and the *Steganographia* of Trithemius.

(2) *The Spiritual Diary,* or *Liber Mysteriorum,* divided by Dee into separate books, each dealing with a special epoch. The first five books, with an appendix to the fifth—dating in all from December 22, 1581, to May 23, 1583—are comprised in Sloane MSS. 3188, at the British Museum. The remaining books, actually twelve but not consecutively numbered, were printed by Dr. Meric Casaubon in *The True and Faithful Relation,* etc., 1659, fol. Three of these are entitled "Libri Mystici Apertorii Cracoviensis Sabbatici" ; three "Mysteriorum Pragensium Confirmatio" ; and the two last "Liber Resurectionis" and "Mysteriorum divinorum memorabilia." This ends on May 23, 1587. About a

dozen pages of occurrences taking place in 1607 are printed by Casaubon at the end of his book, from stray papers.

Dee's autobiographical *Compendious Rehearsall* ranks next in importance. The original MS. was partly burned in the fire in the Cottonian Library, but a transcript made by Dr. Thomas Smith (author of a life of Dee, see below) was printed by Hearne in the Appendix to *Johannis Glastoniensis Chronicon* (Oxford, 1726). This printed version was collated with Ashmole's transcript of the original (Ashmolean MS. 1788), and edited by James Crossley for the Chetham Society, in *Autobiographical Tracts of Dr. John Dee, Warden of the College of Manchester*, 1851. In his preface, the editor promises another volume of correspondence and selections of Dee, which never appeared.

The Latin life of Dee, *Vitæ Eruditissimorum et Illustrium Virorum*, by Dr. Thomas Smith (1707); the article in the *Biographia Britannica*, edited by Kippis (1778, etc.), largely based upon the foregoing, and upon Strype's *Annals* (1725, etc.); some account in Wood's *Athenæ Oxonienses* (Bliss), i. 639, 640, and *Fasti*, i. 143; in Foxe's *Acts and Monuments*, ed. Townsend, vii., 77, 85, 349 n., 638, 641, 642, 681, 734, 756, 783, 784; and in Ashmole's *Theatrum Chemicum Britannicum* (1652), pp. 478—483; with Aubrey's *Lives*, ed. by Dr. A. Clark (1898); and *A Treatise of Religious and Learned Men* (1656), by Edward Leigh, are further sources. For the Manchester years Hibbert and Ware's *Foundations of Manchester* (1833) is useful; and for Dee's descendants, see a *General Account of Families derived from Bedo Dee*, by H. B. Wilson (1815), and his *History of Merchant Taylors' School* (1812—14). Later writers who have descanted more or less at large upon the romantic episode of Dee's partnership with Kelley, as apart from any other achievement of his long life, are William Godwin, in his *History of the Necromancers* (1834); Charles Mackay, *Memoirs of Extraordinary Popular Delusions* (1841); Isaac Disraeli, *Amenities of Literature* (1841); W. Cooke-Taylor's *Romantic Biography of the Age of Elizabeth* (1842); A. E. Waite in his *Lives of Alchemical Philosophers* (Edinburgh, 1888), *Studies in Mysticism* (1906), and *The Alchemical Writings of Edward Kelley* (1893); Thomas Seccombe, *Twelve Bad Men* (1894); Adelung's *Geschichte der Menschlichen Narrheit* (1785—9); Lenglet de Fresnoy's *Histoire de la Philosophie Hermétique* (1742); Manget's *Bibliotheca Chemica Curiosa* (Geneva, 1702), and Louis Figuier's *L'Alchémie et les Alchémistes* (1856).

Purely fictitious accounts are those in *John Dee, Astrologer of Queen Elizabeth*, by "Hippocrates, jun." (1899), and "John Roby's" *Traditions of Lancashire* (1906).

For the study of witchcraft in the sixteenth century the following may be consulted: George Gifford, *Subtle Practices of Witches* (1587); T. A. Spalding, *Elizabethan Demonology, etc.* (1880); James I., *Demonologie* (1603); Meric Casaubon, *Treatise on Spirits, Witches, etc.* (1672); Reginald Scot, *Discoverie of Witchcraft* (1584, 3rd edition 1605); Sir Walter Scott, *Letters on Demonology and Witchcraft* (1830); Henry Howard, Earl of Northampton, *Defensative against Poyson* (1583), and many other kindred works.

For the history of crystal gazing see Caspar Peucer, *Les Devins* (Antwerp, 1584); M. A. del Rio, *Disquisitionum Magicarum*, 1599; Pierre de l'Ancre, *L'Incredulité et Miscréance du Sortilège* (Paris, 1622); Guido Bonatus, *The Astrologer's Guide* (1866); Andrew Lang, in *Psychical Research of the Nineteenth Century* (1901), and Introduction to Northcote's

Crystal Gazing (1905); Mrs. de Morgan, *From Matter to Spirit* (1863); Sir William Crookes, *Psychic Force and Modern Spiritualism* (1871), and his *Researches in the Phenomena of Spiritualism* (1874); Miss Goodrich Freer's *Essays in Psychical Research* (1899), where she compares the revelations of the spirits to Dee with the work "of a lady novelist of the eighties"!; M. Camille Flammarion's popular and numerous works; F. W. Myers' *Phantasms of the Living* (1886) and his *Human Personality* (1903); with the *Proceedings* of the Psychical Research Society, will all afford information upon psychical and spiritualistic progress. The consummate description of John Inglesant's tragic and pregnant vision of his brother's murder, seen beforehand in the crystal, as related by J. H. Shorthouse, will occur to everyone.

Dee's own writings were extraordinarily numerous. In his *Rehearsall* he enumerated forty-nine. There is a list of seventy-nine in Cooper's *Athenæ Cantabrigensis*, vol. ii., pp. 505—509; but some of these are doubtful: *e.g.*, No. 66, *Treatise of the Rosie-Crucian Secrets*, etc.; for the Rosicrucians only came into existence about the time of Dee's death. Others are but notes from among Ashmole's manuscripts. One (No. 75) is the horoscope or nativity of Kelley, drawn or erected by Dee, which Ashmole has printed in his *Theatrum* (p. 479). To add to Mr. Cooper's list there are some Latin verses in Henry Perry's *Egluryn Phraethineb* (1595).

All the printed books by Dee are extremely rare. There is much information about them in Ames, *Typographical Antiquities* (ed. Herbert). Copies of thirteen are in the British Museum Library, including those of other writers to which he contributed prefaces, additions and notes, as Recorde's *Grounde of Arts* (many editions); Billingsley's *Euclid*; Roger Bacon's *de Secretis operibus artis et naturae, etc.*

and various *Ephemerides.* There are three copies of the "*General and Rare Memorials pertaining to the Perfect Art of Navigation;*" and both the editions of his *Letter . . . Apologeticall, etc.,* addressed to the Archbishop as a protestation and plea for the course of "the philosophicall studies and exercises of a certaine studious gentleman" (1599, 1603). The petitions addressed to the House of Commons and the King are printed on broadsides (1604). There are also three copies of Casaubon's *True Relation* in the British Museum, one of them collated with the original MS. by William Shippen, of Stockport, 1683.

No adequate idea of the remarkable doings of Dee and Kelley over the crystal can be entertained without a study of Dee's manuscript "Book of Enoch" in *Sloane MSS.* 663, 120, and 2,599, 1—45; and his "Claves Angelicæ," 3191 in the same collection. The diagrams of complicated arrangement of letters and figures, their neatness of execution, mathematical precision and etymological intricacy are no less amazing than the clear bold text in which the descriptions are written in printing hand. Regretfully it was decided not to reproduce an example, owing to the lack of pictorial value.

The Portrait of Dee, now in the Ashmolean Museum at Oxford, reproduced as Frontispiece to this volume, was painted when he was 67; it belonged to his grandson, Rowland Dee, and at his death it passed to the possession of Elias Ashmole and was by him bequeathed to the University of Oxford. It has been engraved by Scheneker and W. P. Sherlock. Engraved portraits of Dee and Kelley, by Francis Cleyne, are included, with Roger Bacon; Paracelsus; the prophet Mahomet; and Apollonius of Tyana, on the title-page of Casaubon's volume. Dee's is the same as an anonymous engraving in the Print Room, British Museum, from a younger (German) portrait, in a furred gown and peaked cap; the globe and compasses are in his right hand.

A number of stones and crystals, purporting to be Dr. Dee's, have from time to time been exhibited. Two were at the Tudor Exhibition; another was sold at Sotheby's in 1906, and is now in Dresden. That formerly in the possession of Lord Londesborough (once Horace Walpole's) appears to have been actually the Doctor's; also the globe of smoky quartz now in the British Museum.

The Pedigree which Dee made, tracing his descent from the mythical times of King Arthur, and showing Queen Elizabeth, through her Welsh ancestry, as related to the same source, is illuminated with coats of arms and a small coloured profile portrait of "John Dee, philosophus," in a cap and furred gown. He here (*Cotton Charter*, xiv. 1) describes his grandfather, Bedo Dee, as a soldier fighting under the Emperor Maximilian I., in 1512; his father, Rowland Dee, armiger, as gentleman sewer to King Henry VIII.; and himself as a philosopher.

INDEX

THE END